THE SL/ & EAST EU REVI...

Volume 101, Number 3 — July 2023

ARTICLES

Literature

History

REVIEW ARTICLE

REVIEWS

Maria Renata Mayenowa and the Forgotten Legacy of Polish Theory of Literature and Poetics

TOMASZ ZARYCKI

Reading Mayenowa's biography against the background of the history of literary theory

The twentieth century witnessed two periods of dynamic development in the humanities and social sciences in Central and Eastern Europe which fell roughly between the 1920s and 1960s. In two creative waves, which especially concerned the fields of literary studies and linguistics, the most significant prominence was enjoyed by the intellectual circles of Russia (later the Soviet Union) and Czechoslovakia. However, these groups maintained numerous transnational contacts and were characterized by considerable diversity. Polish scholars could be considered an important component of this wider intellectual exchange network. Although Polish academic circles did not produce such renowned theorists as their Czech and Russian counterparts, being an important part of the broader milieu they are also worthy of attention. Let me, however, first draw a larger context for their relevance. As it has been rightly pointed out by Galin Tihanov,[1] the discussion of the legacy of literary theory in twentieth-century Central and Eastern Europe is signifanctly greater than just its historical dimension. This is because many of the ideas that emerged during that

Tomasz Zarycki is a Professor in the Robert Zajonc Institute for Social Studies (ISS), University of Warsaw.

I am indebted to Teresa Dobrzyńska and Danuta Ulicka for their extremely helpful and detailed comments on draft versions of this text. I would also like to thank the two anonymous reviewers for *SEER* and other readers of the manuscript for their useful suggestions and comments. I am grateful to Ruby Lal and Jerzy Axer for their encouragement to write this text. Needless to say, all its weaknesses are, of course, the sole responsibility of the author. It was written as part of research projects funded by the National Science Center (NCN, grants no. 2015/17/B/HS6/04161 and 2020/39/B/HS6/00211).

[1] Galin Tihanov, *The Birth and Death of Literary Theory: Regimes of Relevance in Russia and Beyond*, Stanford, CA, 2019.

time have entered permanently into the circulation of several disciplines of contemporary humanities worldwide, including philosophy, semiotics and cultural studies. A number of other ideas that were initially outlined are still waiting for more profound recognition and in some cases, rediscovery. As Tihanov has shown, the dynamics of intellectual life were related particularly to the tension between what can be called pre-structuralism (including formalism as one of its currents) and Marxism. Today, this tension has become less obvious and less clear institutionally. However, it still seems to be one of the key axes in disputes driving contemporary critical thought and, more broadly, the reflexive sectors of social sciences and the humanities. In this context, the history of Polish circles as part of the aforementioned broader wave of creative intellectual ferment that came from Central and Eastern Europe, but proved to be important for the entire Western humanities, has become doubly marginalized. It could be said that Poland suffered a defeat of the second degree: it lost both within a current whose dynamism diminished over time, and also developed in a country that found itself strongly marginalized on the intellectual map of Europe after 1968. In fact, 1968 could be seen as a moment of intellectual marginalization of the entire region, while Poland suffered a particular defeat due to the so-called March events.[2] A key consequence was the expulsion of many intellectuals of Jewish origin from Polish academia in the fields of the humanities and social sciences, many of whom were also forced or strongly encouraged to emigrate.

In my recent book on the history of Polish language and literature sciences,[3] I attempted an extensive analysis of the trajectory of the Polish humanities and social sciences from the late nineteenth century to the present. I also tried to explain the sources of its successes in the 1960s and its significant achievements in the first two decades of the twentieth century. In this article, however, I want to focus more on the sources of the comparative failures and disappointments of twentieth-century Polish theory of literature and poetics. The fate of Polish social sciences and humanities during this period is fraught with paradoxes that are largely representative of the entire region and its intellectual dynamics. However, some of them are characteristic mostly of Poland because of the unprecedented role played by the intelligentsia in Polish society.[4] These

[2] Piotr Osęka, 'Dissidents and Police: The Polish March 1968 and a Tale of Two Generations', *East European Politics and Societies*, 33, 2018, pp. 861–80.

[3] Tomasz Zarycki, *The Polish Elite and Language Sciences: A Perspective of Global Historical Sociology*, Cham, 2022.

[4] Tomasz Zarycki, Rafał Smoczyński, Tomasz Warczok, 'The Roots of Polish Culture-

paradoxes can be presented and studied on the basis of the biographies of prominent researchers of the period. Therefore, this article will examine the figure of an outstanding Polish philologist — Maria Renata Mayenowa, to whom I have already devoted some attention.[5] Here, however, I would like to present a much more detailed analysis of Mayenowa's biography, which I will conduct according to the guidelines of modern prosopography,[6] attempting to look at her life and work with the help of sociological tools. I hope they will help to show the largely forgotten transnationality not only of the significant part of the research networks of the time but also of the biographies and identities of the researchers themselves. At the same time, this study will show how this transnationalism was fading at the end of the century, both at the level of academic cooperation as well as in the dimension of individual biographies.

Mayenowa's biography is significant and of particular interest in the context of the history of Polish, as well as Eastern European intellectual thought, for several reasons. Three of these reasons are worth highlighting. First, an analysis of Mayenowa's biography can be helpful in the reconstruction of Polish involvement in the development of social theory in the twentieth century. I am referring, in particular, to the Polish schools of structuralism, which may be seen as a relatively diverse field. In particular, one may note a considerable difference between the Warsaw circle, which will be discussed in more detail below, and the more historically oriented Poznań school, which included such figures as Edward Balcerzan (b. 1937) and Jerzy Ziomek (1924–1990), both prominent theoreticians but also historians of literature. As Danuta Ulicka notes, what some term 'Polish formalism' can be also be seen as a school of Polish pre-structuralism.[7] In any case, most of these schools can be seen as not particularly successful, given their limited lasting influence and lack of wider international recognition. Still, they are important for understanding the broader dynamics of the development of European intellectual humanities and social sciences. Looking for the reasons for the weakness of the Polish efforts to contribute to the global theory-building

Centered Politics: Toward a Non–Purely Cultural Model of Cultural Domination in Central and Eastern Europe', *East European Politics and Societies*, 2017, 31, pp. 360–81.

5 Zarycki, *The Polish Elite and Language Sciences*, pp. 381–85

6 Christophe Charle, *Prosopographie des élites françaises (XVIe–XXe siècles): guide de recherche*, Paris, 1980.

7 Danuta Ulicka, 'At the Crossroads of Marxism and Structuralism in Modern Polish Literary Theory (1918–1939): The Case of Warsaw and Vilnius Student Circles', *Thesis Eleven*, 159, 2020, pp. 64–77.

effort may also help answer the question posed by Ulicka,[8] namely why a fully-fledged Polish school of literary theory (or linguistic theory) failed to emerge during the twentieth century, or at least did not gain wider visibility outside Poland, while such schools were established and became internationally recognized in both Russia and Czechoslovakia. A second, important reason to study Mayenowa's biography is the insight it provides into Polish-Russian, and more broadly, Polish-Eastern European intellectual relations in the twentieth century. Finally, the third reason why I want to introduce her figure here is the non-obvious forms in which the history of Eastern European Jewish elites, and in particular the Jewish bourgeoisie, manifested itself in her biography. The main point of reference for the analysis presented in this article is the biography of the renowned literary theorist Roman Jakobson. The starting point for comparing his career with Mayenowa's will be the similarity of their social backgrounds, as well as their interests, and finally their long-standing intellectual friendship. At the same time, the juxtaposition of the life trajectories of Mayenowa and Jakobson is a useful way of pointing out the differences that not only divided these two scholars (generational difference, difference in the degree of political involvement or academic career strategy), but also divided the dynamics of the broader national intellectual fields, in particular the Polish, and on the other hand the Soviet, Czech and finally the American.

Maria Renata Mayenowa: Turning points

Maria Renata Mayenowa was born on 1 December 1908 in Białystok, then part of the Russian Empire, as Rachela Gurewiczówna, daughter of Benjamin-Lejb Gurewicz (Gurievich) and Szejna Barasz. After the outbreak of the First World War, she moved with her parents to Kharkiv, where she entered a gymnasium in 1917. Her studies there were interrupted by the outbreak of the Bolshevik Revolution. In 1922, Rachela Gurewiczówna returned to Białystok, where from 1923 she attended the fourth grade of the David Druskin Gymnasium, from which she graduated in 1927. In September of that year, she was accepted to study Polish philology at the Department of Humanities at Vilnius University, from which she graduated in 1932, receiving her 'master of philosophy degree in the field of Polish philology'. It should also be noted that she was forced to interrupt her studies for a year for lack of funds. Her academic teachers included well-known professors — the literary scholar, historian and theorist

[8] Danuta Ulicka, 'Przegapiona okazja', *Teksty Drugie*, 6, 2018, pp. 217–30.

Manfred Kridl (1882–1957), and philosopher Tadeusz Czeżowski (1889–1981). In 1934 she received a master's degree in pedagogy as well as a high school teacher diploma and took up a job at the State Jewish Gymnasium. At the same time, at Vilnius University under Kridl's supervision, she wrote a doctoral dissertation, 'Zagadnienia kompozycji *Wesela* Stanisława Wyspiańskiego' (The Problems of the Composition of *The Wedding* by Stanisław Wyspiański), on the basis of which she received her doctoral degree. The thesis defence took place in May 1939, and the doctoral promotion on 13 December 1939, that is, after the fall of the Polish state, under the Lithuanian administration. After obtaining her doctorate she initially held a post as a voluntary assistant, and then — until the outbreak of the German-Soviet war in 1941 — an assistant at the Department of Polish Philology at Vilnius University. During the German occupation she went into hiding with her second husband, Józef Mayen (born Mayer, 1896–1978), in the Belarusian countryside. She survived, thanks in part to the help of her professor, Tadeusz Czeżowski. Shortly after the war, she worked as a librarian at the Białystok City Library. She did her supplementary studies in Prague from 1946 to 1948, where her husband was employed at the Polish embassy. When Stefan Żółkiewski (1911–91) founded the Institute of Literary Research (Instytut Badań Literackich, or IBL) in 1948, a large state institution designed to guide the expansion of Polish literary and linguistic studies, Maria Renata Mayenowa was given employment there. Originally IBL was designed as a central state institution imposing Marxist canons in all branches of research on language and literature. However, Żółkiewski was able to shape the intstitute in such a way as to provide space for research in a wide range of intellectual orientations. This was essentially due to the high position he held in the Communist party which enabled him to hire a number of his pre-war colleagues and peers, many of whom maintained a distance from Marxism, or at least from its orthodox forms. Of course, not all of his pre-war colleagues from the Warsaw and Vilnius circles were able to join the IBL. One of the most promising young theoreticians, Dawid Hopensztand (1904–43), as well as Franciszek Siedlecki (1906–42), did not survive the war, while one of the main mentors — Manfred Kridl — remained in exile in the United States. Andrzej Karcz has provided a detailed analysis of the development of this intellectual field in the last decade of the interwar period.[9] Significant to the development of the environment in which Mayenowa found herself between the wars

[9] Andrzej Karcz, *The Polish Formalist School and Russian Formalism*, Rochester, NY and Kraków, 2002.

was the intellectual atmosphere of Vilnius. As Adam Kola points out, the city, with its cultural and political diversity and multiplicity of academic as well as state research institutions, provided much intellectual stimulus. Also important was the relationship between the circles of critical literary studies and the political left and the then broader relevance that literary theory enjoyed at that time in both public and media spaces.[10]

In the post-war period, Mayenowa, as a member of a diverse group of Żółkiewski's friends, was offered an attractive research position at the newly founded Institute. At IBL, she was the founder and head of the Laboratory of Theoretical Poetics and Literary Language, and from 1957 until 1969 was the Institute's deputy director for academic affairs. From 1953 she was editor of the book series, 'Biblioteka Pisarzów Polskich' ('Library of Polish Writers', a collection of carefully compiled new editions of classic Polish writers). From 1954 until 1968 she was also a professor at the University of Warsaw. She lost her position there in the wave of antisemitic repression after the events of March 1968 but regained it, at least symbolically, in 1981, after the so-called 'Solidarity revolution', when she returned to the university as an invited lecturer. However, her advanced age prevented her from returning to her position as a university professor. She died in Warsaw on 7 May 1988.

The rise and fall of the Polish School of Literary Theory

Mayenowa had a wide range of intellectual interests covering empirical and theoretical linguistics and literary studies. In particular, in the post-war period, she became one of the most prominent specialists on the great Polish writer of the Renaissance period — Jan Kochanowski. Among other achievements, she was the editor-in-chief of the collective edition of Jan Kochanowski's works. She also developed, with great success, the broader field of research on the sixteenth-century Polish language. Her main accomplishment in this area was the *Dictionary of Sixteenth-Century Polish*, which she edited for many decades (and which is still being compiled today).[11] Parallel to these interests, an extremely important strand of Mayenowa's research work comprised her theoretical studies dating back to the pre-war period. In the late 1930s, while writing her doctoral dissertation at Vilnius University, she joined a circle of young Polish

[10] Adam F. Kola, 'Zwrot dokonany niedopełniony: Z dziejów nowoczesnego literaturoznawstwa polskiego okresu międzywojennego', in Jacek Kowalewski and Wojciech Piasek (eds), *'Zwroty' badawcze w humanistyce: Konteksty poznawcze, kulturowe i społeczno-instytucjonalne*, Olsztyn, 2010, pp. 237–84.

[11] See <http://spxvi.edu.pl/o-slowniku/historia> [accessed 2 July 2022].

scholars active there. It operated under the supervision of Kridl, becoming the nucleus of the original Polish pre-structural group. Andrzej Karcz has called it a Polish formalist school,[12] although this is a controversial label, as the very coherence of the given milieu was rather low, so, as some argue, it should not even be considered as such. In any case, it functioned in close cooperation with a similar circle of young scholars of Polish literature active at the University of Warsaw, whose main organizer was Stefan Żółkiewski. Żółkiewski was head of the University of Warsaw Polonists' Circle for only a very short time, between 1932 and 1934, while it included other more prominent activists and scholars, like Franciszek Siedlecki (1867–1934) and Kazimierz Budzyk (1911–64). However, Żółkiewski's role as a coordinator of the circle was crucial.[13] The main tangible achievement of the cooperation of these two groups was the publication of a large collective work dedicated to Kazimierz Wóycicki (1876–1938), a pioneer of Polish literary theory and a specialist in verse studies and stylistics, under the title, *Prace ofiarowane Kazimierzowi Wóycickiemu* (Works Dedicated to Kazimierz Wóycicki).[14] The volume remains to this day an important reference for the history of Polish literary study. In particular, it indicates the potential of the developing cooperation not only of the Vilnius and Warsaw circles but also of foreign connections. A trace of the latter is the presence in the book of representatives of the Prague School milieu, in particular Roman Jakobson, Nikolai Trubetskoi and Josef Hrabák.

After the war, several former members of the Warsaw and Vilnius circles joined the IBL. The situation for many of them turned out to be very ambivalent. On the one hand, after 1945, they were offered significant promotions; in particular, they were given excellent working conditions at the IBL. On the other hand, important political restrictions on their work were imposed. The Institute had a huge budget, a great number of full-time positions and undertook many research projects that had been either initiated or outlined before the war, both empirical and theoretical. In particular, the theoretical work of the milieu in which Mayenowa participated continued. She attempted to synthesize its achievements and chart further avenues of research by defining them within the field of poetics. She did this in particular in the form of a book entitled 'Descriptive Poetics: Description of a Literary Work'.[15] Mayenowa's interpretation —

[12] Karcz, *The Polish Formalist School and Russian Formalism.*

[13] Ibid.

[14] *Prace ofiarowane Kazimierzowi Wóycickiemu*, Wilno, 1937.

[15] Maria Renata Mayenowa, *Poetyka opisowa. Opis utworu literackiego: Książka pomocnicza dla nauczyciela*, Warsaw, 1949.

because of the Stalinist doctrine's condemnation of formalism — was a compromise. She tried to present the achievements of the school from which she grew, fitting them into the current framework of an orthodox form of Marxism. Similar efforts on a higher, purely ideological level were made by Stefan Żółkiewski himself. On the one hand, by virtue of his positions (in particular, sitting on the Central Committee of the Polish United Workers' Party), he became a key ideologue of Stalinism. On the other hand, as director of the IBL, he tried to protect both his former friends and the intellectual legacy of their milieu. Thus, his interpretations neutralized attacks on formalism which, although condemned during Stalinism, did not become the subject of open rebuke in Poland as it was in the USSR. Mayenowa became, at that time, one of the leaders of the dynamic circle centred at the IBL. It is also in this milieu that the new Polish school of structuralism began to develop in 1956, for which the pre-war traditions of formalism remain an important inspiration. This was when Polish-Czech cooperation flourished, in which Mayenowa was an important player. She also popularized the achievements of the Prague school in Poland by publishing a selection of classic works.[16] She dealt, in particular, with the issue (so important to Czech scholars) of textual coherence. She also tried to introduce the work of Russian and Soviet theorists who inspired the work of her circle before the war.[17] In this way, between 1956 and 1968 Mayenowa became one of the key figures in the development of Polish humanities. As Ulicka argues, 'Mayenowa's role in the popularization of the literary theory developed in the Russian-Czech-Polish space from the 1920s onwards is comparable to Jakobson's role in its globalization, especially given that Mayenowa imported to Poland some works of the Prague Circle written in 1926–48'.[18]

Mayenowa's career in the golden '60s

From the point of view of many disciplines in the Polish social sciences and humanities, the years between 1956 and 1968 can be called 'golden'. This largely unique period was defined, first of all, by the geopolitical conditions of the era, and more specifically — the emergence of a

[16] Maria Renata Mayenowa (ed.), *Praska szkoła strukturalna w latach 1926–1948*, Warsaw, 1966.

[17] Maria Renata Mayenowa and Saloni Zygmunt (eds), *Rosyjska szkoła stylistyki*, Warsaw, 1970.

[18] Danuta Ulicka, 'Spaces of Theory', in Michał Mrugalski, Schamma Schahadat and Irina Wutsdorff (eds), *Central and Eastern European Literary Theory and the West*, Berlin, 2023, p. 91.

configuration in which Poland acquired a status that can be described after Stein Rokkan in terms of 'interface periphery'.[19] Specifically, this refers to the competition for intellectual influence in Poland that began to develop in 1956 between the USSR and the United States (and, to a lesser extent, other Western countries). Although Poland was then part of the Soviet bloc and was tightly controlled by Moscow, primarily in military and economic terms, after 1956 it gained (for Eastern bloc countries) a considerable degree of autonomy: less so in the political dimension but more significant in the cultural dimension. This liberalization was also an opportunity to explore the region which was seized by Western actors, led by American foundations (in particular, the Ford Foundation) and intellectual elites interested in engaging in cooperation with researchers from behind the Iron Curtain. This resulted in a dynamic development of academic exchange between Poland and the United States, and also France, which included an influx of Western literature into the country. Together with political liberalization and a significant weakening of restrictions on foreign travel, as well as censorship, Poland became relatively attractive to both Western scholars and researchers from Soviet bloc countries. Poland thus became a meeting place for researchers and intellectuals from East and West, which resulted in the significant development of Polish humanities and social sciences and their increased visibility on a global scale. The international attractiveness of Polish intellectuals and scientists also increased, particularly those who tried to take advantage of the relative freedom of research and oriented themselves toward theoretical frameworks distant from Marxist orthodoxy. Many of them introduced approaches that were original from the Western point of view at the time, often being a synthesis of different ideological and theoretical orientations. A large proportion of these highly motivated researchers devoted themselves to ambitious projects. The intensity of intellectual life and theoretical debates was also significant. This happened, among other reasons, because an academic career was the most attractive path of advancement for the intelligentsia elites who wanted to avoid political engagement at that time. In particular, it granted social prestige, did not involve the need to compromise too far politically with the authorities, and often allowed international travel. The fields of humanities and social sciences also became a key platform for intellectual debates, which often

[19] Stein Rokkan, 'Territories, Centres, and Peripheries: Toward a Geoethnic-Geoeconomic-Geopolitical Model of Differentiation within Western Europe', in Jean Gottmann (ed.), *Centre and Periphery: Spatial Variations in Politics*, Beverly Hills, CA and London, 1980, pp. 163–204.

had the aspect of veiled or, to use Bourdieu's language, refracted ideological disputes. This is because, thanks to their relative abstractness, the language of science, especially of social theory, allowed for the expression of voices critical of the authorities that would not have been allowed in other forums by the censors.

Mayenowa's biography seems to be an excellent illustration of how the social macro-mechanisms mentioned above operated at the level of the careers of specific academics. The trajectory of her professional career seems to be a spectacular example of how the individual biography of even a highly original intellectual can be strongly conditioned by the structural configuration of geopolitical forces, for it was Mayenowa who proved to be a key *spiritus movens* of the great and unprecedented revival of theoretical work within Polish linguistics and literary studies that took place after 1956. Structuralism was the strongest trend in that period and it was well represented at IBL by such scholars as Janusz Sławiński (1934–2014), Aleksandra Okopień-Sławińska (b. 1932), Michał Głowiński (1934–2023), Edward Balcerzan, Kazimierz Bartoszyński (1921–2015) and several others. As mentioned, a key aspect of this revival was the favourable international configuration, which turned Poland into a platform for exchange between the West and the Soviet Union. First and foremost, Poland, as the most open country in the Soviet bloc, began to attract in large numbers representatives of Western academic centres. At the same time, a significant number of the Polish intelligentsia was, as it were, prepared to meet with them, especially the liberal sectors of the social sciences and humanities, members of which often received an excellent education in the interwar period and even managed to develop their first intellectual ideas during that time, subsequently passing the Stalinist years by following, informally, Western intellectual life.[20]

Mayenowa and Jakobson: Intersecting trajectories

In this context, the collaboration between Mayenowa and Roman Jakobson (1896–1982) — one of the key figures in post-war linguistics — was paradigmatic. Their first meeting took place in January 1958 when Jakobson came to Warsaw to attend a meeting of the International Slavists' Committee, which was preparing a Moscow congress planned for September, which they also both attended. Later that year, at Mayenowa's

[20] This mechanism in the history of Polish social sciences was well described in the case of the field of historical sciences by Valentin Behr, *Powojenna historiografia polska jako pole walki: Studium z socjologii wiedzy i polityki*, Warsaw, 2021.

invitation, Jakobson came to Poland for a seminar in Krynica Górska, where he delivered a series of lectures in Russian.[21] This was also where Jakobson met his third wife — Krystyna Pomorska (1928–86), a graduate of Polish studies from University of Warsaw, later professor of Russian literature at MIT.[22] Contacts between Jakobson and Mayenowa, however, predate this time. Mayenowa first wrote to Jakobson as early as October 1946, which proved to be the beginning of a correspondence that lasted more than thirty years.[23] Although both Mayenowa and, in particular, Jakobson, were outstanding and unique scholars, it is also possible to look at them in a structural, and therefore sociological, way, pointing to their trajectories as socially constructed life paths. In this sense, one can analyse their biographies in terms of Pierre Bourdieu's 'epistemic individual'.[24]

Both Jakobson and Mayenowa were recognized academic leaders in their respective countries (and Jakobson even globally), and were interested in opening their academic fields to international contacts. For Mayenowa, Jakobson was the key door-keeper to the global and particularly American realm.[25] For Jakobson, visits to Poland were an opportunity to open more widely the door to the Communist-Slavic world from which he emerged, and whose own vision he propagated in the American and then global academy. He could now also act as a guide to its contemporary incarnation for a number of Western scholars, whom he invited to Poland for conferences he organized with Mayenowa. Jakobson's trips to Poland were, in fact, numerous in the 1960s, with the last one taking place in 1973.

Jakobson was twelve years older than Mayenowa. He received his diploma in 1918 in Petrograd (although he undertook most of his studies in Moscow, where he was born), while Mayenowa did not begin hers until 1927 in Vilnius. They shared a similar social background. Both came from Jewish bourgeois families of the Russian Empire. Both families entered Russian culture and language in the second half of the nineteeth century.

[21] According to Głowiński, at the Krynica Górska seminar Jakobson presented his paper, 'Poetics in the Light of Linguistics', which was published in 1960 in *Pamiętnik Literacki*. The paper discussed the concept of a hierarchical arrangement of linguistic functions in an utterance. See Michał Głowiński, 'Pani Mayenowa – próba portretu', in Bożena Chodźko, Elżbierta Feliksiak and Marek Olesiewicz (eds), *Obecność: Maria Renata Mayenowa (1908–1988)*, Białystok, 2006, pp. 17–32.

[22] Ibid.

[23] Jakobson's letters to Mayenowa from 1947–86 have been preserved in Poland. Mayenowa's letters to Jakobson deposited at the Massachusetts Institute of Technology, Institute Archives and Special Collections cover the years 1946–79. See Danuta Ulicka, 'Role społeczne uczonych. Roman Jakobson i Polacy', *Teksty Drugie*, 2, 2021, pp. 260–80.

[24] Pierre Bourdieu, *Homo Academicus*, Paris, 1984.

[25] Ulicka, 'Role społeczne uczonych', pp. 260–80.

When Jakobson and Mayenowa were born it was Russian that was their first language, their mother tongue. Mayenowa, who was born in Białystok, had more contact with traditional Jewish culture and the Yiddish language in the wider family-neighbourhood circle of her childhood. Jakobson, whose parents were graduates of Russian universities, including his father Osip, a graduate of the Riga Polytechnic and originating from Austria-Hungary,[26] may not have had much contact with traditional Jewish culture. Interestingly, both Mayenowa's father and Jakobson's father were merchants of the first, and therefore highest capital guild.[27] They therefore came from the same milieu, the wealthy Russian-speaking Jewish bourgeoisie whose dynamic growth was associated with the Russian Empire's economic boom in the late nineteenth century. Danuta Ulicka has pointed out that several other members of the given wider network were the descendants of the wealthy bourgeoisie and entrepreneurs of the Russian Empire. In particular, Osip Brik, whose wealthy father financed the publication of the book series, 'Sborniki po teorii poeticheskogo iazyka' (Collected Works in Poetic Language Theory).[28]

It can be also recalled that Russian was the language of early education for both future linguists. In Mayenowa's case, it lasted almost until the end of World War One, when she studied in Kharkiv's gymnasiums. Geographically, it is possible that their paths on a structural level may have already crossed before the revolution. In particular, before the First World War they may have passed each other as children on the streets of Moscow. Indeed, in Mayenowa's memoirs, she describes her visits to Moscow as a child to see her grandfather, who lived there.[29] Mayenowa did not enter the realm of the Polish language until after the Great War,[30] when she studied in the Jewish gymnasium of Białystok, the Druskin

[26] Henry Kučera, 'Roman Jakobson', *Language*, 59, 4, 1983, pp. 871–83.

[27] Małgorzata Baranowska reports that Mayenowa herself mentioned in passing that the notion of the first guild is 'now a name without a designator'. These words seem significant, because they indicate a conviction that the memory of basic social status designators of the bourgeois world in which she grew up had completely disappeared. Małgorzata Baranowska, 'Koniec Świata', in Bożena Chodźko, Elżbieta Feliksiak and Elżbieta Konończuk (eds), *Okna Pamięci: Maria Renata Mayenowa (1910–1988)*, Białystok, 2003, p. 90.

[28] Danuta Ulicka, '"Archiwum" i archiwum', *Teksty Drugie*, 4, 2017, pp. 273–302.

[29] Specifically, Mayenowa recalls walking with her grandfather 'through a cold Moscow street to a flower shop'. See Baranowska, 'Koniec świata', p. 92.

[30] According to Baranowska, the young Rachela Gurewiczówna did not learn Polish until she was about 13 years old. Her father wanted her to learn Hebrew because he had no son and dreamed that his daughter would receive the education expected of the oldest male descendant of a Jewish family. See ibid., p. 91.

Gymnasium for the Humanities, which had Polish as its main language of instruction and was an expensive school.[31] However, over time she lost her knowledge of Yiddish, which after the war, she supposedly was no longer able to use.

There are several other structural (that is, sociological) similarities between the biographies of Jakobson and Mayenowa. As a result of the Bolshevik Revolution, their families lost huge fortunes, but they themselves were able to move into elite intelligentsia positions. Thus, in the language of Pierre Bourdieu's social theory, we can say that they managed to convert their family's economic capital, particularly through parental expenditures on elite education and broader socialization, into cultural capital. In Mayenowa's case, this process was somewhat prolonged in a manner characteristic of the course of social change in interwar Poland. While Jakobson, since 1918, could be considered as a member of the intelligentsia elite, even as capitalism in Russia had collapsed, Mayenowa remained partly in the bourgeoisie in the first half of the interwar period. Despite the fact that her father lost most of his wealth in the Russian Revolution, she married a prosperous businessman, the chemical engineer Yefim Kaplan.[32] According to Głowiński, Kaplan was a factory owner. Baranowska recounts that Mayenowa mentioned once that her first husband provided her with a very high standard of living, and she took advantage of the opportunities to benefit from the luxuries he financed for her.[33] In the latter part of the interwar period, however, she seems to have lived primarly in the world of the intelligentsia. She worked as a Polish language teacher at the Gymnasium of the Central Committee for Education in Vilnius (a Bund-party controlled institution).[34] Her second husband, Józef Mayen, was also a typical member of the intelligentsia. His father, Alexander Mayer, was a lawyer. He also came from a Jewish family, but one which had Polonized earlier than Mayenowa's and joined the elite of Lviv's intelligentsia. Their wedding took place in Vilnius Cathedral during the war. According to Sławiński (1934–2014), the Polish literary

[31] For a review of archival documents of Mayenowa's pre-war education, see Tomasz Chachulski, 'Maria Renata Mayenowa. Dokumenty z lat studenckich w archiwum Uniwersytetu Stefana Batorego w Wilnie', *Teksty Drugie*, 2017, 4, pp. 318–35. Some useful information on Mayenowa's early years is also provided by Zygmunt Saloni, 'Wspomnienie o Marii Renacie Mayenowej', in Bożena Chodźko, Elżbieta Feliksiak and Elżbieta Konończuk (eds), *Okna Pamięci. Maria Renata Mayenowa (1910–1988)*, Białystok, 2003, p. 63.

[32] Ibid.

[33] Baranowska, 'Koniec świata', p. 89.

[34] Saloni, 'Wspomnienie o Marii Renacie Mayenowej'.

theorist and historian,[35] Mayen was active in the Polish underground Home Army (AK). Although Mayenowa and Jakobson were unlikely to have met during the interwar period, they appear on the pages of the same publication, namely the aforementioned collection, *Works Offered to Kazimierz Wóycicki*, which was published in Vilnius in 1937. A chapter by Roman Jakobson also appeared in this volume.[36] Mayenowa, still as Rachela Kapłanowa, contributed a chapter on the realist novel.[37]

The great congresses of the 1960s

During the 1960s, contacts between Jakobson and Mayenowa became regular and proved to be central to a wide network of international cooperation, which can be seen in terms of the effect of Poland's interface peripherality, which became clearly apparent between 1956 and 1968. The team of researchers collaborating with Jakobson and Mayenowa, under the patronage of Stefan Żółkiewski, organized successive international conferences attended by numerous prominent foreign scholars. The scale and global reach of these projects is difficult to imagine in present-day Poland in which, after the fall of Communism, much of the social sciences underwent significant downgrading in international hierarchies of prestige and visibility.[38] The first series of the conference co-organized by Jakobson and Mayenowa was devoted to poetics (1960, 1961, 1964 and 1967), while the second to linguistics and semiotics (1965, 1967, 1968). The inaugural grand International Conference on Poetics was held in Warsaw in August 1960, attended by scholars from twelve countries who presented fifty-one papers published in a collected volume.[39] Among those present (or at least who contributed to the post-conference volume) were Roger Caillois, Victor Erlich, Mac Hammond, Dmitrii Likhachev, Bruno Markwardt, Thomas Sebeok, Paul Zumthor, Lubomir Doležel

[35] Janusz Sławiński, 'MRM', in Bożena Chodźko, Elżbieta Feliksiak and Elżbieta Konończuk (eds), *Okna pamięci: Maria Renata Mayenowa (1910–1988)*, Białystok, 2003. pp. 11–21.

[36] Roman Jakobson, 'Z zagadnień prozodji starogreckiej', in *Prace ofiarowane Kazimierzowi Wóycickiemu*, Wilno, 1937, pp. 73–88.

[37] Rachela Kapłanowa, 'W sprawie tendencji w powieści realistycznej', in *Prace ofiarowane Kazimierzowi Wóycickiemu*, Wilno, 1937, pp. 467–82.

[38] Tomasz Warczok and Tomasz Zarycki, 'Polish Political Sciences in a Global Context', in William R. Thompson (ed.), *Oxford Research Encyclopedia of Politics*, Oxford, 2018 <http://politics.oxfordre.com/view/10.1093/acrefore/9780190228637.001.0001/acrefore-9780190228637-e-872> [accessed 12 June 2022].

[39] Donald Davie, Ivan Fónagy, Roman Jakobson, Dmitrii S. Likhachev, Maria Renata Mayenowa, Wolfgang Steinitz, Kazimierz Wyka and Stefan Żółkiewski, *Poetics, poetyka, poetika*, Warsaw, 1961.

and, of course, Roman Jakobson. On the Polish side, in addition to literary scholars such as Stefania Skwarczyńska, Czesław Zgorzelski, Kazimierz Wyka and Julian Krzyżanowski, linguists such as Zenon Klemensiewicz, Jerzy Kuryłowicz, and philosophers such as Roman Ingarden and Władysław Tatarkiewicz took part. The plenary session featured Jakobson and Ingarden, representing the two main streams of poetics defined by Mayenowa in her *Poetyka teoretyczna*,[40] which first identified the phenomenological current represented by such scholars as Roman Ingarden, Juliusz Kleiner, Stefan Kołaczkowski and Eugeniusz Kucharski. It focused on the question of how the subject constitutes and feels aesthetic objects, relating them to aesthetic, existential and world-view values. The second stream discerned by Mayenowa was the structural current with sociologizing tendencies. The second stream attempted to establish the principles of linguistic organization of texts and propose a consistent programme for studying the linguistic structure of meaning of literary works. The first to attempt to propagate its theses were members of the Warsaw circle, in particular, Kazimierz Budzyk, Dawid Hopensztand, Franciszek Siedlecki and Stefan Żółkiewski, who all recognized Kazimierz Wóycicki as their patron. This current, according to Mayenowa, was distinctive, as it differed from others in international circulation in its distancing from phenomenology (also ironically called 'spiritualology'). The given division, according to Mayenowa, was already clear in the works of Kazimierz Wóyciki, who called them subjective and objective, respectively, and also proposed their synthesis. The conferences of the 1960s were therefore not only a meeting of the main currents of global intellectual networks, but also an unprecedented opportunity to present the achievements of Polish researchers from several generations to an international audience.

Thanks to the aforementioned series of semantic conferences, the International Semiotic Society was established in 1966, as is mentioned by the official website of the International Association for Semiotic Studies (IASS-AIS).[41] According to this source, Żółkiewski became the president of the society, while Algirdas Greimas became its secretary. Mayenowa was a member and at the same time joined the board of the nascent Polish Semiotic Society. She also organized seminars for young Polish scholars.

[40] Maria Renata Mayenowa, *Poetyka teoretyczna: Zagadnienia języka*. Wrocław, Warsaw, Kraków and Gdańsk, 1979, pp. 7–8; Saloni, 'Wspomnienie O Marii Renacie Mayenowej', pp. 318–35.

[41] For a short history of IASS-AIS, see <https://iass-ais.org/presentation-2/short-history/> [accessed 12 June 2022].

Participants included Viktor V. Zhirmunskii, Pierre Guiraud and Roman Jakobson.[42] Other well-known names who came to Warsaw through Mayenowa's efforts included Dmitrii Likhachev, Roland Barthes, Émile Benveniste, Umberto Eco, Pierre Guiraud, Oscar Ducrot, Yuri Apresjan and Boris A. Uspenskij.

In August 1968, a major Semiotic Congress was held in Warsaw, on which Mayenowa and her circle placed great hopes. The congress was held just after the Warsaw Pact forces' invasion of Czechoslovakia and for this reason was boycotted by representatives of some Western countries. This had a more than symbolic significance, as Poland then fell out of the global field of this emerging discipline, in which Mayenowa had planned Poland would be central. In purely institutional terms, the failure of the Congress doomed the chances of the International Association for Semiotic Studies (IASS) to be established (and headquartered) in Warsaw, and thus for Poland to be given a prominent role in the field. To Mayenowa's great disappointment the association was established a year later in Paris.[43] It never organized a congress in Poland, although its second president after Émile Benveniste (1902–76) was Jerzy Pelc (1924–2017) of the University of Warsaw. Poland's contribution to semiotics was then quite modest, and Pelc was unable to achieve much international publicity or wider recognition for his work. There are few contemporary traces outside Poland of the contributions of these developments that ended abruptly in 1968. French researcher Lucile Dumont,[44] writing about the history of the development of literary theory and semiotics internationally, only briefly mentions Poland's contribution during the 1960s. She mentions, for example, an international semiotics conference in Kazimierz Dolny in 1966, at which a plan for the establishment of the International Semiotic Association was adopted. Members of the Polish organizing committee included Kuryłowicz, Mayenowa and Żółkiewski.[45]

In addition to this impressive series of conferences that directed streams of global thought circulation toward Warsaw, Mayenowa's own unusually far-reaching network of contacts is also noteworthy. Michał

[42] Lucylla Pszczołowska, 'Maria Renata Mayenowa', *Biuletyn Polonistyczny*, 32, 113, 1989, pp. 168–74.

[43] Teresa Dobrzyńska, 'Maria Renata Mayenowa', Bożena Chodźko, Elżbieta Feliksiak and Elżbieta Konończuk (eds), *Okna pamięci: Maria Renata Mayenowa (1910–1988)*, Białystok, 2003, pp. 73–85.

[44] Lucile Dumont, 'Théories sans frontières? Les Théories Littéraires en France et la construction d'un espace transnational, années 1960-années 1970', *Actes de la recherche en sciences sociales*, 4, 224, 2018, pp. 46–63.

[45] Dumont, 'Théories sans frontières?', p. 61.

Głowiński recalls that Mayenowa 'had extensive contacts, she took care of them, knew how to maintain them, and had been to the US several times'.[46] It is worth mentioning that she was a grantee of the Ford Foundation in the 1960s, thanks to which she visited Jakobson in the US, where she also had an opportunity to listen to lectures by Noam Chomsky and Morris Halle. She was therefore the beneficiary of a generous stream of American scholarship funds which at the time flowed mainly to Poland, and also to Hungary, as the most liberal countries of the bloc.[47] As the study by Jarosław Kilias, among others, shows, this was a stream that was largely geopolitically conditioned, and had specific political considerations in decisions about its distribution.[48] Individuals who were able to benefit from Ford scholarships during this period very often became intellectual leaders in their academic fields for many years, and usually assumed the role of propagators of 'advanced', ' international' thought in Poland, and sometimes in other countries of the Communist camp. Another of the beneficiaries of this American support for Polish academia was Jerzy Kuryłowicz (1895–1978), who had already benefited from the first wave which took place on a smaller scale in the interwar period. Thanks to the Rockefeller Foundation, he visited Yale University in 1931 and 1932, and met Edward Sapir and Bronisław Malinowski, among others, there. He then travelled again to the United States as part of the big wave of Ford Foundation-funded internships during the 1960s.

In addition to her trips to the United States, Mayenowa also frequented Western European universities. In particular, she taught at the University of Amsterdam, where Jan van der Eng invited her to join the Slavic Studies department. Also significant were Mayenowa's, and by extension an important part of the IBL community's, contacts with researchers from Soviet Russia, as well as Czechoslovakia, Bulgaria and East Germany.[49] Thanks to these contacts, Polish researchers were able to become acquainted with both the achievements of the Moscow school (Yuri Apresian, Aleksandr Zolkovsikii) and the Tartu school, namely

[46] Głowiński, 'Pani Mayenowa - próba portretu', p. 24.

[47] Johanna K. Bockman and Gil Eyal, 'Eastern Europe as a Laboratory for Economic Knowledge: The Transnational Roots of Neoliberalism', *American Journal of Sociology*, 108, 2, 2002, pp. 310–52.

[48] Jarosław Kilias, 'Not Only Scholarships: The Ford Foundation, Its Material Support, and the Rise of Social Research in Poland', *Serendipities. Journal for the Sociology and History of the Social Sciences*, 5, 1–2, 2021, pp. 33–46.

[49] Most of these exchanges were financed by the Foreign Office of the Polish Academy of Sciences (PAN). The bureau also financed part of the exchanges with Great Britain, France and the Netherlands. I am indebted to Teresa Dobrzynska for this information.

Yuri Lotman, Vyacheslav Ivanov and Vladimir Toporov, as well as such prominent scholars as Vladimir Propp and Mikhail Bakhtin, although with the latter her contacts were only indirect.[50] In fact, after the Moscow congress of 1958, Mayenowa played the role of an intellectual messenger, passing on information from Russian researchers, many of whom were introduced to her by Jakobson who knew them from his youth in Russia, to their Polish and Western colleagues. Later on, she established personal contact with Lotman, whom she met during one of her many trips to the USSR. Lotman proposed her candidacy for the post of editor-in-chief of the journal *Semiotica*. As Adam Kola and Danuta Ulicka mention, 'Lotman believed that — due to her friendship with scholars from all over the world — Mayenowa could bind Eastern (especially the Tartu-Moscow School) and Western scholars'.[51] She also managed to invite Viktor Zhirmunskii to Warsaw.[52] The fact that Mayenowa was referred to by her Russian-speaking colleagues as 'Maria Lvovna', instead of 'Pani Maria', as members of the Russian intelligentsia who want to show courtesy to Poles usually do, seems to confirm that she was considered by them as belonging to their own cultural sphere.[53] It is worth noting that Polish and Russian were the only languages she was fully fluent in, while she hardly spoke any other foreign languages easily, although she read in several. Because of the importance Mayenowa attached to Russian culture, Głowiński refers to her as a 'Russophile'.[54] As Głowiński writes, 'she nourished the conviction that it was in Russia that modern humanities was born, and above all the currents she considered most important'.[55] He adds that this kind of attitude was rare in those days, and from the tone of his remarks, it seems such a way of perceiving Russian culture was not entirely convincing to him. It is not clear whether Głowiński realizes that Russian was the family language for Mayenowa prior to Polish. This does not change the fact that Głowiński, like a whole group of then-young scholars working mainly at

[50] Teresa Kostkiewiczowa, 'Rola działalności organizacyjnej Marii Renaty Mayenowej w rozwoju polskiej nauki o literaturze po 1956 roku', in Bożena Chodźko, Elżbieta Feliksiak and Marek Olesiewicz (eds), *Obecność: Maria Renata Mayenowa (1908–1988)*, Białystok, 2006, pp. 37–44.

[51] Adam F. Kola and Danuta Ulicka, 'From Circles to the School (and Back Again): The Case of Polish Structuralism', in Marina Grishakova and Silvi Salupere (eds), *Theoretical Schools and Circles in the Twentieth Century Humanities: Literary Theory, History, Philosophy*, New York and London, 2015, pp. 80–81.

[52] Saloni, 'Wspomnienie o Marii Renacie Mayenowej'.

[53] Teresa Dobrzyńska, *Maria Renata Mayenowa i jej pracownia: W 25. rocznicę śmierci*, Warsaw, 2013.

[54] Głowiński, 'Pani Mayenowa – próba portretu', p. 25.

[55] Ibid.

the IBL around Mayenowa, succumbed in the 1960s to her enthusiasm for semiotics, text linguistics and the sociology of language. As Janusz Sławiński wrote, his generation came into close contact with Mayenowa's generation (born around 1910): 'Our youth established communication with their youth and found in them a model of ourselves.'[56] According to Sławiński, the two generations were united by, among other things, anti-psychologism. What also brought the two generations together was an orientation toward linguistics. During the 1960s, therefore, elements of the non-Marxist intellectual tradition of the left of the 1920s and 1930s resonated with the new younger generation of Polish scholars. In turn, the older generation was inspired by the linguistic thought of earlier generations, in particular Baudouin de Courtenay (1845–1929), the famous Polish linguist and Slavist.

The 1970s and retraditionalization

The year 1968, with its antisemitic campaign and the defeat of the liberal faction within the Communist Party elite, marked the end of the 'golden 1960s' in the Polish social sciences and humanities. It can be said, however, that the March 1968 moment was the de facto culmination of a process that had begun earlier, at least in 1964. At that time, there were clear signs of a limitation of the relatively liberal political climate that had prevailed since October 1956. For Mayenowa's circle, this had various negative effects, such as the Jagiellonian University abandoning its intention to confer an honorary doctorate on Roman Jakobson, which had been planned for the university's 600th anniversary celebration in 1964. March 1968 was also a very clear and painful caesura for Mayenowa. She was forced to resign from a number of positions, including the editorship of *Pamiętnik Literacki*, an established quarterly journal of Polish literary history, literary theory and literary criticism founded in 1902 in Lviv, as well as her position as deputy-director of the IBL, and her full-time position at the University of Warsaw in the Department of Literary Theory. The department was established in 1955 by Kazimierz Budzyk and after 1968 it was demoted from the status of chair to one of unit (*zakład*) following a general reform of the university system. After these dramatic events, when many of Mayenowa's colleagues were demoted or dismissed and some forced to emigrate, she lost confidence in the effectiveness of her work. Although the wave of antisemitic rhetoric was a psychologically difficult experience for her, she decided to stay. She consciously chose to remain in Poland despite offers to

[56] Sławiński, 'MRM', p. 13.

move to the United States made to her primarily by Jakobson and Wiktor Weintraub (1908–88), the Polish literary historian and diplomat, who had been teaching at Harvard since 1950.

From the sociological point of view, 1968 was a moment of an obvious, one might say homologous, overlap of international and domestic crises. In the former dimension, Poland was pushed out of the earlier international constellation in which it played the role of a relatively liberal interface periphery, and as a result a country attractive to Western scholars. An important aspect of this crisis was the subsequent participation of Polish troops in the intervention in Czechoslovakia. Domestically, Poland saw the failure of the liberal intelligentsia as a sphere of influence. A part of it was pushed more or less forcibly abroad, while another was removed beyond the home academic and intellectual fields.

Interestingly, in addition to the administrative repression of people of Jewish origin and members of the liberal intelligentsia, which were the most brutal, there were also social meta-forces at work. They were perceived by many in the liberal camp that was marginalized in 1968 as a 'social atmosphere' (tedious or even 'suffocating') or as a psycho-physical condition ('a sense of fatigue' or 'boredom'). This drove many people during the first half of the 1970s into emigration. Others were pushed towards opposition activity, the stronger centres of which, as is well known, begin to crystallize around 1977.

This political activation of intelligentsia elites interfered more and more explictly with academia, especially in the social sciences and humanities. Thus, a new dimension of the division of the field into those who entered into open opposition activity and those who did not want to get involved, even if they were critical of the authorities, emerged. The latter included Andrzej Walicki (1930–2020), a Polish historian who believed that the increasing pressure for political involvement was detrimental to academia. It led him to the decision to go into exile in 1981 where he lectured first in Australia, then at the University of Notre-Dame.[57] Although Mayenowa never considered emigrating, and was not a member of the Polish United Workers' Party, she clearly assumed a sceptical position concerning the open politicization of academia. This is pointed out by Głowiński who appreciates her earlier opposition to Jakubowski's circle,[58] that is, her critical attitude toward Jan Zygmunt Jakubowski (1909–75) from the Department of Polish Studies at the University of Warsaw, whom

[57] Robert Krasowski, 'Czekając na odwilż, czyli umysł nadal zniewolony', *Życie*, 29, 6, 2002.

[58] Głowiński, 'Pani Mayenowa – próba portretu', p. 30.

Głowiński identifies as the leader of the nationalist faction in the field (related to the faction led by Mieczysław Moczar in the party leadership). Głowiński, who himself has taken a political stance since 1977 by becoming involved in such oppositional activities as the Society for Educational Courses (Towarzystwo Kursów Naukowych or TKN),[59] was disappointed that in the 1980s Mayenowa criticized the 'Solidarity' trade union for opposing the authorities too harshly.[60] He described her reluctance to become politically involved and her fear of retaliation from the authorities in the 1980s as a result of her older age.[61] However, it is worth noting that during the period of the so-called first Solidarity, that is, in late 1980 and early 1981, she became involved in the wave of criticism of the language of propaganda that was developing at the time. As Teresa Dobrzyńska has mentioned, 'even Mayenowa, who was cautious by nature, took part in a conference organized in early 1981 on newsspeak — a degenerate type of discourse that was a product of the Communist system'.[62]

At the same time, as Małgorzata Baranowska points out, Mayenowa did not express much interest in Jewish topics, which began to be popular at that time. She was even irritated by the texts appearing more and more frequently in the Catholic weekly, *Tygodnik Powszechny*, that dealt with the Holocaust and Jewish traditions. As Baranowska recalls, she believed that 'a well-bred man does not talk about misfortunes, either private or national'.[63] Such a reaction can be interpreted in terms of not giving in to the process that was gaining momentum at the time, which can be referred to as retraditionalization. By this notion, which I have developed at length elsewhere,[64] I mean, in particular, the gradual replacement of theoretical debates that occupied a central place in the Polish social sciences and humanities in the 1960s by a turn to emotionally and morally charged historical themes, a return to 'forgotten' traditions and previously forbidden topics. This turn correlated, of course, with the global 'cultural turn', and its derivatives had two main currents which gradually became mutually polarized due to their homologous ties in an emerging political

[59] Głowiński's engagement, however, compared to some other IBL researchers (e.g., Jan Józef Lipski or Roman Zimand) who engaged in openly political projects, was not as an activist. Rather, he took a position that, while not radical, nevertheless proved more pronounced in its distancing from the Communist authorities than Mayenowa's more insular stance.

[60] Głowiński, 'Pani Mayenowa – próba portretu', pp. 31.

[61] Ibid.

[62] Dobrzyńska, *Maria Renata Mayenowa i jej pracownia*, pp. 12.

[63] Baranowska, 'Koniec świata'.

[64] Zarycki, *The Polish Elite and Language Sciences.*

division into 'Catholic conservatives' and 'cosmopolitan liberals'. For the first of these camps in the humanities, the key figures became Cyprian Kamil Norwid (1821–83), the famous Polish poet, dramatist, painter and philosopher, and Stanisław Brzozowski (1878–1911), the notable Polish philosopher, writer, publicist, literary and theatre critic, who were considered as exemplary 'forgotten' patriots with a special spiritual sensitivity. Also significant for this orientation is the 'recovery of memory' of the so-called Kresy or Eastern borderlands. For the opposite pole of the humanities, in turn, the memory of the Holocaust and the history of Jews of Polish lands, as well as other national or ethnic and religious minorities and their cultures have become significant topics. Even after the fall of Communism, the profile of the 'Laboratory of Theoretical Poetics' at the IBL, once headed by Mayenowa, also fitted into this trend. Its most important areas of research become Holocaust studies and 'cultural semiotics', which could be seen as one of the new forms of retraditionalization. On the other hand, the laboratory's research profile currently includes neurosemiotics, the analytical philosophy of language, and cognitive science more broadly.[65] The current head of the laboratory is Jan Kordys who specializes in cognitive and neural research.

In the late 1970s a clear turn to the study of culture and language can be identified, which displaced the earlier structural paradigm (based on the idea of the autonomy of the literary work). Among the traditions abandoned at that time was the Polish school of formalism and later structuralism with their unique interest in the sociological research of literary work. In the pre-war period its most promising representative was Dawid Hopensztand who, however, died in the Warsaw Ghetto in 1943.[66] After the war Stefan Żółkiewski tried to develop this direction of research, although he did not devote much effort to it due to his political career. Only after it ended in 1968, when he was stripped of all his positions because of his firm support for the protesting students and criticism of antisemitic rhetoric, did he write a number of ambitious studies on the sociology of literature.[67] However,

[65] At the same time, it should be noted that research that came out of Mayenowa's programme remains at the core of her former Lab's activity in areas such as stylistics, verse studies and discourse theory. In recent decades, this has been led in particular by Teresa Dobrzyńska, Lucylla Pszczołowska, Elżbieta Janus and Grzegorz Grochowski. See *Pracownia Poetyki Teoretycznej i Semiotyki Kultury* <https://ibl.waw.pl/pl/o-instytucie/pracownie-i-zespoly/pracownia-poetyki-literackiej> [accessed 1 September 2022].

[66] Ulicka, 'At the Crossroads of Marxism and Structuralism', pp. 64–77.

[67] They included Stefan Żółkiewski, *Kultura Literacka (1918–1932)*, Wrocław, 1973, as well as his comprehensive Stefan Żółkiewski, *Wiedza o kulturze literackiej: główne pojęcia*, Warsaw, 1980.

they made little traction, which was mainly due to the aforementioned ideological changes that were taking place in the 1970s. Thus there was a shift from theoretical interests (which were best represented by a waning interest in structuralism) to cultural and historical themes (conservative or liberal, but always presented as 'recovered' after a period of 'oblivion' thanks to the special commitment of a new generation of researchers characterized by courage and dedication), as well as displacement of sociological inspirations by psychological insights. At the same time, analysis in terms of social classes and other inequalities was gradually replaced by theories of motivation or theories of attitudes that resonated better with the ideology of 1970s technocratism. Another important trend that occurred in the 1970s was the apparent divergence of the paths of linguistics and literary theory, which for Mayenowa's generation were inseparable. This separation made it all the more difficult to maintain the earlier synergies and develop theoretical meta-reflection.

Perhaps it is these changes, which intensified in the second half of the 1970s, and whose effects are still felt today, that can explain both the generally lower international visibility of the achievements of Polish linguistics and literary studies from before 1968, and in particular the relative oblivion of Mayenowa's work. It is also hard not to agree with the comments of Danuta Ulicka, who points out that an important reason for the poor global recognition of Polish theorists was also the neglect, in the 1960s, of publication activity in international circulation by the Polish academic community.[68] Today, if we try to identify scholarly publications from Poland that attract particular attention in the wider international scene, they are not so much theoretical but rather historical works with clear moral aspects, in particular dealing with Jewish topics, such as studies on the Holocaust and antisemitism.[69]

[68] Ulicka, 'Przegapiona okazja', p. 217–30.

[69] In France, for example, a collective work on the 'new Polish school of Shoah studies' has recently been published: Audrey Kichelewski, Judith Lyon-Caen, Jean-Charles Szurek and Anette Wieviorka, *Les Polonais et la Shoah: Une nouvelle école historique*, Paris, 2019. This new wave of Western interest in violence on Polish soil during the twentieth century, about which the works of Timothy Snyder is also a good illustration, can be seen as one more dimension of the global retraditionalization of the region. Central and Eastern Europe is thus seen less and less as a potential centre of theoretical thought and increasingly as a generator of discourses in the genre of historical reflection of an ethical nature.

Structural and individual factors in the marginalization of the School of Polish Structuralism

However, when we look at the weakness in memory related to the achievements of Mayenowa,[70] and more broadly the Polish formalist and then structuralist milieu, it is possible to separate individual from structural factors. It should be noted that Mayenowa's output did not include many works with clearly formulated innovative arguments. Rather, they were synthesizing works, of which her impressive *Theoretical Poetics*[71] was foremost, but numerous shorter commentaries and contributions predominated in her output. Although sometimes innovative and daring, they did not openly put forward theses that would allow a clear delineation of her proposed theoretical path. Her main contribution to literary theory remains the aforementioned syntheses. These presented the state of the art of text theory with great erudition, and took care to identify the roots of the development of this field of knowledge, in particular the Czech, Russian and, above all, Polish schools.

Mayenowa's relatively limited influence as a theorist was also due to her dedication to meticulous documentary and interpretive work.[72] It seems that this tendency of hers can be read as a disposition typical of the Polish intelligentsia, in that she devoted herself to important tasks for the benefit of national culture while not caring excessively about chasing fame. Michał Głowiński, in particular, points to this, writing that she seemed much more concerned with the fate of the *Dictionary of Sixteenth-Century Polish* and the edition of Jan Kochanowski's works, which she coordinated and devoted most of her energy to in the last two decades of her life, than with her own career ambitions.[73] Also, of great importance in Mayenowa's *oeuvre* was her work on Slavic Comparative Metrics, which was led by a team formed on her initiative, modelled on Jakobson's ideas.

[70] By writing about the certain oblivion of Mayenowa's achievements, I am not suggesting that her works are completely forgotten, particularly in Poland. They continue to be cited, and some of her theoretical and organizational ideas, starting with the *Dictionary of Sixteenth-Century Polish,* and the conventions of editing sources that she developed, continue. My thesis is mainly concerned with the fact that she is no longer a canonical theorist, and her works did not enter wider international circulation. Meanwhile, I am convinced that their inspirational potential would definitely deserve such a promotion. I am referring in particular to her contributions to her approach to the study of literary texts based on linguistic analysis, that is, the theoretical programme of linguistic poetics that she developed.

[71] Mayenowa, *Poetyka teoretyczna.*

[72] Elżbieta Janus, 'A Page from the History of the University of Vilnius: Selected Biographical Threads', *Vilnius University Open Series,* 2021, pp. 314–27.

[73] Głowiński, 'Pani Mayenowa – próba portretu', p. 30.

The Metrics network also had political significance, as researchers from Czechoslovakia, Bulgaria and the USSR, critical of the authorities, came to workshop meetings.[74]

However, the structural factors that contributed to the certain oblivion of her achievements seem no less important. These are, first, the aforementioned shift away from structuralism toward traditionalist themes, which clearly did not draw Mayenowa in. The move away from structuralism and, more broadly, the abandonment of 'grand theories' was also a trend with global dimensions, specifically related to the process of the 'death of literary theory', that is, its loss of social relevance, as pointed out by Galin Tihanov.[75] Interestingly, on the global scene, certain elements of structural analysis returned with the emergence of discourse analysis in the 1970s. They re-emerged, for example, in the pages of *Poetics*, a journal founded in 1971 by Teun A. van Dijk. Mayenowa was referred to twice in the early issues of the journal, but no text of hers appeared on its pages. In English, she contributed to *Russian Literature* by presenting a brief synthesis of structuralist thought in Poland.[76] At the same time, at the turn of the 1970s and 1980s, on the same pages of *Poetics* there were a number of references to authors from the Prague and Russian schools. One should, however, also note that a redefinition of the dominant meaning of 'poetics' took place roughly during this period and was most clearly reflected in a change in the profile of the journal. In particular, from a periodical initially devoted to language and its structures, it became a journal focused on issues of the sociology of knowledge and science.

In turn, when discourse analysis, as a new incarnation of text analysis came to Poland (with a noticeable delay), its main points of reference were almost exclusively authors publishing in the West. It was rather through them that Prague and Russian references also returned to Poland, while the work of Mayenowa herself and her colleagues, which could have served as significant inspiration for the development of discourse analysis, became relatively marginalized. This weakness is particularly evident in citation patterns, especially during the renaissance in the interest in text theory which happened in the 1990s. This phenomenon is particularly well illustrated by Anna Duszak's (1950–2015) synthesis,

[74] Danuta Ulicka, 'Rzut oka na nowoczesne polskie literaturoznawstwo teoretyczne', in Ulicka (ed.), *Wiek teorii: Sto lat nowoczesnego literaturoznawstwa polskiego*. Warsaw, 2020, p. 87.

[75] Tihanov, *The Birth and Death of Literary Theory*.

[76] Maria Renata Mayenowa, 'Structural Thought in Poland', *Russian Literature*, 13, 3, 1983, pp. 313–31.

Text, Discourse, Communication,[77] which introduced discourse analysis to the Polish academic field. Duszak, who was a prominent professor of English at the University of Warsaw, but had much wider recognition in the field of linguistics, refers to Mayenowa and several other authors of her generation, but only mentions the existence of their works in passing. The key points of reference are Western figures such as Teun van Dijk and Norman Fairclough who dominated over the Polish authors, as well as the key proponents of the Czech school. Neither does Duszak refer to the works of Żółkiewski which could be a useful source of inspiration. This does not mean of course that Mayenowa's works are not evoked in the writings of her disciples, many of them eminent scholars who remain active to this day. However, this influence is mainly limited to Polish researchers and selected traditional subdisciplines of linguistics. It seems, therefore, that we are dealing here with a rather typical peripheral 'forgetting' of native traditions, instead drawing parallel inspiration from the global circulation of ideas. Similar ways of referring to the achievements of Mayenowa and her circle can also be observed in the younger generation of researchers.[78] The memory of Mayenowa's generation is restored only marginally in the form which could be seen as typical for peripheral academic fields, that is of works devoted to 'forgotten precursors'.

Sociological conclusion

Let me summarize my attempt at a sociological interpretation of Maria Renata Mayenowa's life trajectory. She was a descendant of the bourgeois elite of the Western periphery of the Russian Empire, which after its disintegration and the Bolshevik Revolution became part of the reborn Polish state, one which can be treated as a republic of the intelligentsia,[79] for in the Second Republic it is no longer the bourgeoisie that becomes the dominant faction of the elite (or to use Pierre Bourdieu's terms, the field of power). As I have suggested above, Mayenowa's trajectory, especially in her teenage years, can be read as a period of intense conversion of her parents' economic capital (which was significant only until World War One, but after that she could count on her first husband's economic resources) into cultural capital. It was a successful conversion, in the sense that the aforementioned economic capital facilitated her receiving

[77] Anna Duszak, *Tekst, dyskurs, komunikacja międzykulturowa*, Warsaw, 1998.

[78] See, for example, Waldemar Czachur, *Lingwistyka dyskursu jako integrujący program badawczy*, Wrocław, 2020.

[79] Zarycki, Smoczyński, Warczok, 'The Roots of Polish Culture-Centered Politics'.

higher education and also studying and preparing her doctorate at Vilnius University. After World War Two, she was a representative of the young generation of the intelligentsia who occupied dominant positions in the academic field (and often also in politics, as the biography of her colleague Stefan Żółkiewski shows), which she owed both to her family resources (including the financial resources of her parents) and to the investments made by the Second Republic in the elite research universities to which Vilnius University belonged in the interwar period. This generation invested all of its energies and resources, particularly its cultural competence, but also its social, and therefore its contacts, as well as its material, in their academic careers. This contributed to the significant development of Polish humanities and social sciences in the post-war period. It found special conditions for its development in the 'golden 1960s', when both the national political and international environments favoured them. At the same time, the field was being developed by a generation aspiring to participate in international academic life and which was also making ambitious attempts at theory-building in the social sciences and humanities. Forward-looking, it worked within the paradigm of modernization that was most often inspired by left thought in its various variants. Among its strengths was a creative combination of diverse strands of structuralism and variants of non-orthodox Marxism originating both from East and West.

There was no small number of discontinuities in the life of this generation. In Mayenowa's biography, there is at least a triple rupture: a break with bourgeois identity, a break with Jewish identity and a break with Russian culture. With the former, the rupture appears to be the strongest, while the last appears to be relatively limited. In the first two cases, perhaps even 'rupture' is not the best description, because it was not so much a matter of renunciation as of moving these identities and cultures to the private sphere. In any case, in Poland bourgeois identity as a group identity, not to mention class, completely disappeared. This contrasts with the tradition of aristocratic or landed gentry families, which often maintained, at least, their cultural identity, even if they moved completely to intelligentsia positions in the structural/class sense.[80] As far as Jewish identity on the collective level is concerned, it can be said that Mayenowa, with her choice to keep it as an element

[80] Rafał Smoczyński and Tomasz Zarycki, 'The Extended Family: Descendants of Nobility in Post-Communist Poland', *Communist and Post-Communist Studies*, 54, 4, 2021, pp. 157–75.

of her private identity, belonged to a generation that was divided, on the one hand, into those adopting such a tactic and, on the other, into those choosing Jewishness as their central identity and therefore usually leaving Poland sooner or later. Towards the end of her life, from the late 1970s, a revival of Jewish identity was initiated by a new generation of the intelligentsia.[81] The activities of these usually much younger circles can be related to the aforementioned broader wave of retraditionalization. Thus, this was a Jewishness not only reconstructed, but also designed in a completely different paradigm from the one in which Mayenowa lived during her childhood. An important component of the new project of Jewish identity in Poland was the rejection of the modernizing leftist project, linked in one way or another to the intellectual trends developing in Russia and then the USSR with a clear emancipatory aspect. The new Jewishness, in which Mayenowa was clearly not interested, was and still is, on the one hand, oriented toward the West as the only source of intellectual inspiration, which marginalized aspects of the Jewish heritage related to Russian and secular culture. On the other hand, it turned strongly toward tradition, including religion, and was strongly focused on the memory of the Holocaust.

The unequivocal turn to the West, as the sole source of modernity, social theory, intellectual innovation and social progress, was an important element of the changes that took place in the 1970s. This tendency can be seen as being structurally at odds with the perception of Russian culture, and Russian intellectual traditions in particular, as valuable and inspiring, which was an attitude close to Mayenowa. Not only was Russian her first culture, but on an intellectual level it remained an important source of her intellectual inspiration and an object of fascination. It was against this background that she built many contacts, primarily with Russian intellectuals and émigrés, including Roman Jakobson. The development of relations with Russians and the fascination with their achievements, especially after 1968, appeared to be less and less understood in circles of the Polish intelligentsia. The understanding of Russian culture which Mayenowa shared was perceived as increasingly odd in the last decade of Communism, when the dominant intellectual tendency was to recover Poland's 'forgotten' cultural ties with the West. Hence, the most recent waves of interest in the traditions of Russian

[81] Stanisław Krajewski, 'My wszyscy z niej: Dezasymilacja polskich Żydów', in Urszula Kurczewska, Małgorzata Głowania, Wojciech Ogrodnik and Dominik Wasilewski (eds), *Co się dzieje z polskim społeczeństwem? Księga jubileuszowa dedykowana Profesorowi Ireneuszowi Krzemińskiemu*, Warsaw, 2019, pp. 297–309.

theoretical schools came to post-Communist Poland again rather via the West than directly from Russia, and were not particularly strong, while the native intermediaries between the worlds of Polish and Russian culture, the generations of close Polish friends of Russian intellectuals to which Mayenowa belonged, became no longer interesting or relevant.

Repetition, Ageing and End of Life in Liudmila Ulitskaia's *The Body of the Soul*

BENJAMIN M. SUTCLIFFE

The Body of the Soul (*O tele dushi*), Liudmila Ulitskaia's 2019 volume of stories, humanizes the end of life and counters harmful mythologies about ageing as well as dying. Born in 1943, Ulitskaia published mainly in the 1990s to early 2000s and is the first woman to receive the Russian Booker Prize. She received the honour for *The Kukotsky Enigma* (*Kazus Kukotskogo*, 2001), a novel using the body to depict the darkest moments of Soviet history. Dying a natural death is an ordinary miracle in her prose, which portrays the USSR's political repression with a particular focus on Stalinism. In picturing old age, *The Body of the Soul* repeats topics and images from the writer's previous works. These deliberate recurrences, a culmination of previous themes, emphasize beliefs about the body and ideas that Ulitskaia values as a voice of the liberal intelligentsia.[1]

The author envisions ageing as inextricable from the bonds between flesh and soul. Ulitskaia is fascinated by this part of life, a phase defined by the present in addition to past memories. The volume's title makes clear that Ulitskaia believes the body to be spiritual (as opposed to merely corporeal) while the soul has a physical presence; these two components are complementary, not antagonistic. Ulitskaia's experience, shaped by the death of first her great-grandfather and then her mother, influences

Benjamin Sutcliffe is Professor of Russian at Miami University where he is Faculty Associate with the Havighurst Center for Russian and Post-Soviet Studies.

[1] For one of Ulitskaia's many comments supporting the intelligentsia, see 'Liudmila Ulitskaia: Rugat′ intelligentsiiu — uzhasnaia poshlost′′', interview with Ol′ga Mozgovaia, *Vecherniaia Moskva*, 29 May 2005, p. 5. Ulitskaia's latest volume of stories has been translated into English: Ludmila Ulitskaya, *The Body of the Soul: Stories (The Margellos World Republic of Letters)*, trans. Richard Pevear and Larissa Volokhonsky, New Haven, CT, 2023. In this article all translations from Ulitskaia's prose are my own unless otherwise indicated.

Slavonic and East European Review, 101, 3, 2023

the writer's views of dying. She notes that her own health is slowly failing. One of the few critics to address *The Body of the Soul* deems it her goodbye to readers.[2] However, this farewell is a surprisingly prolonged process in Ulitskaia's writing: in 2004, after the publication of her novel, *Sincerely Yours, Shurik* (*Iskrenne vash Shurik*), she speculated that she would abandon the genre. Instead, a string of acclaimed novels followed. The latest, *Jacob's Ladder* (*Lestnitsa Iakova*, 2015), summarized Ulitskaia's recurring themes of family, genetics and Stalinism. *The Body of the Soul*, like *Jacob's Ladder*, connects death to reconciliation and acceptance alongside loss.[3] The volume of stories illuminates how *telesnost′* (corporeality) is its own cosmos of meaning that can encompass ideas but does not depend on them. This axiom in Ulitskaia's writing contradicts two assumptions dominating Russian culture over the past century. The first is Orthodoxy's dichotomy between the eternal soul and mortal flesh; the second is the state's demand that the body serve ideology.[4]

These stories pair ageing with repetition. *The Body of the Soul* demonstrates that recurrence is a deliberate, creative and culturally significant part of the author's writing. In his seminal study of repetition, J. Hillis Miller succinctly explains it as 'one instance which then in one way or another reappears in another instance'.[5] This flexible definition shows that repetition is a creative component allowing literature to depict the connections that underpin the world, a world that begins with the body. Hillis discusses recurrences within a single novel. This approach fits Ulitskaia's *oeuvre*, which critics have compared to one overarching, unified work.

Natasha Sankovitch, exploring repetition in Russian literature, argues that it is 'the ability to recognize similarities' and is key to understanding

[2] E. Moroz, 'Ne govori s toskoi — ikh net…', *Znamia*, 5, 2020, pp. 216–19 (p. 216) <https://znamlit.ru/publication.php?id=7606> [accessed 14 June 2023].

[3] Liudmila Ulitskaia, *Iskrenne vash Shurik*, Moscow, 2005. For Ulitskaia's claim that *Sincerely Yours, Shurik* might be her last novel, see Ulitskaia, 'Liudmila Ulitskaia napisala, vozmozhno, svoi poslednii roman', *Newsru.com*, 8 April 2004 <https://www.newsru.com/cinema/08apr2004/uli.html> [accessed 14 June 2023]. Ulitskaia, *Lestnitsa Iakova*, Moscow, 2015. For a recent study of *Jacob's Ladder* and its place in her *oeuvre*, see Tünde Szabo [Tiunde Shabo], *Stat′i po poetike L. Ulitskoi*, Moscow, 2022. Concerning Ulitskaia's biography and her ties to the intelligentsia, see this early but insightful study, Maria Litovskaia, 'Lyudmila Ulitskaya', trans. Seth Graham, in Marina Balina and Mark Lipovetsky (eds), *Russian Writers since 1980*: *Dictionary of Literary Biography*, 285, Detroit, MI, 2004, pp. 329–35.

[4] On the importance of *telesnost′*, see Elizabeth Skomp and Benjamin Sutcliffe, *Ludmila Ulitskaya and the Art of Tolerance*, Madison, WI, 2015, pp. 66–67.

[5] J. Hillis Miller, *Fiction and Repetition*: *Seven English Novels*, Cambridge, MA, 1982, p. 1.

oneself and the world.[6] She notes how recurrence draws attention to likeness yet underscores each instance's individuality. *The Body of the Soul* uses repetition in three ways. Recurring themes accentuate the humane values of the intelligentsia: respect, honesty and altruistic intellect. Repetition also recalls the violence reverberating through Soviet culture and Ulitskaia's writing. Its third purpose is to uncover connections between characters. These three functions are a summation of Ulitskaia's previous works. They likewise help the volume portray ageing and the end of life, focusing on the body as a repetition of the life it has lived.[7]

The problem with death: Ageing, dying and Russian culture

The Body of the Soul represents how ageing leads to the end of life, a truism that Ulitskaia renders as nuanced and intriguing. In the process she negotiates two interrelated issues: giving the body its own identity while honouring the past of her characters. As Peter Öberg notes, society often views the ageing body as problematic; Elisabeth Bronfen and Sarah Webster Goodwin, for example, decry the cultural and political symbolism that obscures the act of dying.[8] Loss of life is key to literature's portrayal of the USSR but also implies a subordination of *telesnost´* to the state. Helena Goscilo and Andrea Lanoux contend that Russian culture often limits the body to being a victim or loyal servant of political efforts to remake society.[9] Ulitskaia's prose gives a graphic example when it depicts the mass suffocations as crowds rushed to view Stalin's corpse in 1953. She deems this scene important enough to repeat the portrayal in two novels. The dictator's funeral reifies the results of forcing the flesh to serve ideology: Stalin's policies ended the lives of millions, then even his body compelled people to trample others.[10]

[6] On Ulitskaia's *oeuvre* as a single work see, for instance, Radostina Veleva, 'Romanite na Liudmila Ulitskaia — mezhdu traditsiiata i novata slovesnost', *Bol´garskaia rusistika*, 1–2, 2010, pp. 154–60 (p. 155); Natasha Sankovitch, *Creating and Recovering Experience: Repetition in Tolstoy*, Palo Alto, CA, 1998, p. 5.

[7] For one discussion of intelligentsia values, see Dmitrii Likhachev, 'O russkoi intelligentsii', in O. V. Panchenko et al. (eds), *Vospominaniia, razdum´ia, raboty raznykh let*, St Petersburg, 2006, vol. 2, pp. 382, 389.

[8] Peter Öberg, 'Image versus Experience of the Aging Body', in Christopher Faircloth (ed.), *Aging Bodies: Images and Everyday Experience*, Walnut Creek, CA, 2003, pp. 103–42 (p. 103); Elisabeth Bronfen and Sarah Webster Goodwin, 'Introduction', in *Death and Representation*, Baltimore, MD, 1993, pp. 3–35 (p. 4).

[9] Helena Goscilo and Andrea Lanoux, 'Introduction: Lost in the Myths', in Helena Goscilo and Andrea Lanoux (eds), *Gender and National Identity in Twentieth-Century Russian Culture*, DeKalb, IL, 2006, pp. 3–29 (p. 20).

[10] On the deaths at Stalin's funeral, see Ulitskaia, *Kazus Kukotskogo*, Moscow, 2002,

Soviet culture politicized ageing as well as death. Every year on 9 May ranks of older veterans remind the world of the USSR's victory over Hitler, implying that the individual physical form mattered because it symbolized something greater. At the same time, as Susan Grant and Isaac McKean Scarborough explore, for policymakers 'pensioners were [...] a "problem" or "crisis" to be solved' as the state struggled to care for its ageing population.[11] Ulitskaia's images of the older body in *The Body of the Soul* react against such misconceptions but also have a more specific source. Her style and topics belong to women's prose (*zhenskaia proza*), a diffuse trend that shaped late- and post-Soviet literature. She follows the precedent of Natal′ia Baranskaia and I. Grekova (pseudonym of Elena Ventsel′), whose images of ageing *intelligentki* influenced fiction in the Brezhnev era.[12] Some critics assailed women's prose for alleged lack of originality, not realizing that its themes recurred because they were ongoing problems ignored by society. (Ulitskaia's writing was similarly attacked.)[13] Her characterization of older people emulates the ways *zhenskaia proza* associates the body, daily life, the past and trauma.

The USSR's collapse changed conceptions of ageing and death but the body remained a troubling symbol. In the 1990s older people exemplified the socialist past that had been lost, as opposed to the Soviet cult of the future that preferred youth. The ageing population became simply another sign of a crisis where declining birth rates and high mortality raised the xenophobic fear that ethnic Russians could become a minority in 'their own' country. The poverty, hopelessness and vulnerability ascribed to older citizens stoked what Serguei Oushakine labels a 'patriotism of despair'.[14]

p. 138, and Ulitskaia, *Zelenyi shater*, Moscow, 2011, pp. 67, 69, 73.

[11] Susan Grant and Isaac McKean Scarborough, 'Introduction: Ageing in a Soviet Context', in Susan Grant and Isaac McKean Scarborough (eds), *Geriatrics and Ageing: Medical, Political and Social Contexts in the Soviet Union*, London, 2023, pp. 1–14 (p. 2).

[12] On ageing and death in the works of Baranskaia and Grekova, see Benjamin Sutcliffe, *The Prose of Life: Russian Women Writers from Khrushchev to Putin*, Madison, WI, 2009, pp. 24–57. Goscilo surveys how Ulitskaia builds on earlier writing by other women. See 'Perestroika and Post-Soviet Prose: From Dazzle to Dispersal', in Adele Barker and Jehanne Gheith (eds), *A History of Women's Writing in Russia*, Cambridge, 2002, pp. 297–312 (pp. 303, 309–10).

[13] Pavel Basinskii gives an early, misguided critique of women's prose as recycling previous topics: 'Pozabyvshie dobro? Zametki na poliakh "novoi zhenskoi prozy"', *Literaturnaia gazeta*, 7, 1991, p. 10. On repetition in Ulitskaia's earlier writing, see Ol′ga Rychova, 'Knizhnik. Damskie shtuchki', *Literaturnaia gazeta*, 39–40, 2005, p. 13.

[14] Serguei Oushakine, *The Patriotism of Despair: Nation, War, and Loss in Russia*, Ithaca, NY, 2009, pp. 5, 101–03. Michele Rivkin-Fish analyses the links between xenophobia and declining birthrates in 'From 'Demographic Crisis' to 'Dying Nation': The Politics of Language and Reproduction in Russia', in Goscilo and Lanoux (eds), *Gender and National*

Gerontologist Irina Grigoryeva argues against such apocalyptic associations, countering that ageing is a rich period of life defined by far more than state neglect or economic suffering. *The Body of the Soul* moves beyond what Öberg critiques as culture's 'misery perspective' on ageing. Even Ulitskaia's dying characters evince hope, focusing more on a variegated past than the infirmity of the present.[15] In the 2000s Vladimir Putin appealed to the older generation and others left behind by El′tsin's shock therapy. Putin, far from young when he took office, nonetheless promised vigour, masculine resolve and respect for the USSR's history. Ulitskaia fiercely rejects Putin's supposedly revitalized body politic, which co-opts older citizens through a falsely heroic vision of the Soviet past.[16] In the 2022 invasion of Ukraine the state used the image of an older woman brandishing a Soviet flag, welcoming Russia's so-called liberation, a gesture that conflated ageing, nostalgia for the USSR and support for the occupiers.[17]

Ulitskaia reclaims ageing and the end of life as more personal than political. Death, she maintains, imparts significance (*bytie*) and connects us to those we love. Her belief illuminates the body's central place in everyday life, a scenario Christopher Faircloth defines as the 'corporality of mundane practice'.[18] In Ulitskaia's prose preparing for death is a process that begins long before the final days. This is one reason why she supports the charity Hospice, an organization which aids patients and their families

Identity in Twentieth-Century Russian Culture, pp. 151–73.

15 'Introduction', in Irina Grigoryeva, Lyudmila Vidiasova, Alexandra Dmitrieva and Olga Sergeyeva, *Elderly Population in Modern Russia: Between Work, Education and Health*, Cham, 2019, p. 5; Öberg, 'Image versus Experience of the Aging Body', p. 103. Christopher Faircloth underlines the need to understand that the lives of the ageing are not defined only by growing older. Faircloth, 'Introduction. Different Bodies and the Paradox of Aging: Locating Aging Bodies in Images and Everyday Experience', in *Aging Bodies*, pp. 1–28 (p. 17).

16 On Putin's carefully crafted image, see Helena Goscilo (ed.), *Putin as Celebrity and Cultural Icon*, New York, 2013. For one of Ulitskaia's earlier critiques of Putin and the Soviet past, see the interview 'Ia ne khochu golosovat′ za men′shee zlo', *Russkii kur′er*, 10 March 2004, p. 1.

17 In 2022 Ulitskaia fled Russia for Berlin, where she harshly condemns Putin's aggression in Ukraine. See Sil′viia Noinraiter, 'Esli voinu ostanoviat, to eto budet zasluga zhenshchin', interview with Liudmila Ulitskaia, *Deutsche Welle*, 1 April 2022 <https://www.dw.com/ru/ljudmila-ulizkaya-esli-vojna-budet-ostanovlena-eto-budet-zasluga-zhenchin/a-61326679> [accessed 14 June 2023]. On the symbolism of the 'grandmother' with the Soviet flag, see '"Babushka s sovetskim flagom" — novyi simvol rossiiskoi propagandy. 9 maia ee skul′ptury ustanoviat v mnogikh rossiiskiikh gorodakh', *Meduza*, 5 May 2022 <https://meduza.io/feature/2022/05/05/babushka-s-sovetskim-flagom-novyy-simvol-rossiyskoy-propagandy-9-maya-ee-skulpturu-ustanovyat-vo-mnogih-rossiyskih-gorodah> [accessed 14 June 2023].

18 For discussion of death and *bytie*, see Ulitskaia, *Sviashchennyi musor*, Moscow, 2012, p. 412; Faircloth, 'Introduction', p. 14.

at the end of life. It models itself on the notion that it is the duty of the intelligentsia to help the less fortunate, transforming this abstract ideal of altruism into tangible actions. For Ulitskaia death should elicit kindness and understanding that join the dying to those around them; it must not become a moment that furthers state control.[19] *The Body of the Soul* continues this concern, using repetition to depict ageing and dying as interconnected phases that draw on recurring images from the past.

The beauty of ageing and life's end

Long before her 2019 collection, Ulitskaia broke new ground with images focusing on ageing where younger female characters bathe older women or accompany them to the *bania*. These moments connected scarred and sagging bodies to difficult lives, a pairing that Soviet culture shunned in favour of strength and fecundity. Ulitskaia regrets that Russian lacks an appropriate lexicon to describe sexuality, worrying that language veers toward the extremes of degrading obscenities or coldly medical terminology.[20] Scholars have overlooked how the same gap exists for ageing; Ulitskaia's writing fills this lacuna. Beginning with her earliest stories, she portrays the bodies of older characters in a complex, sympathetic manner. Many critics misunderstand this stance, mocking Ulitskaia for emphasizing life's physical and banal aspects. These detractors disregard how, in depicting the body as the heart of everyday existence, she uncovers the astounding in the corporeal and quotidian.[21] For Ulitskaia ageing is not a condition to be disparaged. Instead, her prose reveals it to be a difficult, essential process that builds on the past yet adds meaning to both flesh and spirit.

The Body of the Soul opens with a poem — 'I Do Not Need Any Others... Instead of a Foreword' ('Mne ne nado drugikh... Vmesto predisloviia'). The title is fitting given that many of the stories that follow are dedicated

[19] Ulitskaia discusses preparing for death in Mariia Bashmakova, 'Liudmila Ulitskaia: 'Smert′ tozhe prinadlezhit zhizni': Znamenityi pisatel′ — o mnogolikosti tela i dushi', *Novaia gazeta*, 17 November 2019 <https://novayagazeta.ru/articles/2019/11/17/82761-lyudmila-ulitskaya-smert-tozhe-prinadlezhit-zhizni> [accessed 14 June 2023]. For a discussion of Hospice, see Ulitskaia, *Sviashchennyi musor*, p. 463.

[20] See the bathing scenes in Ulitskaia, *Kazus Kukotskogo*, pp. 395, 410 and 442, and *Zelenyi shater*, pp. 350, 340. In *Jacob's Ladder* one of the protagonists bathes her grandmother's body in preparation for burial (*Lestnitsa Iakova*, pp. 21–22). On the limits of the Russian language and sex, see Ulitskaia, *Sviashchennyi musor*, pp. 210–11.

[21] For criticism of the physiological and mundane in Ulitskaia's prose see, among others, Lev Kuklin, 'Kazus Ulitskoi', *Neva*, 7, 2003, pp. 177–89 (p. 179), and Nikolai Aleksandrov, 'Chuda ne proizoshlo. "Liudi nashego tsaria" Liudmily Ulitskoi', *Izvestiia*, 27 July 2005.

to the author's friends. Its verses celebrate girls and women, beginning with childhood in post-war Moscow, then describing a woman who uses a cane after a stroke.[22] Accepting ageing and its various travails, the poem contextualizes growing older within a variety of friendships over almost eight decades. The lines recall one of Ulitskaia's first short-story cycles, *Girls* (*Devochki*), which explores the warmth and rivalry between children in Moscow during Stalin's last years. *The Body of the Soul* finishes what those much earlier works begin: investigating how *telesnost′* develops, changes and ages. Ulitskaia's prose thus depicts the body in all its stages, suggesting that *telesnost′* is a continuing part of existence.

Even death has its own beauty. 'Autopsy' ('Autopsiia'), the volume's penultimate story, makes this clear as it opens with the aged pathologist Kogan praising the corpses he examines:

> Kogan loved his nightmarish work, especially his corpses that had died at their own pace [*svoevremenno ushedshikh*] — old, worn out by life, bald, having lost the lively vegetation under armpits and on groins, the well-trodden heels, rough and calloused, their flaccid breasts and scrotums. [...] In Kogan's thoughts a pathologist was a priest of all that was purely of the body [*sviashchennikom chistoi telesnosti*], the last cleaner of the cathedral that the soul had abandoned.[23]

In this story the corpses are far less important than the individuals' past lives. Despite many deeming the pathologist's work 'nightmarish', the narrator quickly establishes the opposite: the pathologist's gaze is precise yet respectful as it discerns the personal histories written on the deceased. The body in death is a specific form of repetition: a corporeal recurrence of the life it has lived, where 'well-trodden heels' and callouses indicate their owners' hardships. Kogan is one of Ulitskaia's benevolent doctors, combining care for others with extensive knowledge of *telesnost′*. Like the gynaecologist Pavel Alekseevich in *The Kukotsky Enigma*, he finds beauty in those facets of the physical ('flaccid breasts and scrotums') that Russian literature eschews. Analysing repetition, Miller observes that recurrence highlights essential beliefs shared by humanity. By this logic Kogan's similarity to previous characters implies that Ulitskaia believes the physical form is itself a thing of beauty.[24] The narrator deems Kogan

[22] Ulitskaia, 'Mne ne nado drugikh... Vmesto predisloviia', *O tele dushi. Novye rasskazy*, Moscow, 2019, p. 6.

[23] Ulitskaia, 'Autopsiia', *O tele dushi*, p. 63.

[24] Miller, *Fiction and Repetition*, p. 15. Kogan's eulogy continues the theme of another

a cleric of what is 'purely of the body'; the phrase hints that spirituality, dying and corporeality are complementary. They form the 'cathedral' of the flesh, an image that resembles the 'body of the soul' giving the collection its title.

The volume's first story, 'Dragon and Phoenix' ('Drakon i feniks'), relays how Armenian Musia sits by the bedside of her Azerbaijani wife, Zarifa, who is dying of cancer in a Cyprus hospital. Musia cries because 'Zarifa had not eaten for a week, would not take a bite, just drank a lot and into the plastic bag trickled no longer a rose-coloured liquid but something violently red'.[25] Musia is not repelled by the contents of the catheter but is worried by the colour of the body's waste: Zarifa's urine is another indication that death is near. This scene recalls *Medea and Her Children* (*Medeiia i ee deti*, 1996), whose Greek Orthodox protagonist cares for her Jewish husband after an unsuccessful operation for stomach cancer. Medea, inspecting Samuel's bedpan, is alarmed that his excrement contains food barely digested as the disease weakens him:

> Samuel at first turned away squeamishly, embarrassed at the exposing of this unpleasant physiology, but then he detected that Medea was not having to make the slightest effort to conceal revulsion, and that she was much more concerned about the inflamed edge of the wound or a delay in the outpouring of porridge which had only slightly changed its appearance than about the unpleasant smell coming from the wound.[26]

Medea, a former nurse, pays close attention to the collapse of Samuel's body. Worry for her husband eclipses any reaction to his 'unpleasant smell'. Her care conveys to readers that the problems of *telesnost'* are an appropriate topic for literature even when removed from politics. Discussing age studies, Stephen Katz explains that the field looks at 'the 'inside of aging'; in Ulitskaia's prose what the dying and their caregivers experience reminds us that such statements have a physical as well as metaphorical meaning.[27]

story in the volume. 'Alisa Purchases Death' ('Alisa pokupaet smert'') opens with the observation that 'When life had been lived to perfection, old age began'. The story details the love that defines Alisa's final years: she marries a doctor under the condition that he will help end her life when she feels the time is right. It is the doctor who dies first; Alisa then adopts his grandchild, discovering that yet another unexpected phase has begun for her. Ulitskaia, 'Alisa pokupaet smert'', *O tele dushi*, pp. 16, 22.

25 Ulitskaia, 'Drakon i feniks', *O tele dushi*, p. 9.

26 Ludmila Ulitskaya, *Medea and Her Children*, trans. Arch Tait, New York, 2002, p. 187.

27 Stephen Katz, 'What is Age Studies?', *Age Culture Humanities*, 1, 2014, pp. 17–23 (p. 20).

Following a pattern in Ulitskaia's writing, Samuel, Medea, Musia and Zarifa represent how cultural and religious differences are less important than decades of life together. The ailing, ageing body manifests this truth while hinting that older characters grew up in a time kinder than the Soviet era. In *Medea and Her Children*, for instance, the protagonist preserves the pre-revolutionary culture the USSR tried to destroy. Medea is 'the last pure-blooded Greek of a family settled since time immemorial on the Tauride coast' of Crimea; she escaped the deportations that rocked the region under Stalin.[28] The narrator of 'Dragon and Phoenix' recalls how Zarifa and Musia attended the first school for girls in what later became Nagorno-Karabakh, before the Armenian genocide and the Bolsheviks' conquest of the Caucasus. The two characters come from an epoch when knowledge of Greek and Pushkin was more important than ethnic or ideological identity. The early bond of education provided a common heritage that lingers on despite Zarifa's approaching death.[29]

Ulitskaia depoliticizes death and illness. Unlike Solzhenitsyn, whose *Gulag Archipelago* construed the camps as a cancer metastasizing throughout the USSR, Ulitskaia does not make disease into social commentary. 'Dragon and Phoenix' gives no hint, for instance, that Zarifa's malady comes from the psychic toll Musia and Zarifa paid as the first lesbians from Russia to marry in Amsterdam. They are forced to live abroad due to Putin's homophobic policies; for the same reason they would be shunned (or worse) in the Caucasus. Cancer and the characters' response to it contribute to the story's unusually strong sense of conviction, which sets the tone for the volume.[30] 'Dragon and Phoenix' legitimates morality and mortality as virtues that are personal, not ideological.

Aside from *Medea and Her Children*, 'Dragon and Phoenix' draws on two other Ulitskaia works. All emphasize the 'low-key' role of *telesnost'* which Helena Goscilo admired in the author's early writing. They also reinforce what David Van Tassel sees as a core tenet of ageing: it is a lifelong process that does not begin at a certain moment.[31] The account of Zarifa's

[28] On Medea representing a more civilized era, see Anja Grothe, 'Medusa, Cassandra, Medea: Re-inscribing Myth in Contemporary German and Russian Women's Writing', unpublished PhD thesis, City University of New York, 2000, p. 267. Ulitskaya, *Medea and Her Children*, p. 3.

[29] Ulitskaia, 'Drakon i feniks', p. 8.

[30] On this sense of conviction, see Moroz, 'Ne govori s toskoi', p. 217.

[31] Goscilo, 'Introduction', in Ayesha Kagal and Natal′ia Perova (eds), *Present Imperfect: Stories by Russian Women*, Boulder, CO, 1996, pp 1–10 (p. 6); David Van Tassel, 'Introduction', in David Van Tassel (ed.), *Aging, Death, and the Completion of Being*, Philadelphia, PA, 1979, pp. ix–xix (p. x).

last days inherits the themes of growing older from 'Gulia' (1994), where the protagonist sleeps with a younger man who has long been attracted to her.[32] 'Dragon and Phoenix' depicts ageing and death as only part of a long, eventful life, just as 'Gulia' does not let its unusual romance overshadow the main character's many friendships and time in the gulag.

The third source for 'Dragon and Phoenix' is 'March 1953' ('Vtorogo marta togo zhe goda...', 1991). In this story Lily's great-grandfather Aaron is dying of cancer, which coincides with the death of Stalin and Lily's first menstruation. Like most older Ulitskaia characters, Aaron is a member of the intelligentsia. He finds peace within his family, which compensates for declining health and the mounting antisemitism of early 1953. Aaron in turn distracts Lily from the simmering hatred of the Doctors' Plot and the unstoppable changes within her own body. She takes comfort in his stories and smell, which resembles camphor and old books, as her great-grandfather's tales transport the girl to another world:[33]

> Aaron would tell her of Daniel, or Gideon, of legendary heroes of the past and fair virgins, of wise men and czars with obscure names, all of them long-dead members of their tribe, until Lily was firmly persuaded that her great-grandfather, himself so ancient, must have known and personally remembered some of them at least.[34]

The old man and the teenager draw strength from each other. Aaron's stories give Lily a sense of her 'tribe' and become a substitute for her father, who is a warden in a distant labour camp. This absent parent belongs to the totalitarian culture trying to erase Judaism and supplant the bonds between family members. Aaron, however, emphasizes the importance of humanely shaping the next generation — in Ulitskaia's prose the way one completes life is a moral act that influences those who remain. Storytelling is crucial to this process; indeed, for Faircloth personal narratives are important to age studies. They convey knowledge, shape identity and reveal that how one thinks about ageing is as important as the physical aspects of growing old.[35]

[32] Ulitskaia, 'Gulia', *Bednye, zlye, liubimye. Povesti i rasskazy*, Moscow, 2002, pp. 33–94 (p. 93).

[33] Ulitskaia, 'Vtorogo marta togo zhe goda...', *Bednye, zlye, liubimye*, pp. 163–77 (pp. 163–67, 176). Skomp and Sutcliffe discuss the ways Aaron and Ulitskaia's older characters preserve the past: *Ludmila Ulitskaya*, pp. 54–55, 60.

[34] Ludmila Ulitskaya, 'March 1953', in *Present Imperfect*, pp. 11–24 (p. 12).

[35] Faircloth, 'Introduction', pp. 20–21.

Aaron's decline also draws on Ulitskaia's own experience. She had herself recovered from a tumor in her breast while several close relatives died from the disease. The writer's great-grandfather had been a bulwark similar to Aaron. When he passed away from cancer, she mourned, but death made a 'good impression' on the future author. As Ulitskaia explains, '[m]y great-grandfather died the wonderful death of a prophet. And I, it is important to remember, received his blessing [*blagoslovenie*]'.[36] His cancer was not excessively painful, which formed Ulitskaia's understanding that dying is the natural conclusion of life, as opposed to something to be feared. Because she was the only great-grandchild, her great-grandfather gave her his 'blessing'. Ulitskaia notes that her grandmother also peacefully died from cancer. Her mother's struggle was more difficult, leaving the author with bad memories of Moscow's radiation institute.[37]

'March 1953', *Medea and Her Children* and 'Dragon and Phoenix' repeat similar themes and protagonists. They also have a less evident commonality, as Ulitskaia's characters all escape violent ends during the purges, the Holocaust and the post-Soviet conflicts in the Caucasus. Their peaceful deaths, however, hint at the bloody alternative that befell many in the intelligentsia. This disturbing possibility is another function of recurrence in Ulitskaia's prose: repetition draws the reader's attention to an absence shaping what is present in her works. As Cathy Caruth notes, trauma is an event that is suffered again and again as victims try to repair their lives. Oushakine argues that this repetition becomes part of life for those who lived through the Soviet era. Zarifa's death recalls Samuel's, which resembles Aaron's — all die from cancer yet could have perished at the hands of the state.[38] *Jacob's Ladder* gives one such harrowing example as it depicts the destruction of the intelligentsia in the gulag. The narrator describes the Abez camp's 'gigantic cemetery — almost four hectares. [...] In the winter snow mercifully covered the graves that had been dug during

[36] Ulitskaia, *Sviashchennyi musor*, p. 409.

[37] On Ulitskaia's cancer and the death of her grandmother, see ibid., pp. 427, 410. The writer discusses her mother in 'Liudmila Ulitskaia: "Smert′ tozhe prinadlezhit zhizni"'. Ulitskaia's mother was only 53 when she died: 'Liudmila Ulitskaia rasskazyvaet o novoi knige "O tele dushi. Novye rasskazy"', *Litres*, 27 May 2020 <https://www.youtube.com/watch?v=tKhxwaTfGFw> [accessed 14 June 2023]. Ulitskaia describes Moscow's radiation institute in *Sviashchennyi musor*, p. 423.

[38] Cathy Caruth, 'Introduction,' in Cathy Caruth (ed.), *Trauma: Explorations in Memory*, Baltimore, MD, 1995, pp. 3–12 (pp. 4–5). Sergei Ushakin, '"Nam etoi bol′iu dyshat′?" O travme, pamiati i soobshchestvakh', in Sergei Ushakin and Elena Trubina (eds), *Travma: punkty*, Moscow, 2009, pp. 5–41 (pp. 8–9).

the year, each one for fifty corpses, but in spring when the snow receded, the thawed dead men poked up through the ground'.[39] The mass grave was the fate of many *intelligenty* whose final resting place is unknown or forgotten. By contrast, Ulitskaia's depictions of dying in peace make each death into a monument that unites generations.

Ageing, acceptance, compassion

While Ulitskaia does not idealize the approach of death, she implies it brings characters together as they come to terms with dying. Her 2005 nonfiction story, 'What For and For What' ('Za chto i dlia chego') pairs the Orthodox virtue of acceptance (*smirenie*) and the ageing body. Nadezhda Konstantinovna, daughter of the Silver Age poet Konstantin Bal′mont, is accidentally pushed off a crowded bus while taking food to be blessed before Easter. The bus drives over her leg, which then must be amputated. Nadezhda Konstantinovna reconciles herself with this tragedy, believing she needs to 'sit and think' instead of being constantly on the move.[40] An unintended, humble imitation of Christ on the cross, the protagonist's 'coming to peace' (*primirennost′*) astounds the narrator. Reconciled with her fate, the older woman subtly models acceptance for ensuing generations: this virtue unites flesh and spirit through the Orthodoxy that Ulitskaia embraced decades after her secular Jewish upbringing. She stresses that it is everyday actions — not Church dogma — that define her sense of Christianity, a statement that reinforces how living rightly is more important than adhering to ideas.[41]

Accepting the final phase of life is a concept that recurs in Ulitskaia's recent interviews. Discussing *The Body of the Soul* and her own ageing, she observes:

> I am one of those people who gets wiser over the years, it seems to me. Ageing is a rather disgusting process [*dovol′no otvratitel′noe iavlenie*]

[39] Ulitskaia, *Lestnitsa Iakova*, pp. 677–78.

[40] Ulitskaia, 'Za chto i dlia chego', *Liudi nashego tsaria*, Moscow, 2005, pp. 257–58. On Nadezhda Konstantinovna's identity, see Ulitskaia, *Sviashchennyi musor*, p. 88. Her novella, *The Funeral Party*, elaborates on acceptance and the dying body. *Veselye pokhorony*, Moscow, 2000.

[41] While she criticizes Christianity's links to wealth and power, her fiction praises *smirenie* as one of the religion's enduring positive values. For a comment castigating this faith's ties to the rich, see Ulitskaia, *Daniel′ Shtain, perevodchik*, Moscow, 2006, p. 498. On actions versus dogma, see Ulitskaia, 'Mladshaia shestidesiatnitsa', interview with Mariia Sedykh, *Obshchaia gazeta*, 20, 2002, p. 8.

> and one needs to apply a certain amount of strength to resist biological degradation. On the whole I have internally reconciled myself with ageing [...]. You learn acceptance [*smireniiu*].[42]

Ageing makes one 'wiser' as we practice 'acceptance' while also trying to forestall 'degradation'. Ulitskaia bemoans the body's changes as death approaches but believes we can 'resist' despair while also being 'internally reconciled' with the end of life. The decline of one's physical state coincides with the wisdom accrued over previous decades.

The Body of the Soul also defines this period as a time for mending broken ties. 'Dragon and Phoenix' relates how Zarifa calls Said, her estranged brother. Knowing death is close, she wants to see him, despite Said and other relatives having left her wedding when they discovered she was marrying Musia. Said forgets his abhorrence of homosexuality and arrives from the Caucasus with the heirloom rug that is one of Zarifa's last requests. His sister's impending death makes him understand that family is more important than prejudice, a simple realization whose recurrence shows how key it is to Ulitskaia's world-view.[43]

Caring for others is another moral lesson. The story 'Blessed Are Those, Who...' ('Blagoslovennye te, kotorye...') references a prayer that scholar Aleksandra Vikent′evna translates after seeing a statue of the Virgin Mary as intercessor for the aged. Vikent′evna's daughters, Lidiia and Nina, discover the text among her mother's papers in Italy where she stayed before her death. The lines enumerate a litany of thanks:

> Blessed are those who look on me with compassion [*uchastie*],
> Blessed are those who adjust their pace to mine, tired and slowed,
> Blessed are those who speak loudly into my deafened ear,
> Blessed are those who tenderly squeeze my trembling hands,
> Blessed are those who listen with interest to the stories of my long-departed youth,
> Blessed are those who understand my thirst for companionship,
> Blessed are those who give me their valuable time,

42 Nataliia Lomykina, '"Blizost′ k smerti — khoroshee ispytanie': Liudmila Ulitskaia o novoi knige, zhenskoi druzhbe i otnosheniiakh s vozrastom', *Forbes Woman*, 18 November 2019 <https://www.forbes.ru/forbes-woman/387365-blizost-k-smerti-horoshee-ispytanie-lyudmila-ulickaya-o-novoy-knige-zhenskoy> [accessed 14 June 2023].

43 Ulitskaia, 'Drakon i feniks', pp. 11, 14. On family and Ulitskaia's philosophy, see Sutcliffe, 'Everyday Life and the Ties that Bind in Liudmila Ulitskaia's *Medea and Her Children*', in David Ransel et al. (eds), *Everyday Life in Russia: Subjectivities, Perspectives, and Lived Experience*, Bloomington, IN, 2015, pp. 311–25.

Blessed are those who remember about my loneliness,
Blessed are those who are beside me in the minutes of my suffering,
Blessed are those who make me happy in the last days of my life,
Blessed are those who will hold my hand at the moment of my departure.[44]

The lines laud the ordinary goodness of those that comfort the dying. The prayer's repeated phrase ('blessed are those') requests God's favour not for the speaker, but for the people who assist her. Here recurrence is a stylistic device that mimics the patience needed again and again by speaker and friends. Companionship and 'compassion' are precious gifts that the cold and distant Aleksandra Vikent′evna craved in her old age. The prayer astounds Lidiia and Nina. The sisters now comprehend that, by blaming their mother for ignoring them earlier in life, they overlooked Vikent′evna's loneliness in her final days. The sisters likewise understand that they unjustly accused each other of receiving more of their mother's love. Critic Il′ia Nichiporov emphasizes how this story encapsulates two of the volume's main themes: reconciliation and the approach of death.[45] Another is compassion, which connotes recognizing and trying to reduce another's suffering. Aleksandra Vikent′evna posthumously asserts the value of mercy and togetherness through words, the only medium the scholar knows to impart emotions. Yet the prayer is grounded in old age's 'deafened ear' and 'trembling hands'; the speaker depends on others as the flesh weakens. This story demonstrates that reassuring daily contact helps those in the the final period of life. The repeated invocation, 'Blessed are those', accentuates Ulitskaia's belief that all deserve dignity and compassion as death approaches. The body is the core of these experiences. Without *telesnost′* the story's prayers and thanks are nothing more than elaborately empty abstractions.

Death and commemoration

Ulitskaia's prose focuses less on important events than how these fit into long lives; death is no exception. *The Body of the Soul* depicts this point as the time when memories about the deceased take the place of their actions. 'Dragon and Phoenix' deemphasizes the moment of Zarifa's passing. The narrator states only:

[44] Ulitskaia, 'Blagoslovennye te, kotorye…', *O tele dushi*, pp. 43, 41–42. For the Italian text, see 'Cantico di un anziano' <https://www.dominicanes.it/predicazione/briciole-di-luce/780-cantico-di-un-anziano.html> [accessed 14 June 2023].

[45] Il′ia Nichiporov, 'Predmetnyi mir v sbornike rasskazov Liudmily Ulitskoi "O tele dushi"', *Art Logos (Iskusstvo slova)*, 3, 2020, pp. 84–91 (p. 88) <https://istina.ips.ac.ru/publications/article/331850702/> [accessed 14 June 2023].

> That night [she] died. Musia sat by her until the very last minute. The doctor was also there, watching the monitor more than the departing patient. The line on the monitor shivered occasionally and then stopped moving and Zarifa was no longer [*Zarify ne stalo*].[46]

Death is integrated into a scene where Musia is at Zarifa's side; the doctor and screen that officially mark the end of life are overshadowed by the women's years together. 'Autopsy' offers a similar message. The reader never learns exactly when Kogan passes away; he dies dreaming of the miraculous flautist whose corpse he examined. The deceased young man beckons the pathologist to follow his music:

> The next morning his wife called twice for him to come to breakfast but he did not come. She went into his study. Kogan lay dead under the checked plaid blanket and was smiling.[47]

The volume's concluding story, 'Serpentine' ('Serpantin') takes a seemingly different approach as it chronicles librarian Nadezhda Georgievna's slide into dementia. The story is dedicated to one of Ulitskaia's longtime friends, Ekaterina Genieva, who headed Moscow's Library of Foreign Literature.[48] This institution is a favourite place of the capital's liberal intelligentsia, symbolizing how the shared knowledge between countries and cultures enriches readers. Nadezhda Georgievna's memory becomes as ephemeral and fragile as a serpentine streamer, a word that initiates the plot when she forgets the term:

> Words, last names, numbers slipped away. Words and numbers were not the problem. What was worse was how she noticed that, going to the kitchen to get some water, on the way she forgot why she was going and went back to where she came from, remembered, then set out for the kitchen once again. Numerous trips to get a cup, dish, a towel. She lost her passport although, truth be told, she then found it.[49]

[46] Ulitskaia, 'Drakon i feniks', p. 14.

[47] Ulitskaia, 'Autopsiia', p. 67.

[48] On Ulitskaia's friendship with Genieva and the library's (now endangered) role in promoting tolerance and understanding, see 'Chelovek kul´tury: Liudmila Ulitskaia o Ekaterine Genievoi', *Piatnichnyi Gor´kii*, 10 July 2017 <https://gorky.media/intervyu/chelovek-kultury/> [accessed 14 June 2023].

[49] Ulitskaia, 'Serpantin', *O tele dushi*, p. 69.

The narrator knows what Nadezhda Georgievna will not admit: this is the beginning of dementia's merciless onslaught. Many of Ulitskaia's longtime readers might also be aware of this because of their own advancing age or experience with older relatives.[50] During the final stages of dementia, Nadezhda Georgievna is in an expensive nursing home near Moscow. One morning she sits with a feeling of calming blankness (*belizna*) within her that blends with the snow outside:

> And she sat in concentrated stillness until the moment when an entire burst of blue lightning tore apart that blankness and one of its bolts hit her in the head. This blow destroyed her comforting blankness, she cracked with a thin ringing and suddenly became nothing more than a curtain, and that curtain fell.
>
> Nadezhda Georgievna cried out. The picture opening up before her was much bigger than the world in which she had lived. There were no gaps, no emptiness — the cosmos was a thick and amazing fabric in which Earth and everything living on it, and all the knowledges [*vse znaniia*] of its plants, microbes, ants, elephants and humans were gathered together and communicated, flowing into each other. It was complete, perfect and constantly growing knowledge.[51]

While the plot details the moment the protagonist dies, what comes after is more important. Leaving dementia's 'stillness' and 'blankness', Nadezhda Georgievna enters a realm of 'constantly growing knowledge'. Endless freedom and awareness replace the mental and physical constraints that bound her. Georgievna's life ends with her yell, a brief shock replaced by a sense that real existence is just beginning. This recalls the passing of Tolstoi's Ivan Il′ich, whose fear and pain first intensify then dissolve into the better afterworld that God provides. Ulitskaia praises this moment in the classic novella as literature's best depiction of death: even the unworthy receive divine forgiveness.[52] Unlike Ivan Il′ich, Nadezhda Georgievna devotes herself to the immaterial riches of knowledge, which now have multiplied to encompass the universe. The story's penultimate sentence suggests that Georgievna possesses infinite understanding: 'There were no boundaries to this shimmering world.' This phrase recalls the Judeo-

[50] The protagonist in 'Alisa Purchases Death' wants to avoid Nadezhda Georgievna's fate. Ulitskaia, 'Alisa pokupaet smert′', p. 17.

[51] Ulitskaia, 'Serpantin', p. 71.

[52] On *The Death of Ivan Il′ich*, see Ulitskaia, 'Smert′ tozhe prinadlezhit zhizni'.

Christian belief that knowledge from God is the basis for all creation, both before and after the short span of human lives.[53]

Those who mourn also shape the nature of death. Gatherings to honour the deceased are the crux of most of Ulitskaia's narratives. *Medea and Her Children* and *The Funeral Party* (*Veselye pokhorony*, 1997), for example, detail how commemorating the dead unites characters and cultures. New and old acquaintances meet, mixing and combining the rituals of Judaism, Christianity and other faiths.[54] This coming together of disparate religions acts as a counterbalance to Russia's entrenched suspicion of Jews and Muslims (as well as Putin's takeover of the Church). Aaron, Zarifa and Musia embody Judaism, Islam and Orthodoxy; these characters evince the mercy and generosity with which the three faiths prepare for and then commemorate death. Ulitskaia's novel, *Daniel Stein, Interpreter* (*Daniel′ Shtain, perevodchik*, 2006), investigates the similarities of the Abrahamic religions. How they care for the dying shows that the sameness of compassion can overcome differences. The author's ecumenical worldview includes a fourth sacred tradition: the intelligentsia. For her it resembles a religious order, safeguarding the education and morality that are the best of culture. Ulitskaia fears *intelligenty* themselves will vanish as its oldest members die; a character in 'Dragon and Phoenix' even asks if the intelligentsia 'still exists'.[55] Ulitskaia's prose, which emerged in the dire 1990s, focused on moral, erudite characters surviving first socialism and then the chaotic, brutal shift to capitalism. The author doubts the intelligentsia's virtues will take root in the next generation, which she believes has a troubling thirst for things. *The Body of the Soul* is a lament for this group as well as for its individual members.[56]

These stories describe commemorating the deceased as mainly a private event. In 'Blessed Are Those Who…', as well as 'Dragon and Phoenix', death

[53] Ulitskaia, 'Serpantin', p. 71.

[54] For one of the critics who discusses Ulitskaia's funerals and wakes, see M. A. Bologova, 'Rozhdenie liriki iz dukha parodii: L. Ulitskaia. "Veselye pokhorony" vs "Medeia i ee deti", "Sonechka" & "Kazus Kukotskogo"', in A. I. Kuliapin et al. (eds), *Parodiia v russkoi literature XX v.: sbornik statei*, Barnaul, 2002, pp. 135–56 (p. 138). See also, Skomp and Sutcliffe, *Ludmila Ulitskaya*, pp. 52–53, 161–62.

[55] Ulitskaia, 'Liudmila Ulitskaia: Rugat′ intelligentsiiu', p. 5; Ulitskaia, 'Drakon i feniks', p. 13.

[56] Skomp and Sutcliffe discuss the intelligentsia and its putative demise in *Ludmila Ulitskaya*, pp. 100–05. For worries about the young and consumerism, see Galina Iuzefovich, 'Gospozha nabliudatel′', *Itogi*, 8, 2011 <http://bukvoid.com.ua/print/?7259> [accessed 14 June 2023]. *The Big Green Tent* (*Zelenyi shater*), with its images of Brezhnev-era dissidents and state oppression, is an extended eulogy for the intelligentsia.

is the opportunity to mend misunderstandings. Lidiia and Nina realize they must care for each other, as opposed to neglecting their mother while competing for her attention. After discovering the prayer she translated, the sisters fly back to Russia from Italy and 'Nina's puny shoulder and entire sparrow-like face was tucked into the side of her sister's large, soft breast. And both fell asleep. Loneliness had left them'. Lidiia and Nina take physical and sororal comfort in each other's presence, a mundane yet touching scene impossible without their mother's death and the daughters' discovery of her translation.[57]

'Dragon and Phoenix' contains the volume's only mention of a memorial service. In the story Said's presence is more important than a large funeral. Coming to Cyprus means he recognizes that love for his sister — and Musia's love for Zarifa — matters more than a 'sinful' lesbian relationship. The memorial service for Zarifa is a rebuttal to the homophobic policies that made her and Musia exiles, yet the story never makes this explicit.[58] The focus of remembrance is the rug Said brings from Azerbaijan:

> Woven into its cloth, a Dragon had entered into a mortal and unending embrace with a Phoenix. [On the rug] in the centre one could make out the thin Dragon, knotted into a circle with the sacred bird. Maybe a Phoenix, maybe Simurg. It was as if the circle were an eternally frozen reminder of a struggle in which no one can gain victory. Teeth and sharp prongs on claws were imprinted forever by the hands of the rugmaker, for as long as the colours do not fade, the wool rot, while time does not rub into dust memory of the artist's labour, of the opposing forces of nature and myth, of the hatred of weak people that lives much deeper than in this handmade picture, in the consciousness of two neighbouring groups, one of which is a terrifying dragon and the other a holy bird, or the opposite, one of which is a holy dragon and the other a terrifying bird. And who is the warrior, who is the sorcerer, who is evil, who is good, is impossible to tell, because they are bound to the same immovable and unbreakable circle.[59]

The rug with its Dragon and Phoenix suggests how Zarifa's life with Musia has overcome the enmity between Armenia and Azerbaijan. Ulitskaia, explaining 'Dragon and Phoenix', notes how she visited Nagorno-Karabakh in 2018 and was outraged by the way Russian policies had exacerbated

[57] Ulitskaia, 'Blagoslovennye te, kotorye…', p. 43.
[58] Ulitskaia, 'Drakon i feniks', pp. 14–15.
[59] Ibid., p. 15.

the conflict.[60] The story, however, has a deeper level of interpretation: the interminable, pointless struggle between the two creatures implies humanity's need to move beyond 'who is evil, who is good'. Abandoning these recriminations permits us to escape the 'immovable and unbreakable circle' that has marked centuries of conflict. The rug reveals the third function of repetition, aside from reiterating values and recalling trauma. *The Body of the Soul*, like Ulitskaia's writing in general, uses recurring images, plots and themes to depict existence as a network of positive interactions, not an endless cycle of hatred. The author's prose explores how bonds between people can support humanity, passing positive morals from one generation to the next.[61]

In 'Dragon and Phoenix' the rug symbolizes a life that has ended but it also gives optimism for the future. The heirloom has a referent in Ulitskaia's previous prose: the icon a parishioner paints to commemorate the protagonist in *Daniel Stein, Interpreter*. Stein escapes the Holocaust, converts to Catholicism, emigrates to Israel, then tries to reconcile Jews, Christians and Muslims. This utopian plan fails but after Daniel's death one of his followers discovers the holy image:

> It was a marvellous depiction of 'Praise the Lord the Highest Heavens.' On the icon the [artist] had represented Adam with a beard and moustache and Eve with a long pigtail, hares, squirrels, birds, and serpents, and all of creation which had formed a long queue to embark on Noah's Ark and was now leaping and rejoicing and praising the Lord. [The icon] envisaged all creation praising the Lord: rocks, plants, animals, and even the iron creations of man.[62]

Death brings sorrow but is part of 'all creation'. Daniel's icon and Zarifa's rug show how hope can transcend the wars that have sundered the Caucasus, Middle East and humanity as a whole. Both objects are works of art whose meaning is revealed after the end of life. 'Dragon and Phoenix', like *Daniel Stein*, emphasizes that hope outlasts tragedy. *The Body of the Soul*, a culmination of patterns in Ulitskaia's earlier prose, illuminates how ageing and dying reaffirm the tangible, emotional and spiritual ties

[60] On Nagorno-Karabakh, see Ulitskaia, 'Blizost′ k smerti'.

[61] This resembles the crossed paths and improbable meetings that underly *Doctor Zhivago*, the most important literary work for the liberal intelligentsia. Skomp and Sutcliffe connect Ulitskaia to the legacy of Boris Pasternak's novel. *Ludmila Ulitskaya*, p. 17.

[62] Ludmila Ulitskaya, *Daniel Stein, Interpreter: A Novel in Documents*, trans. Arch Tait New York, 2011, p. 402.

between individuals. Portraying the final stage of life, these stories repeat scenes from previous works to assert that, even in its most weakened state, the flesh has dignity and significance.

Addressing the Public in Eighteenth-Century Russian Printed Letter Collections

KELSEY RUBIN-DETLEV

ALTHOUGH unlikely to be resolved any time soon, the longstanding debate about whether Russia has ever possessed a public sphere has proven highly productive. Historians have long since demonstrated that Jürgen Habermas's idealized bourgeois public sphere never existed either in Russia or in Western Europe. Yet, the generative potential of Habermas's questions and categories has been recognized from the moment his work began to be used extensively in English-language scholarship.[1] An awareness of grey areas and ambiguities has replaced a rigid contrast between the public and private spheres, and there is growing interest in the particularities of the Russian articulation of these categories as they evolved over time and in different areas of discourse.[2] An emerging

Kelsey Rubin-Detlev is an Assistant Professor of Slavic Languages and Literatures at the University of Southern California.

The author would like to thank the American Council of Learned Societies (ACLS) and the Alexander von Humboldt Foundation for supporting this research, Ekaterina Shubenkina and all the participants in the panel 'Precarious Privacy: Russian Epistolary Culture in the Long Eighteenth Century' at ASEEES 2022 for the opportunity to present and discuss an early version of this article and *SEER*'s anonymous reviewers for their valuable comments.

[1] Craig Calhoun, 'Introduction: Habermas and the Public Sphere', in Craig Calhoun (ed.), *Habermas and the Public Sphere*, Cambridge, MA and London, 1992, pp. 1–48 (p. 41); Harold Mah, 'Phantasies of the Public Sphere: Rethinking the Habermas of Historians', *The Journal of Modern History*, 72, 2000, pp. 153–82.

[2] Andreas Schönle, 'The Scare of the Self: Sentimentalism, Privacy, and Private Life in Russian Culture, 1780–1820', *Slavic Review*, 57, 4, 1998, pp. 723–46; Paul Keenan, 'Creating a "Public" in St Petersburg, 1703–1761', unpublished PhD thesis, School of Slavonic and East European Studies, UCL, 2006; Andrew Kahn (ed.), *Representing Private Lives of the Enlightenment*, SVEC 2010:11, Oxford, 2010; Dmitrii Kalugin, '"A Society that Speaks Concordantly", or Mechanisms of Communication of Government and Society in Old and New Russia', in Nikolai Vakhtin and Boris Firsov (eds), *Public Debate in Russia: Matters of (Dis)order*, Edinburgh, 2016, pp. 52–84; Mikhail Velizhev, 'The Moscow English Club and

consensus affirms that a genuine, active Russian public took shape in the second half of the eighteenth century, although it remained small, socially exclusive and apolitical compared to its European counterparts.[3] The rapid expansion of print culture provided the foundation for educated Russians' new experience of being — and imagining themselves to be — a public.[4] Eighteenth-century texts employ various terms to express this self-awareness: while 'public' (*publika*) emphasized educated society's role as an audience and arbiter (for example, of literary taste and personal reputations), 'society' (*obshchestvo*, *svet*) designated variously defined groups participating in civic and cultural life, sometimes specified by modifiers as in *uchenyi svet* ('learned society').[5] Intensive efforts to translate Western literature, original literary experiments, and shifting social realities all kept the language and conceptualization of publicness in flux.[6]

Published letter collections constitute an exceptionally useful but hitherto neglected source for probing eighteenth-century Russian thinking about these questions: they clarify both the limits of publicness (what

the Public Sphere in Early Nineteenth-Century Russia', in Andreas Schönle, Andrei Zorin and Alexei Evstratov (eds), *The Europeanized Elite in Russia, 1762–1825: Public Role and Subjective Self*, DeKalb, IL, 2016, pp. 220–37; N. T. Pakhsar′ian (ed.), *XVIII vek: intimnoe i publichnoe v literature i kul′ture epokhi*, St Petersburg, 2021; Timur Atnashev, Tat′iana Vaizer and Mikhail Velizhev (eds), *Nesovershennaia publichnaia sfera: istoriia rezhimov publichnosti v Rossii*, Moscow, 2021; Evgenii Akel′ev, 'Rezhimy publichnosti i verkhovnaia vlast′ v Moskovskom tsarstve i Rossiiskoi imperii', *Cahiers du monde russe*, 62, 4, 2021, pp. 785–814.

[3] Simon Dixon, *The Modernisation of Russia 1676–1825*, Cambridge, 1999, pp. 152–88; Douglas Smith, *Working the Rough Stone: Freemasonry and Society in Eighteenth-Century Russia*, DeKalb, IL, 1999; Cynthia Hyla Whittaker, *Russian Monarchy: Eighteenth-Century Rulers and Writers in Political Dialogue*, DeKalb, IL, 2003; Elise Kimerling Wirtschafter, *The Play of Ideas in Russian Enlightenment Theater*, DeKalb, IL, 2003; Colum Leckey, *Patrons of Enlightenment: The Free Economic Society in Eighteenth-Century Russia*, Newark, DE, 2011; Jan Kusber, *Vospitanie elit i narodnoe obrazovanie v Rossiiskoi imperii XVIII–pervoi poloviny XIX veka: diskurs, zakonodatel′stvo, real′nost′*, Moscow, 2018, pp. 28–33; Damiano Rebecchini and Raffaella Vassena (eds), *Reading Russia: A History of Reading in Modern Russia*, 3 vols, vol. 1, Milan, 2020, <https://doi.org/10.4000/books.ledizioni.12681> [accessed 15 July 2023], especially the contributions by Gary Marker, Rodolphe Baudin and Bella Grigoryan.

[4] Gary Marker, *Publishing, Printing, and the Origins of Intellectual Life in Russia, 1700–1800*, Princeton, NJ, 1985; James Cracraft, *The Petrine Revolution in Russian Culture*, Cambridge, MA and London, 2004, pp. 257–76.

[5] D. A. Sdvizhkov, 'Ot *obshchestva* k *intelligentsii*: istoriia poniatii kak istoriia samosoznaniia', in A. I. Miller, D. A. Sdvizhkov and Ingrid Schierle (eds), *'Poniatiia o Rossii': k istoricheskoi semantike imperskogo perioda*, 2 vols, Moscow, 2011–2012, 1, pp. 382–427.

[6] S. V. Pol′skoi and V. S. Rjéoutski (eds), *Laboratoriia poniatii: perevod i iazyki politiki v Rossii XVIII veka*, Moscow, 2022.

is considered public and why) and the meanings attached to publicity (the act of making a text public and the attention it attracts).[7] Printed correspondence reveals how eighteenth-century Russians articulated both types of private/public distinction identified by Jeff Weintraub: the opposition between private and public can be understood as roughly equivalent to hidden/revealed or individual/collective.[8] Letter collections unveil before a potentially unlimited audience texts that were previously hidden from all except a few select individuals. At the same time, the way in which correspondences are presented to the public can explain a great deal about how a given culture understands the relationship between individuals who write or publish texts and the collectivity who might read them.

In Russia as in Western Europe, eighteenth-century readers and writers of letters constantly renegotiated the publicness of epistolary texts. As likely to be written collectively as individually, constantly defying the limits of public and private, letters regularly circulated beyond their named addressee(s).[9] Nonetheless, the decision to print a letter was a weighty one, and each publication had to be agreed with all interested parties or risk violating social and personal bonds.[10] In the eighteenth century as today, the transition to print illuminated and transformed the social relationships embodied in letters, as editors redefined the context in which a letter was read and, in more or less drastic ways, rewrote the text as they transcribed it.[11] By lending letters a new form of publicity, editors projected and constructed a public for epistolary writings. Printed correspondence brings into focus the stakes, meanings and ambiguities of publicity, arguably as no other genre can.

Yet, in the growing body of epistolary scholarship in Slavic studies, the history of published correspondence in eighteenth-century Russia remains

[7] 'Publicness' and 'Publicity', in *Oxford English Dictionary* <https://www.oed.com> [accessed 15 July 2023].

[8] Jeff Weintraub, 'The Theory and Politics of the Public/Private Distinction', in Jeff Weintraub and Krishan Kumar (eds), *Public and Private in Thought and Practice: Perspectives on a Grand Dichotomy*, Chicago, IL and London, 1997, pp. 1–42 (p. 5).

[9] Mary A. Favret, *Romantic Correspondence: Women, Politics and the Fiction of Letters*, Cambridge, 1993; Clare Brant, *Eighteenth-Century Letters and British Culture*, Basingstoke, 2006; Kelsey Rubin-Detlev, *The Epistolary Art of Catherine the Great*, Liverpool, 2019, pp. 263–300.

[10] Antoine Lilti, *Le monde de salons: sociabilité et mondanité à Paris au XVIII*e *siècle*, Paris, 2005, pp. 287–95. Epistolary publication became legally regulated in Britain. See Mark Rose, 'The Author in Court: *Pope v. Curll* (1741)', *Cultural Critique*, 21, Spring 1992, pp. 197–217.

[11] Liz Stanley, 'The Epistolary Gift, the Editorial Third-Party, Counter-Epistolaria: Rethinking the Epistolarium', *Life Writing*, 8, 2, 2011, pp. 135–52 (pp. 141–44).

uncharted.[12] By contrast, literary historians of Western Europe have examined letter collections through numerous lenses. The correspondences of scholars and writers have attracted especial attention, and great emphasis has been placed on the Renaissance tradition of letter writing and letter publishing, in which the manuscript letter and the published letter book were valued as literary forms that ideally lent themselves to the articulation of intimate relationships and unique selves.[13] Recent scholars of English literature have analysed the published letter as a key medium that helped early-modern writers and readers navigate between manuscript and print in a booming print market.[14] These studies raise the question of how Russian letter collections compared to their Western counterparts.

The present article aims to fill this gap by offering the first overview of original and translated letter collections printed in eighteenth-century Russia and by scrutinizing the concepts of publicness and publicity implicit in them. By letter collections I mean books containing a sequence of real, sent letters written and/or received by a single correspondent. Fictional letters, works written only conventionally in epistolary form, single published letters and letter manuals have their own separate histories that fall outside the scope of this article.[15] Through a close reading of the

[12] For overviews of scholarship on Russian epistolarity in this period, see Kelsey Rubin-Detlev, 'Russian Epistolary Writing from the Middle Ages to the Turn of the 19th Century', in Paula Rabinowitz (ed.), *Oxford Research Encyclopedia of Literature*, New York, 2021 <https://doi.org/10.1093/acrefore/9780190201098.013.1245> [accessed 15 July 2023], and Rodolphe Baudin (ed.), *Epistolary Emotions in Early Imperial Russia (1770–1830), Avtobiografija: Journal on Life Writing and the Representation of the Self in Russian Culture*, 10, 2021.

[13] Janet Gurkin Altman, 'The Letter Book as a Literary Institution 1539–1789: Toward a Cultural History of Published Correspondences in France', *Yale French Studies*, 71, 1986, pp. 17–62; Françoise Waquet, 'Les éditions de correspondances savantes et les idéaux de la République des Lettres,' *XVIIe siècle*, 178, 1993, pp. 99–118; Alexandre Stroev (ed.), *Quand l'écrivain publie ses lettres, Épistolaire: Revue de l'A.I.R.E.*, 35, 2009; Kathy Eden, *The Renaissance Rediscovery of Intimacy*, Chicago, IL and London, 2012; Emmanuelle Chapron and Jean Boutier, 'Utiliser, archiver, éditer: usages savants de la correspondance en Europe, XVIIe–XVIIIe siècles', *Bibliothèque de l'École des chartes*, 171, 2013, pp. 7–49; Diana G. Barnes, *Epistolary Community in Print, 1580–1664*, London and New York, 2016.

[14] Melanie Bigold, *Women of Letters, Manuscript Circulation, and Print Afterlives in the Eighteenth Century: Elizabeth Rowe, Catharine Cockburn, and Elizabeth Carter*, Basingstoke, 2013; Gary Schneider, *Print Letters in Seventeenth-Century England: Politics, Religion, and News Culture*, New York and London, 2018; Rachael Scarborough King, *Writing to the World: Letters and the Origins of Modern Print Genres*, Baltimore, MD, 2018.

[15] Preparing this article, I examined approximately thirty eighteenth-century editions that fit my definition of letter collections, alongside numerous borderline cases that render an exact count somewhat futile. For example, an eighteenth-century reader probably did not differentiate between a genuine letter collection and a book such as *Dobroe serdtse i zdravoi razum, ili Pis′ma markizy Pompadur*, u g. Vil′kovskago i Galchenkova, St

publication history, structure and paratexts of correspondence editions, I argue that the proliferation of printed letter collections during the reign of Catherine the Great (1762–96) reflects an expanding definition of publicness and a related eagerness on the part of editors and translators to reconfigure relationships within the public. Although Russians were increasingly acquainted with the Western European tradition of literary letter collections traceable to Antiquity and the Renaissance and with concordant views of correspondence as an aesthetic form opening a window into private selves, original Russian letter collections did not adopt them as primary models. Rather, Russians developed a practice of letter publishing in which the function of correspondence as a medium for constructing social relationships predominated. Late eighteenth-century editors of letter collections expanded state- and church-centred concepts of publicness to encompass a broad array of letter writers, from cultural figures to ordinary citizens. Simultaneously, horizontal relationships of exchange between writers, editors, texts and readers came to rival vertical hierarchies in motivating and shaping epistolary publicity. A previously overlooked element in Catherinian print culture, letter collections provide unique insights into late eighteenth-century Russian thinking about what it meant to be (a) public.

Western European literary letter collections in eighteenth-century Russia: An absent tradition?

When printed collections of real correspondence began to multiply under Catherine the Great, they had no literary tradition on which to rely. The bookmen of Kyivan Rus' and Muscovy did not translate wholescale either ancient model correspondences like those of Cicero and Pliny or the elaborate single-author collections of Byzantine epistolography. Often focused on poetry, the writers in the first half of the eighteenth century who set out to create a modern Russian literature similarly made little effort to absorb the Western epistolary tradition. The first translations of major European literary correspondence collections came remarkably late, in the 1780s and 1790s. Even then, there is little evidence that translators sought to import the European letter book as a literary form to be emulated in original Russian collections.

The relative dearth of translated literary correspondence does not reflect a lack of familiarity. Already in the first half of the century, many of the elites who made up the eighteenth-century Russian reading public

Petersburg, 1787, a partial translation of the correspondence of Mme de Pompadour forged by François Barbé-Marbois in the early 1770s.

had undoubtedly encountered the major European and especially French epistolarians in the original. French-language collections by Marie de Rabutin-Chantal, marquise de Sévigné, could be purchased in the Academy of Sciences bookshop in St Petersburg in the 1730s; in Moscow, editions of both Sévigné and her cousin Roger de Bussy-Rabutin were on sale in the Academy bookshop by the middle of the century.[16] The range of French correspondences available for purchase extended beyond these iconic figures to include those of Huguenot philosopher Pierre Bayle, Louis XIV’s morganatic wife Mme de Maintenon, and the now obscure seventeenth-century French doctor Guy Patin.[17] Anecdotal evidence suggests that at least the most famous writers evoked interest. A prominent diplomat who died in 1739, P. P. Shafirov, owned two different editions of Bussy’s letters; a copy owned by Jean Armand de L’Estocq, a doctor and influential courtier under Empress Elizabeth, ended up in the Academy library; in Ukraine, when Iakiv Andriiovych Markovych — a favourite student of the leading early eighteenth-century churchman, Feofan Prokopovych — decided to learn French in 1729, Bussy’s letters were among the first books he acquired.[18] Most famously, the future Catherine the Great ‘devoured’ Sévigné’s letters in the late 1740s.[19] Nevertheless, to appreciate these European stylistic authorities properly, one apparently had to read them in the original: despite their availability, no individual collections of Bussy’s or Sévigné’s correspondences appeared in eighteenth-century Russian translation.[20]

[16] N. A. Kopanev, *Frantsuzskaia kniga i russkaia kul′tura v seredine XVIII v. (iz istorii mezhdunarodnoi knigotorgovli)*, Leningrad, 1988, p. 131; N. A. Kopanev, ‘Rasprostranenie frantsuzskoi knigi v Moskve v seredine XVIII v.’, in S. P. Luppov (ed.), *Frantsuzskaia kniga v Rossii v XVIII v.: ocherki istorii*, Leningrad, 1986, pp. 59–172 (pp. 121, 165).

[17] P. I. Khoteev, ‘Biblioteka leib-medika Ribeiro Sanshesa’, in S. P. Luppov and N. B. Paramonova (eds), *Knigotorgovoe i bibliotechnoe delo v Rossii v XVII–pervoi polovine XIX v.: sbornik nauchnykh trudov*, Leningrad, 1981, pp. 104–18 (pp. 106, 114); Kopanev, ‘Rasprostranenie frantsuzskoi knigi’, p. 148. Maintenon’s correspondence published by Laurent Angliviel de La Beaumelle in the 1750s includes both genuine and falsified materials: Madame de Maintenon, *Lettres*, ed. Hans Bots and Eugénie Bots–Estourgie, 11 vols, Paris, 2009–18.

[18] N. S. Trofimova and P. I. Khoteev, ‘Katalog biblioteki P. P. Shafirova’, in A. A. Zaitseva (ed.), *Kniga v Rossii v epokhu prosveshcheniia: sbornik nauchnykh trudov*, Leningrad, 1988, pp. 161–68 (p. 164); P. I. Khoteev, *Kniga v Rossii v seredine XVIII veka: chastnye knizhnye sobraniia*, Leningrad, 1989, pp. 26, 94.

[19] A. N. Pypin (ed.), *Sochineniia imperatritsy Ekateriny II na osnovanii podlinnykh rukopisei*, 12 vols, St Petersburg, 1901–1907, 12, p. 105; Khoteev, *Kniga v Rossii*, pp. 12–13.

[20] French Catholic theologians were not translated for the same reason: Ekaterina Kislova, ‘What, How, and Why the Orthodox Clergy Read in Eighteenth-Century Russia’, in Rebecchini and Vassena (eds), *Reading Russia*, 1, pp. 179–218 (para 73).

Under Catherine, a few translations of classical epistolarians emerged from language teaching in educational institutions, but their focus remained on assimilating these models in a foreign language, not on creating a Russian-language epistolary tradition. Cicero's letters were standard texts used for studying Latin rhetoric in seminaries.[21] Accordingly, a seminarian recently promoted from the rhetoric class to that of philosophy decided in 1784 to demonstrate his academic achievements to his patron, Bishop Amvrosii (Podobedov), by publishing eleven letters translated from Cicero's correspondence, with annotations on their rhetorical efficacy and historical context.[22] While this collection implies a certain awareness of the letter as a literary art form, other translations published for didactic purposes suggest, on the contrary, that the emphasis lay elsewhere. A collection of Pliny the Younger's letters in Christoph Martin Wieland's German translation was printed with parallel Russian text in an anthology for the imperial gymnasia in Moscow in 1780: students were meant to learn German, not emulate Pliny's example in Russian.[23] In 1783, another seminarian translated Seneca's letters, but from a Latin edition that had already stripped out all epistolary features to highlight only the moral messages.[24] The European classical tradition, which had instilled in Western European letter collections an emphasis on literary skill and personal epistolary style, had limited resonance in Russia.

Late eighteenth-century translators took more of an interest in contemporary letter collections: the vogue for literary celebrities associated with the language of sentiment, especially Jean-Jacques Rousseau, introduced European understandings of the letter book as revealing private selves and intimate relationships.[25] Translated in 1783, Rousseau's

[21] Ibid., para 58.

[22] *Odinnattsat′ pisem raznago soderzhaniia, a osoblivo uteshitel′nykh, iz druzheskikh Tsitseronovykh pisem vybrannyia, i s latinskago na rossiiskii iazyk perevedennyia Krutitskoi eparkhii obuchaiushchimsia v Lavrskoi seminarii filosofii studentom Kodratom Orlovym*, v Universitetskoi tipografii, u N. Novikova, Moscow, 1784.

[23] F. I. Sapozhnikov, *Izbrannyia mesta iz luchshikh nemetskikh pisatelei dlia upotrebleniia pri Imperatorskikh moskovskikh gimnaziiakh*, v Universitetskoi tipografii, u N. Novikova, Moscow, 1780, pp. 314–71.

[24] *Seneki khristiianstvuiushchago nravstvennyia lekarstva, sostavlennyia iz kratkikh zdravykh razsuzhdenii, kotorymi kazhdyi bez pomoshchi drugago mozhet uvrachevat′ dushu svoiu strazhduiushchuiu porokami, ili Nuzhneishiia nastavleniia sposobstvuiushchiia k ispravleniiu nravov chelovecheskikh i k priobreteniiu istinnago blagopoluchiia, vybrany iz pisem L. A. Seneki, muzha kak uchenostiiu, tak naipache dobrodeteliami v drevnosti otmenno proslavivshagosia*, trans. Aleksandr Mel′gunov, v privilegirovannoi tipografii u Meiera, Moscow, 1783.

[25] On the Russian fascination with Rousseau's biography after his death in 1778, see Thomas Barran, *Russia Reads Rousseau, 1762–1825*, Evanston, IL, 2002, p. 97.

autobiographical letters to the statesman and botanist Chrétien Guillaume de Lamoignon de Malesherbes epitomize the writer's paradoxical rejection of publicity in favour of a spectacular display of private selfhood. In the letters, Rousseau characteristically desires freedom from society while declaring this to be impossible:

> I am not yet free: my last works have not yet been printed [...]. But if, contrary to my expectations, I can reach that point and say farewell to society forever, then I shall be free [...]. Oh, if only![26]

Rousseau's missives depict vividly the strains of a private self that can exist only dialectically with a public. N. M. Karamzin published a different (and stylistically much smoother) translation of these letters in his 1798 anthology *Pantheon of Foreign Literature*; this notable example of competing eighteenth-century translations suggests that the correspondence appealed to Russian readers.[27] Probably prompted by the popularity of Rousseau's *Julie, ou la nouvelle Héloïse* (1761), Aleksandr Dmitriev translated a French volume including Bussy-Rabutin's free translation of the letters of the real Abelard and Héloïse, alongside poetic renditions of their correspondence.[28] Linked directly with the fashion for Rousseau and sentiment, these collections reflect little interest in real correspondence as a literary form.

Likewise, there are few signs that Russians shared Western Europeans' association of letters with women's writing.[29] Such a connection could be found primarily where real correspondence intersected with fiction: it can be discerned, for example, in Dmitriev's choice to dedicate his

[26] *Novyia pis'ma Zh. Zh. Russo*, [Tipografiia Gosudarstvennoi voennoi kollegii], St Petersburg, 1783, p. 21; *Collection complète des œuvres de J. J. Rousseau, citoyen de Genève*, 17 vols, Geneva, 1782–89, 12, pp. 241–65 (pp. 251–52). All English translations are my own.

[27] *Panteon inostrannoi slovesnosti*, 3 vols, v Universitetskoi tipografii, u Ridigera i Klaudiia, Moscow, 1798, 3, pp. 87–154. A third translation by Ivan Martynov appeared in *Filosoficheskiia uedinennyia progulki Zhan Zhaka Russo, ili Posledniaia ego ispoved', pisannaia im samim, s prisovokupleniem pisem ego k Mal'zerbu, v koikh izobrazhaetsia istinnyi kharakter i podlinnyia prichiny postupkov sego slavnago zhenevskago filosofa*, 2 vols, v Imperatorskoi tipografii, St Petersburg, 1802.

[28] *Sobranie pisem Abel'iarda i Eloizy, s prisovokupleniem opisaniia zhizni sikh neshchastnykh liubovnikov*, trans. Aleksandr Dmitriev, v Universitetskoi tipografii, u N. Novikova, Moscow, 1783; *Lettres et épîtres amoureuses d'Héloïse et d'Abeilard*, new edition, 2 vols, Geneva, 1777.

[29] Elizabeth C. Goldsmith (ed.), *Writing the Female Voice: Essays on Epistolary Literature*, Boston, MA, 1989; Elizabeth Heckendorn Cook, *Epistolary Bodies: Gender and Genre in the Eighteenth-Century Republic of Letters*, Stanford, CA, 1996; Christine Planté (ed.), *L'épistolaire, un genre féminin?*, Paris, 1998; Dena Goodman, *Becoming a Woman in the Age of Letters*, Ithaca, NY and London, 2009.

translation of the largely fictional Abelard and Héloïse materials 'to the fair sex', appealing paradoxically to the discourse of female influence softening men's characters that Rousseau abhorred. Likewise, in 1789, when the translator of Laurence Sterne's possibly spurious letters to Eliza Draper and her fictional responses trimmed the prefatory material in the French edition he used, he eliminated considerations of Sterne's style but retained a celebration of Platonic friendship between men and women.[30] The translation of the correspondence volume of German Enlightenment satirist Gottlieb Wilhelm Rabener's collected works offers another example teetering on the border of mystification and reality: the volume opens with Rabener's joking correspondence with two young ladies who decided to correspond with him under a false name.[31] While these translations link women with letter writing, they seem merely symptomatic of what scholars have referred to as the late eighteenth-century 'feminization' of Russian culture under the influence of sentimental literature.[32]

Unlike in the West, where the first French letter collection printed in 1539 was authored by a woman, Hélisenne de Crenne, and where Sévigné reigned as the supreme model epistolarian, letter books did not open doors to publication for Russian women.[33] The sixty-five female translators whom Wendy Rosslyn has identified as active before 1800 in Russia did not find such collections an especially congenial genre.[34] I have unfortunately been unable to locate an extant copy of the work most closely resembling a letter collection translated by an eighteenth-century Russian woman. To judge by the work's title, *Letters of Pope G…*, E. Golenishcheva-Kutuzova published excerpts from Louis-Antoine Caraccioli's falsified editions of Pope Clement XIV (Giovanni Vincenzo Antonio Ganganelli)'s letters:

[30] *Pis'ma Iorika k Elize, i Elizy k Ioriku*, trans. Gavrilo Apukhtin, v Universitetskoi tipografii, u N. Novikova, Moscow, 1789, pp. 7–8; *Voyage sentimental. Par Mr. Sterne, sous le nom d'Yorick. Traduit de l'Anglais par Mr. Frénais. Nouvelle édition, augmentée des Lettres d'Yorick à Eliza, et d'Eliza à Yorick*, 2 vols, Geneva, 1786, 2, pp. 99–104.

[31] *Sobranie sochinenii Gotliba Vil'gel'ma Rabenera*, 8 vols, vol. 6, v Universitetskoi tipografii u V. Okorokova, Moscow, 1793; *Gottlieb Wilhelm Rabeners sämmtliche Schriften*, 6 vols, vol. 6, Leipzig, 1777.

[32] For a bibliography of work in this area, see Ursula Stohler, *Disrupted Idylls: Nature, Equality, and the Feminine in Sentimentalist Russian Women's Writing (Mariia Pospelova, Mariia Bolotnikova, and Anna Naumova)*, with translations by Emily Lygo, Frankfurt am Main, 2016, pp. 45–47.

[33] Altman, 'The Letter Book as a Literary Institution', p. 27; Marie-Claire Grassi, 'Naissance d'un nouveau modèle: l'apparition de Madame de Sévigné dans les traités d'art épistolaire', *Revue d'Histoire littéraire de la France*, 3, 1996, pp. 378–93.

[34] Wendy Rosslyn, *Feats of Agreeable Usefulness: Translations by Russian Women, 1763–1825*, Fichtenwalde, 2000, p. 33.

the texts' moral tenor and Caraccioli's emulation of Rousseau in his characterization of the pope probably justified her choice of source, rather than the epistolary genre.[35]

While echoes of Western epistolary culture can certainly be heard, Russians under Catherine the Great developed their own distinct practice of publishing correspondence that focused above all on the letter's potential to construct social relations. Letter collections were not initially a literary genre in Russia: rather, historical concerns took the lead as editors gradually expanded the definitions of what it meant for letters to be public and how members of the public might interact among themselves and with the correspondences they read.

State, scholarship and publicness in Peter the Great's letter collections

When Catherine the Great oversaw in 1774 the first of eight different editions of Peter the Great's correspondence printed during her reign, she built on an existing practice of publishing epistolary materials that were public in the classical sense of pertaining to the state.[36] Imperial decrees had a basically epistolary structure: signed and dated by the sovereign, they were addressed to the empire as a whole, to subgroups or to individuals. Printed compilations of decrees began to appear in the first third of the eighteenth century.[37] Genuine correspondence was also printed by the Petrine state for propagandistic purposes. During the 1718 investigation of his son Aleksei, Peter made published correspondence a cornerstone of his publicity strategy to justify the persecution of his own family. Peter embedded letters in a manifesto denouncing his first wife,

[35] *Pis'my papy G... k raznym osobam, otkryvaiushchie chuvstvovaniia dobrago grazhdanina, i Zhaloba k zakonodateliam ot vdovy odnogo grazhdanina nakazannago za samoubiistvo poruganiem nad telom, perevedennye s frantsuzskago iazyka devitsei E... Golenishchevoi-Kutuzovoi*, Iaroslavl', 1785; Stéphanie Géhanne Gavoty, *L'Affaire clémentine: une fraude pieuse à l'ère des Lumières*, Paris, 2014; Rosslyn, *Feats of Agreeable Usefulness*, pp. 67–90, 179. Charles-Marguerite-Jean-Baptiste Mercier Dupaty's *Lettres sur l'Italie en 1785* (1788), substantial portions of which were published by a group of female translators in the 1790s, is a travelogue in epistolary form (Rosslyn, *Feats of Agreeable Usefulness*, pp. 148, 184–88).

[36] James Van Horn Melton, *The Rise of the Public in Enlightenment Europe*, Cambridge, 2001, p. 1.

[37] The earliest example I have been able to consult was produced in the reign of Peter II: *1727 goda. Blazhennyia i vechnodostoinyia pamiati Eia Imperatorskogo Velichestva, Ekateriny Aleksievny, sostoiavshiiasia ukazy po konchinu Eia Velichestva. Takozhde manifest o priniatii rossiiskogo prestola, vsepresvetleishago derzhavneishago velikogo gosudaria, Petra Aleksievicha vtorago, imperatora i samoderzhtsa vserossiiskogo, i prisiaga v vernoi sluzhbe Ego Velichestvu, i publichnyiazh ukazy po nyneshnei 728 god*, pri Senate, St Petersburg, 1728.

Evdokiia Lopukhina, for betraying her forced monastic vows and thereby endangering his power: letters of confession from Evdokiia to Peter and, as evidence, three messages from Evdokiia to her lover, Stepan Glebov, as well as a conspiratorial missive written by Evdokiia's supporter, Bishop Dosifei of Rostov.[38] Likewise, on 25 June 1718, the day before Aleksei's death in prison, Peter printed his own correspondence with his son as part of a substantial pamphlet defending Aleksei's death sentence.[39] Despite efforts by Aleksei's son, Emperor Peter II, to ban these pamphlets, they continued to circulate in print and manuscript; Peter's correspondence with his son became well known at home and abroad, and it even re-entered Russian print (in reverse translation from the French) in Stefan Pisarev's translation of Antonio Catiforo's *Vita di Pietro il Grande* (1736), published in 1772.[40] These letters were already in some sense public because they belonged to members of the imperial family and therefore to the state. State interests were also the only justification for adding an additional layer of publicity by revealing the letters to a broad readership.

Catherine transformed this model by supporting the first scholarly editions of Peter's correspondence. In the words of Lindsey Hughes, Peter's image 'remained a central pillar of official ideology' throughout the imperial period, and, despite Catherine's personal competition with Peter, she was a savvy user of his legacy throughout her reign.[41] In September 1763, barely a year after her arrival on the throne, Catherine declared to Voltaire her intention to publish her predecessor's letters: 'It is true that one cannot be sufficiently astonished by the genius of that great man; I am going to go ahead and have printed his original letters, which I have ordered to be gathered from all over.'[42] She gave historians unprecedented access to imperial archives to achieve her goal; she personally read the proofs of Mikhail Shcherbatov's 1774 edition of the cabinet records of

[38] *Manifest ili, ob'iavlenie, kotoroe chteno v stolovoi palate, pri osviashchennom sobore, i Ego Tsarskago Presvetlago Velichestva pri ministrakh, i prochiikh dukhovnago i grazhdanskago china liudekh; leta 1718, Marta v 5 den'*, St Petersburg, 1718.

[39] *Ob"iavlenie rozysknogo dela i suda, po ukazu Ego Tsarskago Velichestva na tsarevicha Alekseia Petrovicha, v Sankt"piterburkhe otpravlennago, i po ukazu Ego Velichestva v pechat', dlia izvestiia vsenarodnago, sego Iiunia v 25 den', 1718. vydanoe*, St Petersburg, 1718.

[40] M. V. Nikolaeva, '"Testament" Petra I tsarevichu Alekseiu', *XVIII vek*, 9, 1974, pp. 93–111; Antonio Catiforo, *Zhitie Petra Velikago [...]*, trans. Stefan Pisarev, pri Imperatorskoi Akademii nauk, St Petersburg, 1772, pp. 360–71.

[41] Lindsey Hughes, *Peter the Great: A Biography*, New Haven, CT and London, 2002, p. 220; Vera Proskurina, *Creating the Empress: Politics and Poetry in the Age of Catherine II*, Boston, MA, 2011, pp. 109–49; Karen Rasmussen, 'Catherine II and the Image of Peter I', *Slavic Review*, 37, 1, 1978, pp. 51–69.

[42] Voltaire, *Œuvres complètes*, 205 vols, Oxford, 1968–2022, 110, p. 407 (Letter D11421).

Peter's early letters and orders.[43] Peter's letters to military commander Count Boris Sheremetev, edited by the academician and head archivist at the College of Foreign Affairs, Gerhard Friedrich Müller, appeared the same year.[44] Catherine did not supervise other publications as closely as Shcherbatov's, but several bore the imprint of her personal involvement. When Count Petr Sheremetev published his father's letters to Peter, he gratefully acknowledged that Catherine had furnished the necessary copies from the Imperial Cabinet; likewise, Admiral Aleksei Siniavin advertised Catherine's approval on the title page of Peter's letters to his father, Vice-Admiral Naum Siniavin.[45]

These more or less official Catherinian editions established the central paradigm for publishing letters in eighteenth-century Russia: combining the publicness of the state with the publicity of print, they also embody a complex idea of the public in which vertical and horizontal relationships between writers, editors and readers coexist. Like much of the period's literature as studied by Iurii Lotman and Kirill Ospovat, Shcherbatov's edition and its imitators were designed to inculcate a service ethic in their readers by modelling the appropriate relationship between the sovereign and his/her devoted nobles.[46] Shcherbatov declares:

[43] W. Gareth Jones, *Nikolay Novikov: Enlightener of Russia*, Cambridge, 1984, pp. 58–59; *Tetrati zapisnyia vsiakim pismam i delam, komu chto prikazano i v kotorom chisle ot Ego Imperatorskago Velichestva Petra Velikago 1704, 1705 i 1706 godov [...]*, v Tipografii Pravitel'stvuiushchago senata, [St Petersburg], 1774, unpaginated preface 'K chitateliu'.

[44] *Pis'ma Petra Velikago pisannyia k general-fel'dmarshalu, tainomu sovetniku, maltiiskomu, S. Apostola Andreia, Belago orla, i Prusskago ordena kavaleru, grafu Borisu Petrovichiu Sheremetevu, po bol'shoi chasti sobstvennoiu gosudarevoiu rukoiu, a inyia s podlinnikov khraniashchikhsia v Imperatorskoi kabinetskoi arkhive spisannyia, skol'ko onykh nashlos' u ego siiatel'stva [...] grafa Petra Borisovicha Sheremeteva [...]*, pri Imperatorskom universitete, Moscow, 1774. In his preface (p. i), Müller confirms that Shcherbatov's collection appeared under the empress's direct supervision. See also, J. L. Black, *G.-F. Müller and the Imperial Russian Academy*, Kingston and Montreal, 1986, pp. 169–71, 183, 194–95.

[45] *Pis'ma k gosudariu imperatoru Petru Velikomu ot general-fel'dmarshala, tainago sovetnika, maltiiskago, S. Apostola Andreia, Belago orla i Prusskago ordena kavalera, grafa Borisa Petrovicha Sheremeteva*, 4 vols, pri Imperatorskom universitete, Moscow, 1778–79, 1, unpaginated preface, 'Blagosklonnyi chitateliu'; *Pis'ma i ukazy Ego Imperatorskago Velichestva gosudaria imperatora Petra Velikago, pisannyia k Naumu Akimovichu Siniavinu, [...] khraniashchiesia u syna ego flota admirala i kavalera Alekseia Naumovicha Siniavina, koego zhelaniem po vysochaishemu Eia Imperatorskago Velichestva vsemilostiveishemu blagovoleniiu izdaiutsia s kratkim opisaniem sluzhby pokoinago roditelia ego*, [Tipografiia Akademii nauk], St Petersburg, 1786.

[46] Kirill Ospovat, *Pridvornaia slovesnost': institut literatury i konstruktsii absoliutizma v Rossii serediny XVIII veka*, Moscow, 2020; Ospovat, 'Reforming Subjects: Poetics and Politics of Reading in Early Eighteenth-Century Russia', in Rebecchini and Vassena (eds), *Reading Russia*, 1, pp. 117–50.

> in a word, I think every Russian who did not have the good fortune of knowing [Peter] tries to come to know his works and thereby to learn their duties, to learn also what can be useful to the fatherland.[47]

Unlike statuary or odes, letters do not promote a mythologized or sacralized hero; rather, they facilitate exceptional intimacy between the ruler and his/her subjects. Introducing the letters to Sheremetev, Müller affirms:

> In these letters, PETER THE GREAT appears without the adornments of might, writes in a friendly manner to a friend, reveals his inner thoughts, gives advice and demands it, shows what He Himself was like, and what the person in whom He had such trust was like.[48]

Printed letters mediate between the sovereign and his/her subjects, establishing a close relationship of trust and affection: now, every literate Russian subject can be as close to the emperor as his most trusted advisers. Publishing Peter's letters exemplified Catherine's 'scenario of power' in which love between the ruler and her subjects should elicit devoted service, allowing a sense of reciprocity without diminishing the empress's absolute power.[49] The classical association of letters with intimacy and love is removed from the private sphere and deployed to reinvent the state's traditional publicness for the age of Enlightenment.

Yet, these editions also express a more horizontal model of the public: as scholarly editions, they aim not just to train imperial subjects, but also to promote the public exchange of knowledge in print among educated Russians. Shcherbatov identifies a dual audience for his edition: 'I thought that I would do a service to all Russians who are grateful to that monarch, as well as to scholarly society.'[50] Petr Sheremetev addresses his edition to 'lovers of Russian history and admirers of illustrious men', concluding his preface by 'professing [his] true respect' for that reading public.[51] While the publicness of the imperial addressee remains an essential justification for publication, the focus shifts from the imperial person to more generalized 'illustrious men' — an unsurprising change given Sheremetev's primary

[47] *Tetrati zapisnyia*, [unpag.].

[48] *Pis′ma Petra Velikago [...] Sheremetevu*, p. i.

[49] Richard S. Wortman, *Scenarios of Power: Myth and Ceremony in Russian Monarchy*, 2 vols, Princeton, NJ, 1995–2000, 1, pp. 110–22.

[50] *Tetrati zapisnyia*, [unpag.].

[51] *Pis′ma k gosudariu imperatoru Petru Velikomu ot [...] Sheremeteva*, 1, [unpag.].

goal of glorifying his own family. Simultaneously, the public comes to be imagined primarily as a society of leisured amateurs whose interest in the correspondence is above all historical and moral and with whom the editor himself identifies: the preface highlights the letters' documentary value, their insights into the 'style and etiquette of correspondence at that time', as well as the noble values of 'loyalty, bravery, and zeal' that their author incarnates.[52] Meanwhile, Müller views Peter's letters through the prism of eighteenth-century language debates, arguing that 'the perfection of the Russian language can be increased by using old letters to learn the words and expressions by which our ancestors expressed themselves on various occasions and which have long since been consigned to complete oblivion'.[53] These collections helped Russians to imagine themselves as scholars exchanging information and opinions about the linguistic, cultural and historical identity of their society.

As editions of Peter's letters multiplied, the ideal of public exchange became ever more visible as the group of editors grew more diverse. These collections contributed to a substantial effort under Catherine to recover and print Russian historical manuscripts — labours most famously exemplified by Nikolai Novikov's *Old Russian Library* (*Drevniaia rossiiskaia vivliofika*, 1773–75, second edition 1788–91). In the 1780s, both Novikov and another publishing entrepreneur of the age, Petr Bogdanovich, took up the endeavour of publishing Peter's letters.[54] Ivan Golikov, who edited around 1,500 of Peter's letters in three volumes of his historical compilation published by Novikov, was a mere merchant who boasted no scholarly qualifications besides passionate admiration for the Emperor.[55] His collection attests to a genuine expansion of the publicness of Peter's letters: seventy years after Peter published his own letters as state propaganda, a common subject felt entitled to lend the former emperor's letters fresh publicity and thereby enter the print sphere himself. The fact

[52] Ibid.

[53] Victor Zhivov, *Language and Culture in Eighteenth-Century Russia*, trans. Marcus C. Levitt, Boston, MA, 2009; *Pis'ma Petra Velikago [...] Sheremetevu*, p. i.

[54] *Pis'ma gosudaria imperatora Petra Velikago k Stepanu Andreevichu Kolychevu, i otvety ego na onyia*, v Universitetskoi tipografii, u N. Novikova, Moscow, 1785; *Pis'ma imperatora Petra Velikago k bratu svoemu tsariu Ioannu Alekseevichu i patriarkhu Adrianu s otvetom na onyia i na otzyvy boiarina i voevody Alekseia Semenovicha Sheina, kniazia Borisa Alekseevicha Golitsyna, i boiarina i voevody Borisa Petrovicha Sheremeteva, na izhd. P[etra]. B[ogdanovicha]*, [Tipografiia Bogdanovicha], St Petersburg, 1788.

[55] I. I. Golikov, *Deianiia Petra Velikago, mudrago preobrazitelia Rossii; sobrannyia iz dostovernykh istochnikov i raspolozhennyia po godam*, 12 vols, vols 10–12, v Universitetskoi tipografii, u N. Novikova, Moscow, 1788–89; Nicholas V. Riasanovsky, *The Image of Peter the Great in Russian History and Thought*, New York and Oxford, 1985, pp. 43–44.

that Golikov's collection ended up in direct competition with another by Ukrainian writer, publisher and historian Fedor Tumanskii highlights the buzz of scholarly activity in which the letter collections participated.[56] The vogue for printing Peter's letters was an imperial initiative, but it became a public conversation involving the full social spectrum of educated Russians.

Tumanskii's collection promotes the ideal of public exchange while underscoring its limits in the Russian context. His ten-volume collection of Petrine documents — including a volume of official correspondence and epistolary materials mixed into other volumes — was funded by subscription, a fact that would seem to attest significant public participation. But Tumanskii complains bitterly about the absence of public support: he had advertised a subscription for a full history of Peter the Great, but, lacking enough subscribers to bring the project to fruition, he printed the materials he had gathered instead. Publishing correspondence and other documents turns out to be an unintended second-best. Nevertheless, Tumanskii reaffirms the concept that such collections can mediate exchange. He concludes his preface by echoing other scholarly publications of the period and calling on the public to share texts: 'if anyone has any manuscripts related to this history, which might have remained unknown to me, they will oblige not only me but also the public by communicating them.'[57] No matter how small the reading public and how insufficient the commercial foundations for a European-style public sphere — and despite Tumanskii's future career as an especially zealous imperial censor under Paul I — Tumanskii and his fellow editors believed in the possibility of public exchange of historical knowledge and in their collections' ability to fuel it.[58]

The largest corpus of correspondence collections by any eighteenth-century Russian author and among the earliest to appear, the Catherinian editions of Peter's letters arguably built the framework underlying the practice of publishing correspondence in eighteenth-century Russia. As print culture bloomed in the second half of the century, imperial example modelled how personal letters could be readdressed to readers of print while leaving room for multiple conceptions of what it meant to be (a) public.

[56] F. O. Tumanskii (ed.), *Sobranie raznykh zapisok i sochinenii, sluzhashchikh k dostavleniiu polnago svedeniia o zhizni i deianiiakh gosudaria imperatora Petra Velikago*, 10 vols, u Shnora, St Petersburg, 1787–88.

[57] Ibid., 1, [unpag.].

[58] Marker, *Publishing*, p. 231.

Epistolary transformations of the Christian community

The state was not the only traditional institution to produce eighteenth-century letter collections that revealed shifting ideas about publicness and publicity. The Orthodox Church had a long history as a site of epistolary circulation. Didactic epistles by East Slavic churchmen had been circulating in manuscript since the eleventh century, appearing less than a century after the adoption of writing in Kyivan Rus'. This religious epistolary culture, of course, built on the biblical epistles and those of the Church Fathers. Eighteenth-century churchmen adapted this tradition to suit new forms of print publicity and embody their vision of Christian community in modern letter collections.

Published in 1772, the first Slavonic translation of the early second-century St Ignatius of Antioch's epistles is the only eighteenth-century letter collection printed in the traditional church type rather than in Peter the Great's modernized 'civil script'. It anticipates the collections of Peter's letters by melding traditional Orthodox approaches to textual community with historical scholarship traceable to the Renaissance Republic of Letters. The translator, Archbishop Amvrosii (Zertis-Kamenskii) of Moscow and Kaluga, seeks both to instruct his readers as members of the communion of saints and to offer an Orthodox response to the scholarly debate about the authenticity and authority of Ignatius's epistles that had been raging in the West since the Reformation.[59] The volume's construction conscientiously pursues that double aim: in a brief prefatory address, Amvrosii announces that 'the reader, in heeding these epistles, will feel directly their sacred antiquity and pure Christian teaching. And if, when these teachings touch his heart, they also produce a striving for virtue, the one who laboured over this translation will already be sufficiently rewarded'.[60] The reading public should be both intellectually satisfied and spiritually edified. Significantly, Amvrosii produced a genre- and author-based volume in a new scholarly translation, rather than a liturgical collection like the Apostol (which contains the biblical epistles along with the Acts of the Apostles) or a medieval miscellany offering multifarious texts assembled for their edifying value. He introduces the text with excerpts from a variety of Church Fathers, beginning with one of Ignatius's addressees, St Polycarp: they attest both to the Church's acceptance of the epistles

[59] John Monfasani, 'The Letters of Ignatius of Antioch as a Philological and Epistemological Issue from the Reformation to Today', in Steven M. Oberhelman, Giancarlo Abbamonte, and Patrick Baker (eds), *Habent sua fata libelli: Studies in Book History, the Classical Tradition, and Humanism in Honor of Craig Kallendorf*, Leiden and Boston, MA, 2022, pp. 299–314.

[60] St Ignatius, *Poslaniia*, Moscow, 1772, unpaginated preface 'K chitateliu'.

as sound doctrine and to the texts' historical circulation. Circumstances added spiritual meaning to the volume that its translator never intended: published a year after Amvrosii's death at the hands of a Moscow mob, the work became an offering from one martyred bishop to another.[61] Outpacing even Rousseau, this was the only Russian letter collection to run to three editions in the eighteenth century, with two further printings in 1779 and 1784. Never meant to be private, Ignatius's letters in Amvrosii's Slavonic translation effectively balanced the Russian public's traditional experience as members of the Orthodox flock with their more recent self-identification as participants in learned society.

A few decades later, the letter collections of St Tikhon of Zadonsk published in the 1780s and 1790s reflect how embedded the Church had become in the contemporary print sphere. The former bishop of Voronezh was the first Russian after Peter to arrange for the publication of his own correspondence, and he exhibited extraordinary self-awareness in negotiating the publicity of his epistolary writings. In 1782, Tikhon petitioned the Holy Synod to review his works for posthumous publication, and, upon his death a little over a year later, his assistant submitted the manuscripts to the Synod and found publishers for them. Among these were two volumes of letters, listed by Tikhon in his petition and both published in 1784.[62] One, entitled *Cloistered Letters*, contained letters that were not actually sent. Rather, according to an early biographer, Tikhon found that the informality and brevity of epistolary writing rendered it the most conducive genre for expressing his thoughts: he wrote these missives either as spare drafts to be addressed to specific recipients when an appropriate occasion arose, or as letters to himself, recording his ideas for future reference.[63] Publication thus made the leap from the secrecy of the monastic cell to the broad publicity of print. The other volume, entitled *Various Letters Sent to Certain Friends*, comprised real, sent letters that

[61] Ignatius was martyred by being thrown to the beasts in Rome.

[62] A. A. Lebedev, *Sviatitel′ Tikhon Zadonskii i vseia Rossii chudotvorets (ego zhizn′, pisaniia i proslavlenie)*, 3rd edn, St Petersburg, 1896, pp. 176–78.

[63] *Pisma keleinyia, sochinennyia preosviashchennym episkopom Voronezhskim i Eletskim Tikhonom pervym, vo vremia prebyvaniia ego na obeshchanii, toi zhe eparkhii v Zadonskom monastyre*, u Shnora, St Petersburg, 1784 (second edition: v Tipografii Korpusa chuzhestrannykh edinovertsov, St Petersburg, 1796); Evgenii (Bolkhovitinov), *Polnoe opisanie zhizni preosviashchennago Tikhona, byvshago prezhde episkopa Keksgol′mskago i Ladozhskago, i vikariia Novogorodskago, a potom episkopa Voronezhskago i Eletskago, sobrannoe iz ustnykh predanii, i zapisok ochevidnykh svidetelei, s nekotorymi istoricheskimi svedeniiami, kasaiushchimisia do Novogorodskoi i Voronezhskoi ierarkhii; izdannoe osobenno dlia liubitelei i pochitatelei pamiati sego Preosviashchennago*, v Tipografii Korpusa chuzhestrannykh edinovertsov, St Petersburg, 1796, pp. 40, 69–70.

Tikhon had selected and edited himself. Devoid of prefatory material and stripped of information identifying the original addressees, *Various Letters* places its emphasis squarely on Christian teaching, with the letters largely constituting sermon-like pastoral reflections on scriptural passages.[64] This vagueness of address paradoxically defines the intended readership: some letters imply monastic or clerical interlocutors, others clearly apostrophize the laity, but most leave the question open and therefore address all Christians as a unified body. The title, evocative of a secular, sociable model of exchange, and the choice to publish all of Tikhon's works in the civil script — rather than the traditional Church type — point to his reconfiguration of the Orthodox understanding of community. These volumes show how one Russian churchman saw in published correspondence an opportunity to open up the holy life of monastics to the laity, drawing educated Russians into a process of individual and collective spiritual renewal.

The interplay between Church tradition and modern print publicity is likewise manifest in the *Remaining Works of the Right Reverend Tikhon*, edited by Evgenii (Bolkhovitinov), later a prominent scholar and metropolitan of Kyiv. Although Evgenii divided his materials into six sections — pastoral instructions to the clergy and to the flock, translations from Greek, reflections on Scripture, instructions to monks and 'Letters to Friends on Various Subjects' — epistolary materials dominate the collection. For example, two of the three translations from the Greek are presented with the text of the personal letters in which they were originally embedded, and several instructions to monks are in epistolary form.[65] The letters are solidly rooted in the tradition of East Slavic didactic epistles. For instance, a missive exhorting a monk to stop looking to change monasteries and instead learn patience has a clear antecedent in the *Patericon* of the Kyivan Caves Monastery (13th–15th centuries), the core of which is formed by a letter from the bishop of Vladimir and Suzdal′ admonishing the monk Polikarp to stop seeking a high-ranking place in the church and learn true monastic humility.[66]

[64] *Raznyia pisma k nekotorym priiateliam posylannyia, sochinennyia Preosviashchennym Episkopom Voronezhskim i Eletskim Tikhonom pervym, vo vremia prebyvaniia ego na obeshchanii, toi zhe eparkhii v Zadonskom monastyre*, u Shnora, St Petersburg, 1784; Evgenii (Bolkhovitinov), *Polnoe opisanie zhizni preosviashchennago Tikhona*, p. 69.

[65] Evgenii (Bolkhovitinov) (ed.), *Ostal′nyia sochineniia preosviashchennago Tikhona, byvshago prezhde episkopa Keksgol′mskago i Ladozhskago; a potom Voronezhskago i Eletskago. Dlia udovol′stviia i dushevnyia pol′zy blagochestivykh chitatelei, a osoblivo dlia liubitelei pamiati sego Preosviashchennago*, v Imperatorskoi tipografii, St Petersburg, 1799, pp. 172–81.

[66] Ibid., pp. 258–62; 'Kievo-Pecherskii paterik', in D. S. Likhachev et al. (eds), *Biblioteka literatury Drevnei Rusi*, 20 vols, St Petersburg, 1997–2020, 4, pp. 296–489 (pp. 354–63).

Simultaneously, Evgenii's introduction invokes the mechanisms of the new print market, depicting his collection as feeding the public's hunger:

> Many pious readers who love the good and who discovered from the description of the life of the Right Reverend Tikhon, published in St Petersburg in 1796, that many of this zealous and virtuous pastor's writings had not been published, eagerly desired their publication too.[67]

Evgenii himself had authored the 1796 biography, in which he presents Tikhon as the antithesis of a state-centred understanding of publicness: in a strikingly Voltairean introduction, Evgenii complains that historiography has traditionally focused on rulers and political figures and argues that Tikhon, by contrast, exemplifies 'the quiet, peaceful virtues of private people', which deserve greater public recognition.[68] Although he never explicitly links the genre of the letter to private virtue in either the biography or the *Remaining Works*, the predominance of epistolary materials and his highlighting of Tikhon's propensity for letter writing imply a connection.[69] Evgenii appeals to contemporary tastes in fiction and typical Western early modern discourses about letters as the genre best revealing the true individual:

> If writings really are the truest mirror of the spirit and heart of an author, and most of all writings that are written not just as a pastime, but rather in social relations about known subjects that arise on particular occasions, then this collection of the works of the Right Reverend Tikhon will, more than his earlier works, show the character of his virtuous soul and his sensitive Christian heart.[70]

Appearing at the very end of the eighteenth century, Evgenii's edition merges multiple paradigms for thinking about letter publication: his projected readership is concurrently a Christian flock, a hungry mass of consumers, and an Enlightenment public interested in both social life and moral improvement.

[67] *Ostal'nyia sochineniia preosviashchennago Tikhona*, p. iii.
[68] Evgenii (Bolkhovitinov), *Polnoe opisanie zhizni preosviashchennago Tikhona*, pp. 2–3.
[69] Ibid., pp. 69–70.
[70] *Ostal'nyia sochineniia preosviashchennago Tikhona*, pp. iv–v.

The shifting boundaries of publicness and the emergence of literary correspondence editions

The practice of publishing correspondence in Russia thus emerged from an expansion of the publicness accorded to letters written by authoritative figures within church and state. The importance of these pre-existing models is especially visible when one turns to the history of published literary correspondences. Initially, printing the correspondence of literary figures was justified by incorporating them into the publicness of the state; only thereafter could Russian writers’ letters begin to acquire publicness in their own right and be juxtaposed with newly translated Western literary correspondences.

The Petrine model of publishing real correspondence in propagandistic pamphlets defending state interests endured under Catherine, but the correspondents were no longer necessarily imperial figures. The new letter writers could also be cultural figures who had won prominence in the European public sphere and thereby became useful to the Russian state. The only eighteenth-century Russian collection of Voltaire’s correspondence fulfilled precisely such a function. In 1769, the bishop of Annecy, Jean-Pierre Biord, published his correspondence with Voltaire as an attack on the patriarch of Ferney during an extended dispute between the two men over a ‘sermon’ that Voltaire gave in his local church. In his three letters, Biord denounces Voltaire for hypocrisy and irreligion; in his two replies, Voltaire defends himself as a virtuous Christian and good landlord to local peasants; a concluding letter from a royal official to Biord confirms the bishop’s objections to Voltaire’s behaviour, albeit lukewarmly.[71] A Russian translator (probably the young Nikolai Novikov) decided to publish the exchange in Russian in 1771, clearly relying on the educated public’s fascination with Voltaire as the greatest literary celebrity of the age. Novikov appended the correspondence to an existing translation of Voltaire’s *Traduction du poème de Jean Plokof, conseiller de Holstein sur les affaires présentes* (1770), a pamphlet exhorting Western powers to ally with Russia against the Ottoman Empire and its primary supporter, France, in the Russo-Turkish War of 1768–74.[72] In a curious reversal, Novikov turned the Catholic bishop’s denunciation of Voltaire into a potent anti-French,

[71] David Adams (ed.), ‘Voltaire’s Correspondence with Jean-Pierre Biord, Bishop of Annecy [Confession de foi de M. de Voltaire]’, in Voltaire, *Œuvres complètes*, 70B, pp. 1–85.

[72] *Perepiska g. Voltera s Episkopom A****, [Tipografiia Sukhoputnogo kadetskogo korpusa], St Petersburg, 1771; *Perevod s poemy o nyneshnikh delakh, Ioganna Plokgofa golstinskago nadvornago sovetnika. v 1770. godu*, [Tipografiia Akademii nauk], St Petersburg, [1770].

anti-Catholic pamphlet: the same French establishment that attacked a virtuous man like Voltaire also sponsored the enemies of innocent Russia.[73] The writer's letters were thus enlisted to represent the state's interests before the public.[74]

A similar example can be found in a translated pamphlet originally published by the British painter Richard Paton to advertise to the British public four prints of paintings representing the major Russian naval victory at Chesme in July 1770. Given to purchasers of the prints as a bonus, the brochure comprises a historical account of the battle; two letters from Paton to Catherine, presenting his work and thanking her for a munificent reward; and one to Paton from Catherine's ambassador in London, A. S. Musin-Pushkin. With a long chiasmus in his thank-you letter, Paton emphasizes the meeting of minds between the British public and its king, on the one hand, and the empress and the Russian public, on the other:

> The favourable Opinion which the Public of this Country entertained of the Paintings [and] the gracious Notice which the King *my* Sovereign condescended to take of them [...] are Favours which I most humbly acknowledge [...]: But your gracious Acceptance of the Pictures [and] the high Honour you have conferred on me, by permitting them to be publicly exhibited [...] fill me with the warmest Sentiments of Gratitude, Veneration, and Respect.[75]

[73] On the literary motif of France conspiring against Russia during this war, see Andrei Zorin, *By Fables Alone: Literature and State Ideology in Late-Eighteenth–Early-Nineteenth-Century Russia*, trans. Marcus C. Levitt with Nicole Monnier and Daniel Schlaffy, Boston, MA, 2014, pp. 61–91.

[74] Novikov published a second edition of the pamphlet in 1787, at the start of Catherine's second Russo-Turkish War (1787–92). Catherine disapproved of the 1787 printing of her correspondence with Voltaire in his posthumous complete works: this apparently impeded further translations of Voltaire's letters despite his stature as one of the century's most celebrated letter writers. Christophe Paillard, 'Ingérence censoriale et imbroglio éditorial. La censure de la correspondance de Voltaire dans les éditions in-8° and in-12 de Kehl', *Revue Voltaire*, 7, 2007, pp. 275–309.

[75] *An Account of the Naval Battle, Fought between the Russians and Turks Off the Coast of Natolia, on the 5th, 6th, and 7th of July, 1770. Extracted from Authentic Papers. To which are Subjoined, Letters Written in Consequence of Four Pictures of the Battle, Being Presented to Her Imperial Majesty the Empress of All the Russias*, [London?], [1773], pp. 23–24; *Skazanie o morskom srazhenii, proiskhodivshem mezhdu rossiianami i turkami pri brege Natolii iiunia 24. 25. i 26. 1770 goda, vybrannoe iz dostoverneishikh zapisok. K semu prilagaiutsia pis′ma pisannye v sledstvie chetyrekh kartin sego srazheniia, podnesennykh Eia Imperatorskomu Velichestvu gosudaryne vserossiiskoi*, v Tipografii morskago shliakhetnago kadetskago korpusa, St Petersburg, [1773], pp. 22–23.

The order of elements in this series is indicative: whereas the British king's notice apparently follows the public's appreciation for the paintings, in Russia the empress alone can render Paton's pictures and letters public. The title page of the Russian translation indicates that Paton's brochure was translated and published at the Naval Cadet Corps in St Petersburg. Emanating from an official institution, the pamphlet highlights how even translating letter collections in the context of language teaching served state interests: the cadets needed to learn English to study and communicate with Britain as the world's leading naval power. In Habermasian terms, these small editions of Voltaire's and Paton's letters mingle the public representation of power by the state with engagement in the Enlightenment public sphere; such an unstable balancing act characterized not just Catherine's reign, but also many eighteenth-century European monarchies.[76]

The ground was thus prepared for the translated literary correspondences that began to appear in Russia from the early 1780s. As we have seen, translations of ancients like Pliny and Cicero grew out of state- and church-driven language teaching, just like that of Paton's letters. Translations of contemporary figures like Rousseau, Sterne and Rabener implied a fascination with varieties of literary fame that allowed publicness to be based on readerly appreciation rather than belonging to the state. Yet, importantly, these translated modern correspondences were joined by others that highlight the ongoing convergence of state and literary ideas of publicness: those of Frederick the Great of Prussia and Henri IV of France.[77] Letters by foreign heads of state fulfilled the same criterion of publicness as Peter the Great's. At the same time, both Frederick and Henri were Enlightenment heroes celebrated by Voltaire.[78] The publicity given to their letters thus had a double justification by the time the translations appeared in the late 1780s and early 1790s.

Nevertheless, published correspondence by Russian writers remained exceptional, and traditional sources of public authority were still necessary

[76] T. C. W. Blanning, *The Culture of Power and the Power of Culture: Old Regime Europe 1660–1789*, Oxford, 2002; Kalugin, '"A Society that Speaks Concordantly"'.

[77] *Ostavshiiasia tvoreniia Fridrikha Vtorago korolia prusskago*, 8 vols, vols 5–8, na izhdivenii I. K. Shnora, St Petersburg, 1789–91; *Perepiska Fridrikha II, prezhde i posle vozshestviia Ego na prestol, s nastavnikom svoim Diuganom Zhandiunom*, trans. Roman Rebinder, v Tipografii P[etra]. B[ogdanovicha]., St Petersburg, 1794; *Dukh Genrika IV, ili sobranie ves'ma liubopytnykh anekdotov, iziashchnykh postupok, ostroumnykh otvetov i neskol'kikh pisem sego Gosudaria*, v Tipografii Kompanii tipograficheskoi, Moscow, 1789.

[78] R. P. Bartlett, 'Catherine II, Voltaire and Henry IV of France', *Newsletter of the Study Group on Eighteenth-Century Russia*, 9, 1981, pp. 41–50.

to justify such publications.[79] Although Leonhard Euler's *Letters on Various Physical and Philosophical Topics, Written to a Certain German Princess*, might be considered the earliest collection of real letters by a modern writer printed in Russia, its primary function as a work of scientific popularization renders its epistolary form a mere convention.[80] Instead, the first true edition of correspondence by a Russian literary or scientific figure coincided precisely with the burst of translated literary correspondences in the 1780s. When the Imperial Academy of Sciences decided to publish some of Mikhail Lomonosov's letters in the first volume of his 1784 posthumous complete works, the editor, O. P. Kozodavlev, proved very self-conscious about this unprecedented act of epistolary publicity. Alluding to a familiar rationale for publishing scholarly missives, Kozodavlev apologizes in a brief introductory note for publicizing texts that do not contain any important scientific information. Instead, Kozodavlev offers three justifications for printing the letters: their novelty, which is announced by the section title, 'Letters to His High Excellency Ivan Ivanovich Shuvalov, which were never before published'; the inherent value of every scrap of Lomonosov's writing ('everything that came from Mr Lomonosov's pen cannot but be precious'); and their autobiographical value ('they reveal to the public certain circumstances in the life of this great writer').[81] Kozodavlev thus imagines his public to be made up of (amateur) scholars who feel at home in the mediatic world of print driven by novelty, adulation and revelation of hidden, private life: the publication of these letters helped to turn Lomonosov into the first Russian scholarly celebrity.[82]

[79] On the status of the Russian author during this period, see V. P. Stepanov, 'K voprosu o reputatsii literatury v seredine XVIII v.', *XVIII vek*, 14, 1983, pp. 105–20; W. Gareth Jones, 'The Image of the Eighteenth-Century Russian Author', in Roger Bartlett and Janet M. Hartley (eds), *Russia in the Age of the Enlightenment: Essays for Isabel de Madariaga*, New York, 1990, pp. 57–74; Ilya Serman, 'Le statut de l'écrivain au XVIIIe siècle', in Efim Etkind et al. (eds), *Histoire de la littérature russe*, vol. 1: *Des origines aux Lumières*, Paris, 1992, pp. 681–89; Viktor Zhivov, 'Pervye russkie literaturnye biografii kak sotsial′noe iavlenie: Trediakovskii, Lomonosov, Sumarokov', *Novoe literaturnoe obozrenie*, 25, 1997, pp. 24–83; Marcus C. Levitt, 'The Illegal Staging of Sumarokov's *Sinav and Truvor* in 1770 and the Problem of Authorial Status in Eighteenth-Century Russia', in Levitt, *Early Modern Russian Letters: Texts and Contexts*, Boston, MA, 2009, pp. 190–217; Irina Reyfman, 'Writing, Ranks and the Eighteenth-Century Russian Gentry Experience', in Kahn (ed.), *Representing Private Lives of the Enlightenment*, pp. 149–66.

[80] Leonhard Euler, *Pis′ma o raznykh fizicheskikh i filozoficheskikh materiiakh, pisannyia k nekotoroi nemetskoi printsesse*, trans. Stepan Rumovskii, 3 vols, pri Imperatorskoi Akademii nauk, St Petersburg, 1768–74.

[81] M. V. Lomonosov, *Polnoe sobranie sochinenii*, 6 vols, izhdiveniem Imperatorskoi Akademii nauk, St Petersburg, 1784–87, 1, pp. 317–18.

[82] On the letters' contribution to establishing Lomonosov's 'myth', see Steven A.

Nevertheless, the distance that separated Russian letter publishing from that in the West remained evident. It can be measured by comparing Kozodavlev's approach to the contemporaneous preface that opened the first of eighteen correspondence volumes in Voltaire's posthumous complete works. Its author, philosopher Nicolas de Condorcet, observes, 'We shall be happy if readers find that, among all the famous men whose letters have been printed after their deaths, [Voltaire] is the first who did not bore them and who could be read for the sole pleasure of reading'.[83] Russian readers certainly did not yet risk feeling bored by the sheer mass of printed correspondence, and the Lomonosov edition, like other Russian and translated editions of writers' letters, downplayed the aesthetic aspects of letters in favour of the social and biographical. Addressed to his patron, the imperial favourite I. I. Shuvalov, and touching on his historical studies and 1755 eulogy of Peter the Great, Lomonosov's letters set a precedent of publishing Russian writers' correspondence by expanding, ever so gradually, the state-centred publicness that governed the editions of Peter's letters.

Although cultural heroes did not replace monarchical ones in either Russia or the West, a broadened definition of the public figure has been identified as a major consequence of the Enlightenment.[84] The evolution of letter collections shows in a nutshell how ideas of publicness expanded in Catherinian Russia. Unsurprisingly, this was not a simple process of translation and emulation of Western models. Rather, the first original published correspondence by a Russian 'great writer' points to an ongoing negotiation within Russian print culture concerning the limits of publicness and publicity.

Usitalo, *The Invention of Mikhail Lomonosov: A Russian National Myth*, Boston, MA, 2013, pp. 27–73. On the concept of celebrity applied to Russia, see Ruth P. Dawson, *Catherine the Great and the Culture of Celebrity in the Eighteenth Century*, London, 2021; K. I. Shneider, 'Fenomen "znamenitosti" v rossiiskom publichnom prostranstve pervoi poloviny XIX veka: teoreticheskie osnovaniia', *Vestnik Permskogo universiteta. Istoriia*, 4, 55, 2021, pp. 5–12; John Randolph, 'Comment: The Utility of "Celebrity"', *Vestnik Permskogo universiteta. Istoriia*, 4, 55, 2021, pp. 25–27.

[83] *Œuvres complètes de Voltaire*, 70 vols, Société littéraire-typographique, Kehl, 1784–89, 52, p. iii; François Bessire, 'Un geste inaugural: la publication de la correspondance dans les premières œuvres complètes de Voltaire', *Épistolaire. Revue de l'A.I.R.E.*, 33, 2007, pp. 23–36.

[84] Jean-Claude Bonnet, *Naissance du Panthéon: Essai sur le culte des grands hommes*, Paris, 1998; Daniel M. Gross, *The Secret History of Emotion: From Aristotle's 'Rhetoric' to Modern Brain Science*, Chicago, IL and London, 2006.

Interacting with the public

There is another sense in which the idea of publicness implicit in original Russian letter collections becomes less state-centric and the horizontal relationship between editors and their public competes with vertical power hierarchies. In some collections, the editor employs an indirect link between his materials and the state publicness of Peter's letters to step forward himself as the object of publicity. These editions echo the function of epistolary publicity as commercial advertisement found in Richard Paton's pamphlet, except that the editor here publishes someone else's rather than his own correspondence. Reversing the state-focused exploitation of cultural clout found in the translated versions of Voltaire and Paton, the editor as cultural figure appropriates the state's publicness and invites readers to affirm his right to be present in the public arena.

Published in 1776, Nikolai Novikov's *History of the Unjust Incarceration of the Innocent Boyar Artemon Sergeevich Matveev* consists almost entirely of historical epistolary materials documenting the life and misfortunes of a Westernizing advisor to Tsar Aleksei Mikhailovich and supporter of the young Peter the Great. As in the collections of Peter's letters, the prefatory materials here express a goal of stimulating scholarly exchange alongside an acknowledgement of Catherine's direct patronage: according to Novikov, 'the book which I today communicate to learned society' was copied from a manuscript in the empress's personal library.[85] As a close confidant of the tsar and a man murdered while protecting Peter, Matveev qualified as a public person within the state; his letters thus deserved publicity both to promote the Petrine and Catherinian visions of the state, and to fuel Russian historical scholarship. Intriguingly, Novikov emphasizes what is lacking from his edition, apparently trying publicly to shame Matveev's descendants into honouring a promise of more materials:

> Very many such letters and other documents [...] can be found in the house of the Princes Meshcherskii, as I heard myself from his late Illustrious Highness Prince Vasilii Ivanovich Meshcherskii, and he promised to send them to me once he had sorted through them. It would be desirable that those letters be communicated to me, so that I could add them to a second edition of this book or begin writing a complete history of this great man.[86]

[85] N. I. Novikov (ed.), *Istoriia o nevinnom zatochenii blizhniago boiarina, Artemona Sergievicha Matveeva, sostoiashchaia iz chelobiten, pisannykh im k Tsariu i Patriiarkhu, takzhe iz pisem k raznym osobam, s priobshcheniem ob"iavleniia o prichinakh ego zatocheniia i o vozvrashchenii iz onago*, [Tipografiia Akademii nauk], St Petersburg, 1776, unpaginated preface 'K chitateliu'.

[86] Ibid.

Even though Prince Vasilii's son and Matveev's great-grandson, Sergei, subscribed to Novikov's publication, the promise apparently remained unfulfilled: in 1785, the second edition reprinted the same challenge.[87] Novikov's audacity suggests the power he ascribed to the Russian public: he thought it worthwhile to make his request in print, so that the weight of a broad readership could perhaps force the revelation of more letters. While reflecting Novikov's somewhat naive optimism about the Russian public that scholars have observed in his work of the 1770s, this demand is nonetheless conceptually significant, as it attests to the moral influence that some Russian editors wanted to ascribe to the Russian public and to the very act of publication.[88]

A more overt attempt to exploit the power of publication occurs in a letter collection edited by the former serf and novelist Matvei Komarov.[89] Printing a small set of seventeenth-century letters exchanged between Russian and Chinese authorities about border and trade disputes, Komarov had no famous correspondent to justify his publication: he did not even know under which tsar the diplomatic missives were composed. Instead, his prefatory materials emphasize the scholarly curiosity and patriotism of the reading public to whom he addresses his work:

> *Dear Compatriots!* As a sign of my gratitude for your gracious reception of the little books I published previously, that is, the *Description of Ancient Royal Weddings* and a few others, I also offer you, for lovers of antiquity, the ancient letters of the Chinese Emperor.[90]

Komarov thus professes to be publishing the letters to contribute to the general effort to make Russian historical documents available to learned society.[91]

[87] *Istoriia o nevinnom zatochenii blizhniago boiarina Artemona Sergievicha Matveeva [...]*, 2nd edn, v Universitetskoi tipografii, u N. Novikova, Moscow, 1785, p. x.

[88] Jones, *Nikolay Novikov*, p. 94; G. J. Marker, 'Novikov's Readers', *Modern Language Review*, 77, 4, 1982, pp. 894–905.

[89] On Komarov as a novelist, see David Gasperetti, *The Rise of the Russian Novel: Carnival, Stylization, and Mockery of the West*, DeKalb, IL, 1998.

[90] *Starinnyia pis′ma kitaiskago imperatora k rossiiskomu gosudariu, pisannyia ot nyneshniago vremeni s lishkom za 150 let, naideny mezhdu ostavshimi pis′mami posle pokoinago grafa Nikity Moiseevicha Zotova, kotoroi, po izvestiiu vernykh rossiiskikh pisatelei, byl u gosudaria imperatora Petra Velikago uchitelem; a nyne izdany v pechat′ byvshim u ego naslednikov sluzhitelem M. K.*, v Tipografii Ponomareva, Moscow, 1787, unpaginated preface 'K chitateliam'.

[91] A parallel can be found in academician Timofei Mal′gin's publication of a seventeenth-century formulary indicating the etiquette to be used in the tsar's epistles: *Chinovnik rossiiskikh gosudarei s raznymi v Evrope i Azii Khristianskimi i Makhometanskimi*

But the main factor driving the release of these letters is Komarov's desire to advertise himself. Unexpectedly freed by his former mistress at her death, Komarov needed a new way to support himself. In pursuit of this goal, Komarov maintains an ambiguity between two editorial identities: he is simultaneously a named individual who serves noble patrons and an anonymous member of a broad national public of readers and writers, of 'lovers of antiquity'. He dedicates the volume to his former mistress's grandson, Prince M. I. Khilkov, and announces on the title page that he found the documents among the papers of his mistress's father-in-law, Peter the Great's mock patriarch, N. M. Zotov. As Viktor Shklovskii has highlighted, Komarov sought the family's patronage by presenting the letter collection as a means of restoring the seriousness of Zotov's historical reputation in the eyes of the Russian public: Zotov is named as Peter's teacher, rather than his fool, and he is shown to have possessed important state papers.[92] But whereas he signs his dedicatory epistle as Khilkov's 'most obedient and most humble servant Matvei Kamarov', the signature on his preface to readers erases his place in the social hierarchy as he blends into the public: 'I remain forever to all of society [...] An inhabitant of the city of Moscow.' Should patronage fail him, Komarov readily turns to the public as a market not just for his book, but also for himself. He made a manuscript addition to the copy of the volume now held in the National Library of Russia: 'The publisher of this book seeks a place to serve in a noble house or with a prominent merchant as a secretary or in another role.'[93] An advert he placed in *Moscow News* (*Moskovskie vedomosti*) listed his two collections of historical documents and his mistress's dog as items for sale, alongside himself as seeking employment.[94] Printing letters for a patriotic and scholarly reading public turns out to be a mechanism for marketing a protean editorial self.

The epistolary public in action

The most brazen example of such editorial self-advertising occurred in the first Russian letter collections to be presented as embodiments of the public's collective voice. This vision of an outspoken and participatory

vladetel'nymi i prochimi vysokimi litsami o vzaimnykh chrez gramoty snosheniiakh izdrevle po 1672 g., kak oboiudnyia mezhdu soboiu titla upotrebliali i znaki druzhestva, pochteniia, preimushchestva i velichiia iz"iavliali, pri Imperatorskoi Akademii nauk, St Petersburg, 1792.

[92] Viktor Shklovskii, *Matvei Komarov: zhitel' goroda Moskvy*, Leningrad, 1929, pp. 19–20, 31, 132–51.

[93] *Starinnyia pis'ma kitaiskago imperatora*, [unpag.].

[94] Shklovskii, *Matvei Komarov*, p. 150.

epistolary public can be found in the most unlikely of places: three volumes of customers' letters published in the early 1790s by a St Petersburg apothecary, D. R. Grodnitskii.[95] In the late 1780s, Grodnitskii began selling a counterfeit version of Johann Georg Kiesow's panacea, known as the Augsburger Lebens-Essenz or, in Grodnitskii's Russian version, Zhiznennaia Essentsiia (Essence of Life). He similarly traded in versions of two other European panaceas: Haarlem oil and Opodeldoc, the latter wonderful name invented by the Renaissance alchemist Paracelsus. He was denounced as a fake by his rival, Ia. E. Danilovskii, who sold medication imported from abroad. Their acrimonious dispute combined epistolary and print media: Danilovskii apparently circulated printed letters and pamphlets censuring Grodnitskii's quackery to provincial postmasters and authorities across the empire.[96] Grodnitskii answered the accusations by printing the letters he received from happy users of his medications; he then circulated copies of the printed volumes to his customers, in turn generating more letters that were published in later books. While Grodnitskii anonymised the letters in the first collection, subsequent volumes provided full names and titles for each writer. Bridging journalism and medical literature in his approach to publishing correspondence, Grodnitskii summons readers not merely to appreciate the letters of prominent individuals: members of the public are invited to become published letter writers themselves. Publicness is no longer an inherent quality of the letter writer on the monarchical model: rather, the letters are public because they belong to a collective that materializes through the very act of print publication.

[95] *Perechni pisem, poluchennykh aptekarem Danilom Grodnitskim, pisannykh k nemu v pokhvalu prodaiushcheisia v ego apteke Zhiznennoi Essentsii, ot raznykh osob toiu Essentsieiu pol'zovavshikhsia*, v Imperatorskoi tipografii, St Petersburg, 1792; *Upotreblenie, deistvie i pol'za trekh lekarstv: Essentsii zhizni, Garlemskikh kapel' i naruzhnago balzama nazyvaemago Opodeldok, izobretennykh i po osoblivomu dozvoleniiu Gosudarstvennoi meditsinskoi kollegii priugotovliaemykh v Sanktpeterburge privilegirovannym aptekarem Danilom Grodnitskim, s prilozheniem perechnei pisem ot raznykh osob v raznye vremena k onomu aptekariu pisannykh, svidetel'stvuiushchikh o pol'ze tekh lekarstv*, v Imperatorskoi tipografii, St Petersburg, 1793; *Prodolzhenie perechnei pisem ot raznykh osob k aptekariu Danilu Grodnitskomu, svidetel'stvuiushchikh o pol'ze lekarstv: Zhiznennoi Essentsii, Garlemskikh kapel' i naruzhago balzama Opodeldok, im Grodnitskim izobretennykh i po osoblivomu dozvoleniiu Gosudarstvennoi meditsinskoi kollegii priugotovliaemykh*, v Imperatorskoi tipografii, St Petersburg, 1794.

[96] Danilovskii added a preface denouncing Grodnitskii's counterfeits and describing his own view of their dispute to both 1793 editions of his translation of a Dutch pamphlet about the efficacy of Haarlem oil: *Poleznoe opisanie upotrebleniia Garlemskikh kapel' ili bal'zama nazyvaemago medicamentum gratia probatum, izdannoe samim izobretatelem onykh g. fan Tilliem*, pri Imperatorskoi Akademii nauk, St Petersburg, 1793, pp. i–xvi.

Grodnitskii's enterprise emulated Western European pamphlets that similarly advertised remedies through printed correspondence from satisfied customers. In the 1780s, for example, British doctors printed numerous collections of their patients' letters that bear evident structural similarities to Grodnitskii's.[97] But Grodnitskii's immediate model was a German tract by Kiesow promoting his original Lebens-Essenz, which Grodnitskii himself translated into Russian in the late 1780s. The bulk of the pamphlet consists of one hundred brief accounts of cures effected by the medication: several take the form of letters, some anonymised and others signed and dated with indications of the author's location and social status. In one case, Kiesow notes his patients' desire for publication: he asserts that an account was submitted 'with the request that it be inserted into this book for the glory of God and the benefit of the human race'.[98] Grodnitskii thus represents an unusual example of an editor whose epistolary publishing project can be traced to a direct Western precedent and who began with translation before emulating his source in an original collection.

Grodnitskii's books are apparently the first of their kind in Russia, although readers had been prepared by letters used in journalism in the earlier decades of Catherine's reign. For example, in *News of the Imperial Foundling Home*, published as a supplement to both *St Petersburg News* (*Sanktpeterburgskie vedomosti*) and *Moscow News* beginning in 1778, representatives of the state used printed letters to stage performances of civic participation and thereby seek investors for the Foundling Home.[99] The newsletter not only presented an ostensible exchange of

[97] *Remarkable Cures, of Gouty, Bilious, and Nervous Cases, related by the Patients themselves, and published at their Desire, in Sundry Letters to John Scot, M. D.*, 7th edn, London, 1784; J. H. Smyth, *A New Treatise on the Venereal Disease, Gleets, Seminal Weaknesses, the Dreadful Effects of Self-Pollution, and the Causes of Impotency, Barrenness, etc.*, 17th edn, London, 1780, pp. 46–51.

[98] *Nastavlenie o deistviiakh i upotreblenii dragotsennago lekarstva, nazyvaemago Essentsieiu zhizni, mnogimi opytami dokazannago, izobretennago i priugotovliaemago v Augsburge kurfirst-bavarskim sovetnikom i doktorom Kizovym, i opisannago v pol′zu obshchestva s prilozheniem sta primerov o raznykh izlecheniiakh proizvedennykh onoiu Essentsieiu po vsemilostiveishe otlichno preimushchestvennoi Privilegii ot Ego Velichestva, imperatora rimskago*, u Vil′kovskago, St Petersburg, 1790, p. 69; *Unterricht von denen Wirkungen und dem Gebrauch der kostbaren, und durch unzählige Proben bewährten Lebens-Essenz, so in Augsburg verfertiget wird von dem Churfürstlich Bayerischen Rath und Doctor Kiesow. Zum Besten des Publici beschrieben und mit hundert Exempeln von allerley Curen, so dadurch gemacht worden, erläutert*, [n.p.], 1770, p. 47.

[99] W. Gareth Jones, 'The *Morning Light* Charity Schools, 1777–80', *Slavonic and East European Review*, 56, 1, 1978, pp. 47–67 (pp. 49–51); Ekaterina Shubenkina, 'Between Literary Training and Literary Service: School Writing Instruction in the Russian Empire, 1780–1860', unpublished PhD thesis, University of Southern California, forthcoming 2024.

correspondence between the Home's director, I. I. Betskoi, and newly selected trustees, but also printed the letters of a deceased benefactor and more minor investors. There is a marked difference between the signed letters — almost all by major grandees — and the other documents, most of which are presented as model texts for readers to imitate in making their own investments: with real names replaced by 'so-and-so' (*imiarek*) or 'My dear sir N. N.' (*Milostivoi Gosudar′ moi N. N.*), the letters are made to resemble the formulae provided in a prayerbook or epistolary manual.[100] Despite the effort to elicit public participation, the underlying model of publicness in the *News* remains that of a court-centred elite representing state power before an anonymous populace invited to provide strictly codified responses.

Fiction offered a more frequent model for published correspondence in Russian journalism. Many different journals invited contributions from the public, but printed responses were typically anonymised, fictionalized, or invented wholescale.[101] The satirical journal overseen by Catherine, *All Sorts* (*Vsiakaia vsiachina*), and its followers present an early, prominent example: most letters from 'contributors' are fictional, constituting elaborate games of literary persona played by the editors.[102] This sort of game was taken to new heights in *Economic Magazine* (*Ekonomicheskoi magazin*, 1780–89), a massive journal of agronomy, medicine and housekeeping, whose editor, the prolific A. T. Bolotov, places epistolary exchange with readers at the heart of his journalistic project. In the first issue, he declares his desire to expand the network of correspondents that had begun forming around his previous journal, *The Village Dweller* (*Sel′skii zhitel′*, 1778–79). He provides detailed instructions for how readers can communicate with him and offers different modalities from simple submission of articles to private correspondence that would not be printed.[103] Later on, he excitedly envisages correspondence with readers as an ever-expanding exchange of information modelled on a market economy:

[100] *Izvestii Imperatorskago vospitatel′nago doma, k udovol′stviiu obshchestva sluzhashchiia*, January–June 1778, pp. 1–36.

[101] In scholarly journalism, see N. I. Novikov's call for contributions in *Sanktpeterburgskiia uchenyia vedomosti na 1777 god*, 1, [6 January 1777], p. [6]. On public participation via letters to the editor in Western Europe, see Elizabeth Andrews Bond, *The Writing Public: Participatory Knowledge Production in Enlightenment and Revolutionary France*, Ithaca, NY and London, 2021.

[102] *Vsiakaia vsiachina*, [Tipografiia Akademii nauk], [St Petersburg], [1769]–70; Jones, *Nikolay Novikov*, pp. 24–56.

[103] A. T. Bolotov, *Ekonomicheskoi magazin*, 40 vols, v Universitetskoi tipografii, u N. Novikova, Moscow, 1780–89, 1, pp. 4–16.

> With what eagerness I, for my part, would try to tell them everything I know that could please them! And how good it would be if we could settle up with one another and pay one another in the same currency.[104]

Articles in epistolary form or labelled as originating with correspondents dominate the journal's early volumes. But no one, not even Bolotov, corresponds under their real name. Published exchanges occur under pseudonyms such as A. Sostradatelev ('A. Sympathetic'), and many letters were obviously written for publication and never mailed in manuscript. The outburst just quoted comes from a series of missives Bolotov purportedly addressed to a certain Uedinennyi (or Uedinen, 'Solitary'), but the letter consists of five public replies to other correspondents. Despite his idealization of public exchange, any real correspondence that Bolotov had with his readers disappears under multiple layers of mystification before reaching print.

Russia's emerging medical literature likewise offers a key context for Grodnitskii's epistolary endeavour. Practically non-existent before Catherine's reign, original and translated medical books became commonplace, encouraged especially by the State Medical College and the aftermath of the 1771 Moscow plague riots.[105] Here one can find staged correspondence that, like Grodnitskii's volumes, seeks to defend a medical reputation before the reading public. In 1789, rebutting an accusation that his malpractice had hastened the demise of Prince P. S. Gagarin, Dr F. G. Politkovskii published a self-defence in epistolary form alongside letters of support from Gagarin's wife and siblings and from medical colleagues.[106] But a pamphlet by another colleague, Engelbert Wichelhausen, reveals the artificiality of this supposed correspondence. Writing in French, Wichelhausen claims that Politkovskii demanded he sign a pre-drafted letter of support, even though Wichelhausen lacked the knowledge of Russian needed to understand Politkovskii's text; when Wichelhausen demurred, Politkovskii extorted a response by adding a footnote to the printed letter of support: 'Dr Wichelhausen was supposed to sign [this letter] as one who was in consultation; but he assured me that he would

[104] Ibid., 1, p. 66.

[105] John T. Alexander, *Bubonic Plague in Early Modern Russia: Public Health and Urban Disaster*, Baltimore, MD and London, 1980, pp. 279–86; S. M. Grombakh, *Russkaia meditsinskaia literatura XVIII veka*, Moscow, 1953.

[106] *Pis′mo ot kollezhskago assessora i doktora Politkovskago k G****, [Universitetskaia tipografiia], [Moscow], [1789]; *Pribavlenie k pis′mu kollezhskago assessora i doktora Politkovskago*, [Universitetskaia tipografiia], [Moscow], [1789].

soon print his explanation.'[107] While Politkovskii's pamphlet accordingly does not qualify as a letter collection, it shows that, under Catherine, published correspondence came to be regarded as a trustworthy form of testimony by private individuals and a potentially powerful means of marshalling public support.

Against this background, Grodnitskii's volumes stand out for their self-conscious attempt to use published letters to generate and depict public opinion. Grodnitskii evinces no doubt that his letter books represent the voice of the true Russian enlightened public. He explains his vision in the foreword to his final volume, where, in a delightful reapplication of Enlightenment vocabulary to the business of charlatanism, he depicts the letters as incontrovertible proof of the progress of Enlightenment in Russia. For him, they show how, under Catherine, 'minds have been purified of the prejudices that forced them to consider everything foreign to be miraculous' and, instead, 'in imitation of their most wise Monarch, the enlightened public (*prosveshchennaia publika*) strives to discover in the depths of the Fatherland and to encourage without bias talents previously oppressed by the former prejudice'. In short, the public are enlightened because they prefer homebrewed rip-offs to foreign products and 'seem to vie with one another to express their satisfaction [with them]'. The decision to publish the letters is therefore presented as a means of fostering individual initiative in a burgeoning civil society:

> through the impartial gratitude that one sees in them, [the previously published letters and those I am herewith publishing] doubtless will incite and encourage others who dedicate their time to the benefit of their fellow countrymen to carry out their well-intentioned undertakings.[108]

Regardless of the authenticity of Grodnitskii's products or of his claims to be enlightened, the reader of his collections watches the public take shape before their eyes. The authors of Grodnitskii's letters constitute a cross-section of literate, largely provincial society: although the genuineness of the texts cannot be conclusively proven, many writers demonstrably existed in real life.[109] Although the service nobility unsurprisingly

[107] E. Wichelhausen, *Sur la maladie de feu le prince Paul de Gagarin, lieutenant général, premier commendant de la ville de Moscou et chevalier de l'ordre St George*, Moscow, 1790, pp. 1–3; *Pribavlenie k pis'mu*, p. 5.

[108] *Prodolzhenie perechnei pisem*, unpaginated 'Predislovie'.

[109] Many correspondents in state service are listed in V. P. Stepanov, *Russkoe sluzhiloe dvorianstvo vtoroi poloviny XVIII veka (1764–1795)*, St Petersburg, 2003. In the 1794 volume,

predominates, the correspondents include women, monks and merchants. The letters began as social interactions between private individuals: in this period, ordering by mail was no impersonal click of a button on Amazon, but rather it entailed forming a personal relationship with Grodnitskii. First-time customers regularly open their letters by apologizing that they 'do not have the honour of knowing' him personally, while recurrent correspondents thank Grodnitskii not just for his products, but also for his friendly letters.[110] These private individuals are quickly constituted as a reading and writing public: although the letter writers included in the first volume may very well have had no idea that their words would be printed, subsequent volumes include correspondents' accounts of reading the published letters, and by the end no one writing to Grodnitskii could have been unaware of the potential for publication. Some correspondents self-consciously decide to write for publication, just like their Western counterparts: Second Major Petr Abaturov in Smolensk proclaims that he 'considers it [his] duty to use this letter to inform the whole world of the astounding effects of the *Zhiznennaia Essentsiia*'.[111] Lieutenant-General Matvei Muromtsov in Dankov expresses his delight at seeing his own letter printed in the 1792 volume and responds directly to a lower-ranking letter writer published alongside him, Collegiate Assessor Ivan Kozelkin from Briansk: Muromtsov corroborates Kozelkin's account of his wife's healing with further examples of women cured and confirms Kozelkin's assertion of the Essentsiia's effectiveness against fever.[112] Grodnitskii's volumes embody the public as a collectivity of various members of society who come together to discuss in print a topic of common interest.

Grodnitskii's primary strategy of self-defence was to situate himself at the heart of a pan-imperial network of real correspondents who form a public by virtue of their participation in printed discourse. Grodnitskii certainly did not miss any opportunity to align himself with imperial power: his later books assert on the title page that he held an imperial privilege and had received special permission from the State Medical College to make his concoctions. He dedicates the books to A. I. Vasil′ev, the director of the Medical College. Yet, the magnitude and authority of Grodnitskii's network formed the core of his argument. Displaying the correspondents' names and titles lends weight to their testimonies as

the censor's approbation states that he compared the letters with the originals (*s podlinnymi svidetel′stvoval*).

[110] For example, *Upotreblenie, deistvie i pol′za trekh lekarstv*, pp. 77, 99.

[111] Ibid., p. 92.

[112] Ibid., pp. 47–51.

trustworthy individuals and as a true representation of Russian society. The 1793 and 1794 volumes include not only an index of ailments that patients claimed his remedies could cure, but also a geographical gazetteer listing all the letters, say, from Kupiansk, Mtsensk or Iakutsk; there is even a letter from an army major who orders the *Zhiznennaia Essentsiia* for an indigenous man in the Transbaikal region.[113] This gazetteer may have allowed provincial readers to identify letter writers who lived nearby and to approach them for confirmation of the printed testimony. Grodnitskii's efforts to enlist society had no oppositional political import: as military personnel and civil servants, many of his correspondents are themselves representatives of the imperial state and its colonizing forces. But his books still stand out in the eighteenth-century print landscape for their remarkable effort to imagine the collective voice of the empire's inhabitants.

Grodnitskii's volumes richly illustrate the permeable border between public and private in this period. Medical discourse in eighteenth-century Europe valued highly the individual subjective experience of illness, and letters to and by doctors circulated patients' stories as both scientific evidence and engaging literary narratives.[114] In this vein, Grodnitskii's volumes integrate the most private aspects of his customers' lives into a discourse about scientific progress and public utility.[115] The printed missives reveal impressively intimate details about their authors. Petr Abaturov unabashedly describes how the *Zhiznennaia Essentsiia* helped him to expel a blockage in his urinary tract — right down to the sound that the obstructing object made when it hit the chamber pot.[116] But publication here does not dramatize the private: rather, personal experience is simply absorbed into the realm of public interest as useful data. Although

[113] Ibid., p. 76.

[114] Wayne Wild, *Medicine-by-Post: The Changing Voice of Illness in Eighteenth-Century British Consultation Letters and Literature*, Amsterdam and New York, 2006; Philip Rieder, 'Writing to Fellow Physicians: Literary Genres and Medical Questions in Louis Odier's (1748–1817) Correspondence', in Sophie Vasset (ed.), *Medicine and Narration in the Eighteenth Century*, SVEC 2013:04, Oxford, 2013, pp. 47–63; Séverine Pilloud, *Les mots du corps. Expérience de la maladie dans les lettres de patients à un médecin du 18e siècle: Samuel Auguste Tissot*, Lausanne, 2013.

[115] On 'utility' in scientific discourse, see Alexander Iosad, '"Sciences Strange and Diverse": Europeanization through the Transfer of Scientific Knowledge in Russia, 1717–65', unpublished DPhil thesis, University of Oxford, 2017, and Iosad, 'Curiosity, Utility, Pleasure: Official Discourses of Natural Philosophy and Their Alternatives in Russia in the Run-Up to 1762', in Schönle, Zorin and Evstratov (eds), *The Europeanized Elite in Russia*, pp. 46–65.

[116] *Upotreblenie, deistvie i pol'za trekh lekarstv*, pp. 96–98.

commercial interests undoubtedly came first for Grodnitskii, rhetorically he presents epistolary publicity as a civic obligation: the sheer number of letters, their usefulness as 'new and diverse medical observations' and his pleasure at helping his neighbour all make publication 'almost [his] duty to the public' (*kak by moim dolgom v razsuzhdenii publiki*).[117] For all the differences between Grodnitskii's project and most other eighteenth-century Russian letter editions, his books remain typical in viewing correspondence as means of assimilating the personal into social relationships and public life.

Conclusion

While representing only a small sample of the publications generated by the printing boom of the second half of the eighteenth century, letter collections constitute a unique source revealing how the expansion of print contributed to changes in Russian thinking about what it means to be (a) public. The traditional institutions of state and church set the initial conditions out of which a practice of publishing correspondence emerged; they also provided a key stimulus to the genre's development. The publicness of published letters originally resided in the status of the letter writer as an embodiment of state or church authority. Catherinian letter collections integrated cultural forms of authority, such as that of artists or writers, by attaching their texts to these older forms of publicness. Only then could Western understandings of correspondence collections as vehicles of literary self-expression and explorations of private life begin to be assimilated, primarily through translation. By the end of the century, even the letters of ordinary people acquired, at least conceptually, a place in print.

Concordantly, state- and church-sponsored letter collections led the way towards a diversification in understandings of the reading public. The indoctrination of readers as zealous and admiring imperial subjects competed even in the most official collections with promotion of scholarly exchange in print. Traditional concepts of the Christian community, in which letters had always figured prominently as foundational texts, proved receptive to print; the success of religious letter collections shows how the idea of the reading public blended effectively with that of the Christian flock. Individual editors turned to letter collections as media for self-promotion, conceiving of the reading public as hungry consumers and patriotic afficionados of history and science, but also as a potentially

[117] *Prodolzhenie perechnei pisem*, unpaginated 'Predislovie'.

powerful court for adjudging personal and professional reputations. Almost every single collection proposes a new, experimental approach to using published letters to form a bond between letter writers, editors, texts and readers. While there is no question that the eighteenth-century Russian public was small and politically powerless, the diversity of approaches to publicity in these collections conveys a certain effervescence. Published correspondence shows that eager exploration of the meanings and possibilities of publicity characterized the Catherinian era. If the literary public sphere is defined by competition between ideas in print, one can certainly find divergent understandings of epistolary publicity jostling for readerly attention in the letter collections of late eighteenth-century Russia.

The Strange Case of the Disappearing Soviet Waiter

DIANE P. KOENKER

THIS article was inspired by my own experience of dining out in Intourist restaurants in the 1970s, where the waiters disappeared after serving the last course, and it seemed impossible to get a bill and to pay; or a whole line-up of tuxedoed waiters could be seen 'propping up the wall' at the back of the half-empty dining room, with no interest in attending to their customers. My research on Soviet consumer culture and the service sector has led me to realize that my foreigner's experience was hardly unique, and it was not simply due to a Soviet contempt for capitalist tourists. Take the example of a trio of customers at the Moscow Volga restaurant in May 1957. Hoping to have dinner, they sat at an uncleared table for fifteen minutes before anyone appeared to remove the dirty dishes; it was another hour before a waiter took their order, and their food came only forty minutes later. 'And we want to note, that all this time while we were not being served, the waiters were sitting and calmly conversing among themselves.'[1] Numerous cartoons in *Krokodil′* confirmed the stereotype of the neglected Soviet restaurant patron.[2] Bad restaurant service is the theme of El′dar Riazanov's 1965 satiric comedy, *Daite zhalobnuiu knigu* (Give me the Complaint Book).[3] Soviet officials acknowledged the problem in their own closed deliberations. Many of the staff in restaurants and cafeterias

Diane P. Koenker is Professor of Russian and Soviet History at UCL School of Slavonic and East European Studies and Professor Emerita of History at the University of Illinois at Urbana-Champaign.

Earlier versions of this article were presented at the 2018 convention of the Association for Slavic, East European and Eurasian Studies in Boston, Massachusetts, at the University of Tallinn and in the SSEES Interdisciplinary Research Workshop. I am grateful to all discussants and participants for their helpful comments.

[1] Tsentral′nyi arkhiv goroda Moskvy (hereafter, TsAGM), f. 224 (Moscow Restaurant Trust), op. 1, d. 108, l. 21.

[2] For example, *Krokodil′*, 8 (20 March 1965), p. 5; *Krokodil′*, 11 (20 April 1965), p. 7; *Krokodil′*, 11 (20 April 1965), p. 7.

[3] *Daite zhalobnuiu knigu* (dir. El′dar Riazanov, Mosfil′m, 1965).

were unwelcoming to customers, admitted the chair of the Trade Union of Trade and Public Catering Employees in 1967. 'There are restaurant patrons who've waited an awfully long time without any attention from the serving personnel.'[4]

Why was service in Soviet restaurants so consistently and uniformly bad? Why did waiters refuse to seat customers when their restaurants were half empty, why did meals take an hour to be served, why did waiters short-change their customers when it came time to pay the bill? There are many explanations, some of which surfaced at the time. The poor performance of Soviet waiters mirrored the Soviet economic system as a whole, and perhaps the problem was socialism itself, where the public ownership of the means of reproduction (nourishing the population) provided neither effective incentive systems (carrots) nor plausible methods of discipline (sticks). Finding the right incentives — a perennial problem of the Soviet economy — played a widely discussed role. Appeals to ideology and enthusiasm clearly failed to motivate workers in the restaurant trade. The endemic scarcity of socialist economic systems was readily observed in Soviet restaurants: the public catering sector lacked sufficient food supplies, tables or serving personnel to serve a growing urban population. But the problem goes deeper than the socialist shortage economy. Other explanations were more specific to the sector. Officials bemoaned the quality of the individuals who staffed the public catering sector, who lacked education and motivation. The best and the brightest Soviet youth preferred to work in production or in glamour fields like physics or medicine.[5] Blame also fell on poorly organized workplaces and incompetent or indifferent management. Underlying these observations was the fact that jobs in restaurant service in particular and in service in general were held in very low esteem. It was difficult to attract people to a sector that was so despised. Beyond the endemic issue of shortages, I would argue that the indifference of waiters toward their customers may have been a logical reaction to low esteem and inadequate rewards. It was also a product of socialist job security, which provided an opportunity to exert control over the workplace in defiance of official norms and prescriptions and without risk of dismissal.

[4] Gosudarstvennyi Arkhiv Rossiiskoi Federatsii (hereafter, GARF), f. 5452 (Trade Union of Trade and Public Catering Employees), op. 37, d. 892, l. 55.

[5] V. N. Shubkin (ed.), *Trudiashchaiasia molodezh′: obrazovanie, professiia, mobil′nost′*, Moscow, 1984, p. 80. For similar concerns with respect to sales clerks, see Diane P. Koenker, 'The Smile behind the Sales Counter: Soviet Shop Assistants on the Road to Full Communism,' *Journal of Social History*, 54, 3, Spring 2021, pp. 872–96.

This article explores the experience of dining out in the Soviet Union of the 1960s, that moment in the consumer history of the USSR in which fulfilling the promises of Communism appeared within reach for the majority urban population of the country. In the century of the cosmos and of atoms, bemoaned another union official, why couldn't the problem of restaurant service be solved?[6] I will examine the role of the restaurant in the dining options of the Soviet urban population, the organization of restaurants, and the culture of service and status of the waitering trade. For reasons of space, I am going to focus on the front of the house, although the failures of the cooks in the kitchen also drew censure and satire. As a waiter in a *Krokodil′* cartoon from 1961 warns, 'If you knew what was awaiting you, you wouldn't ask me to hurry'.[7] I will examine questions of economics and economic reform to investigate how the socialist economic system tried to produce efficient and pleasurable restaurant experiences. Finally, I will attempt to reconstruct the perspective of the Soviet waiter him or herself, to explore how they justified the behaviours decried by officials and customers both domestic and international. This exploration reveals a paradox between competing ideals of the 'good life': one of technologically driven satisfaction of biological needs, and the other of a psychologically rounded balance between work and life, in which the whole person merited respect.

Scholars of post-war socialism have increasingly turned their focus to the question of socialist consumer regimes and whether socialist consumption differed qualitatively from its capitalist counterpart. Under capitalism, theorists argue, consumers purchase goods as much for their sign value — what they convey to others about their status and identities — as for their utility, or use value, inevitably contributing to production and overproduction of goods in order that some might become the 'latest thing'.[8] Rational socialism, however, would avoid this trap of conspicuous consumption through the inculcation of a socialist aesthetic based on utility, simplicity of form and moderate choice. Recent studies of consumer practices in socialist Europe, however, have emphasized that socialist

[6] GARF, f. 5452, op. 37, d. 955, ll. 158–59.

[7] *Krokodil′*, 10 (16 June 1961), p. 14. The Soviet restaurant and stolovaia kitchen is a subject of my further research.

[8] Thorstein Veblen, *The Theory of the Leisure Class: An Economic Study of Institutions*, New York, 1899; Mary Douglas and Baron Isherwood, *The World of Goods: Towards an Anthropology of Consumption*, 2nd edn, London, 1996; Frank Trentmann, *The Empire of Things: How We Became a World of Consumers, from the Fifteenth Century to the Twenty-First*, New York, 2016.

consumers too used their purchasing decisions to express their sense of distinction.[9] They also question the argument that socialist regimes only reluctantly supported consumerism as a concession to their materialist subjects. Rather they argue that consumption was a fundamental element of the original socialist promise. It is my contention that in the decade of the 1960s (which I suggest began in 1957), Soviet citizens and government began to act on this promise, exercising choice, establishing schools of taste, seeking to understand and satisfy consumer demand. They did so in a framework of increasing international consciousness, stimulated by the expansion of international tourist travel, and by the publicity given to the cultural exchange of films, literature and the arts.[10] Soviet dining culture was part of this new socialist consumer regime.

Dining out in the USSR

Soviet public catering had originated in the hungry years of the civil war as a way to optimize scarce food supplies. 'People's catering' (*Narpit*) concentrated on provision of noon meals in factory canteens in the 1920s, to ensure labour productivity and economies of scale, but also as a way to permit women to leave their domestic roles and join the ranks of paid labour. For some visionaries, public catering would eventually replace all domestic meal preparation.[11] By the late 1950s, 'public catering' (*obshchestvennoe pitanie*) had grown into an institutionalized network of eating places ranging from hole-in-the-wall snack bars or *bufets* with

[9] Paulina Bren and Mary Neuburger (eds), *Communism Unwrapped: Consumption in Cold War Eastern Europe,* Oxford, 2012; Cristofer Scarboro, Diana Mincyte and Zsuzsa Gille (eds), *The Socialist Good Life: Desire, Development, and Standards of Living in Eastern Europe,* Bloomington, IN, 2020; Patrick Hyder Patterson, *Bought and Sold: Living and Losing the Good Life in Socialist Yugoslavia,* Ithaca, NY, 2012; Natalya Chernyshova, *Soviet Consumer Culture in the Brezhnev Era,* London, 2013; Susan E. Reid, 'Socialist Modern – This Is Tomorrow! Becoming a Consumer in the Soviet Union', in Anne E. Gorsuch and Diane P. Koenker (eds), *The Socialist Sixties: Crossing Borders in the Second World,* Bloomington, IN, 2013, pp. 25–65; Anna Ivanova, *Magaziny 'Berezka': paradoksy potrebleniia v pozdnom SSSR,* Moscow, 2018; Anna Ivanova, 'Rich Hairdressers and Fancy Car Repairmen: The Rise of a Service Worker Elite in the USSR and the Evolution of Soviet Society in the 1970s', *Journal of Social History,* 56, 4, Summer 2023, pp. 856–81.

[10] Diane P. Koenker, 'The Taste of Others: Soviet Adventures in Cosmopolitan Cuisines', *Kritika,* 19, 2, Spring 2018, pp. 243–72. See also, Anne E. Gorsuch, *All This Is Your World: Soviet Tourism at Home and Abroad after Stalin,* Oxford, 2011; Eleanory Gilburd, *To See Paris and Die: The Soviet Lives of Western Culture,* Cambridge, MA, 2018.

[11] In Moscow, the Public Catering Committee was created in February 1918. Mauricio Borrero, *Hungry Moscow: Scarcity and Urban Society in the Russian Civil War,* New York, 2003, p. 150; Irina Glushchenko, *Obshchepit: Mikoian i sovetskaia kukhnia,* Moscow, 2nd edn, 2015, ch. 2; Julie Hessler, *A Social History of Soviet Trade,* Princeton, NJ, 2004, pp. 177–79.

stand-up tables, to snack bars specializing in *pirozhki, blini*, *pelmeni* or *shashlyk*, to workplace canteens (*stolovaia*) of varying levels of quality and tone, to youth cafés, and to the pinnacle of the public catering pyramid, the restaurant.[12] If the ice cream café had become newly chic in the urban capitals, the stolovaia remained devoted to serving the largest number of patrons in the shortest period of time at the lowest cost. Its standardized offerings and indifferent service became irreparably linked with the word *obshchepit* (public catering) in post-Soviet memory.[13]

The country of 'cosmos and atoms' had pledged in the late 1950s to introduce 'progressive forms' to the retail trade sector to provide consumers with shopping and dining experiences appropriate to a modern developed society. In the public catering sector, progressive forms of trade included the transfer from table service to self-service in stolovaias, the use of semi-prepared foods in restaurant kitchens, the reorganization of restaurant and stolovaia kitchens to provide take-away dishes, and the expansion of restaurant service to cater banquets for work and family celebrations, including jubilees, anniversaries and weddings.[14] In other words, the regime aimed to offer efficiency but also the occasional opportunity for luxury. By 1963, a Moscow official boasted that 90 per cent of its establishments operated on the principle of self-service, and the pages of the industry's monthly journal, *Obshchestvennoe pitanie*, was full of features on the latest technology in cafeteria lines and steam tables.[15] Even more progressive would be the replacement of serving personnel altogether through the expansion of automatic food vending machines. The state planning agency Gosplan had promised in 1960 to produce a half million vending machines by 1965, selling not only carbonated water,

[12] The Moscow restaurant trust, only one of the components of 'obshchepit', enumerated thirty-six *restorany*, sixteen *kafe* and *zakusochnye*, twenty-six *stolovii*, 238 *bufety*, nine *avtobufety* and seven *kulinarnii magaziny* in its network in 1958, with the capacity to serve 17,589 people at a time. TsAGM, f. 224, op. 1, d. 108, l. 5. These numbers exclude the parallel dining institutions that belonged to organizations and agencies, most famously the restaurants of the Union of Writers and Union of Journalists, and including 'Professors' dining rooms' in universities. See also Lynn and Wesley Fisher, *The Moscow Gourmet: Dining Out in the Capital of the* USSR, Ann Arbor, MI, 1974; Alison K. Smith, *Cabbage and Caviar: A History of Food in Russia*, London, 2021, pp. 258–65; Darra Goldstein, *The Kingdom of Rye: A Brief History of Russian Food*, Berkeley, CA, 2022, pp. 58–62.

[13] Anna Mass, 'Moskovskoe kafe', *Smena*, 1, 2, 1968, pp. 8–10. To compare a restaurant to a stolovaia was an insult. TsAGM, f. 224, op. 1, d. 286, l. 70. On cafés, see also, Gleb Tsipursky, *Socialist Fun: Youth, Consumption, and State-Sponsored Popular Culture in the Soviet Union, 1945–1970*, Pittsburgh, PA, 2016. On the stolovaia, see Glushchenko, *Obshchepit*, pp. 184–85.

[14] TsAGM, f. 224, op. 1, d. 164, ll. 139–40.

[15] GARF, f. 5452, op. 37, d. 482, l. 28.

but flowers, pasteurized milk, bread, salt, sugar, groats and conserves.[16] Already in 1958, the journal *Obshchestvennoe pitanie* was reporting on snack bar automats in Gomel′ and Erevan.[17] The waiters' profession was in its last years, mused a journalist in 1965: cybernetics and button-pushing would take over, and customers could just press 'cold appetizers', 'hot dish', 'drinks' and even 'tip'.[18]

Automats aside, promises to consumers also included expansion of the dining-out network. In 1959, the Soviet government threw down its marker for improved consumer life, with a decree that called for the expansion of public catering, to make it mass, convenient and profitable.[19] In 1959 the city of Moscow, the largest in the country, numbered a miserly sixty-four restaurants for its population of six million people, and the Moscow restaurant trust now announced plans to create twenty-three new restaurants between 1959 and 1965.[20] In 1961, the country operated 147,000 public dining enterprises, serving fifteen billion dishes a year. Its goal was to double this number in ten years. The ambitious party programme of 1961 had boasted that by 1980, 80 per cent of all meals would be consumed in public eating places.[21] Most of these new enterprises would be workplace canteens, but expansion plans also included cafés and restaurants.[22] Leningrad public catering officials proudly announced the opening of eighteen new enterprises in time for the fiftieth anniversary of Soviet power in 1967, including the Hotel Sovetskii with a thousand-seat restaurant, two bars, four bufets, a stolovaia and an eighteenth-floor café. The floating restaurant Dolphin opened just in time for the November holiday.[23]

Restaurants would offer Soviet consumers the opportunity for luxury and relaxation on special occasions. In contrast to the midday stolovaia dinner with its limited choice and rapid turnaround, restaurants offered expansive à la carte menus with starters, soup, main courses and dessert,

16 'Tsvety v liubuiu minute', *Literaturnaia gazeta*, 3 November 1960, p. 2; *Obshchestvennoe pitanie*, 3, 1959, p. 62; *Obshchestvennoe pitanie*, 3, 1963, p. 62.

17 *Obshchestvennoe pitanie*, 8, 1958, p. 44 (Gomel′); 10, 1958, p. 24 (Erevan).

18 S. Leonidov, 'Chelovek i professiia. Eto vsegda nuzhno', *Obshchestvennoe pitanie*, 7, 1965, p. 13.

19 'In the Party and Central Committee and the USSR Council of Ministers: On further developing and improving public catering', *Current Digest of the Soviet Press*, 11, 9, 1959, pp. 44-45 (orig. *Pravda* and *Izvestiia*, 28 February 1959).

20 TsAGM, f. 224, op. 1, d. 163, l. 18.

21 G. Korovkin, 'Dlia blaga sovetskikh liudei', *Obshchestvennoe pitanie*, 10, 1961, pp. 4–6.

22 TsAGM, f. 224, op. 1, d. 277, l. 50. There were ninety-four restaurants listed in the 1973 *Moskva 1973: Kratkaia adresno-spravochnaia kniga*, Moscow, 1973, pp. 631–33.

23 TsAGM, f. 224, op. 1, d. 286, l. 36.

and a rich assortment of beverages. Most employed dance orchestras, and a night out in a restaurant was expected to constitute an entire evening's entertainment.[24] But Soviet restaurant dining had its critics. For some Soviet patriots, restaurants represented a throwback to the discredited NEP era of conspicuous consumption. As A. N. Ershov, the head of Moscow's public catering administration, asked in 1961, 'Do we really need restaurants in our current conditions? Aren't they survivals of an old capitalist society?' In the old days, he reminded his audience, restaurants served as sites of debauchery for the rich.[25] Even in more recent times, 'He goes to restaurants' implied someone who earned money illegally, a *stiliag*.[26] By the 1960s, the restaurant had become increasingly identified as a place for heavy drinking rather than eating. As the state cracked down on alcohol consumption, restaurants became a notorious and popular refuge for drinkers.[27] Throughout the 1960s, the sale of alcohol in restaurants often reached 50 to 75 per cent of the total revenue,[28] and rules against serving more than 100 grams of vodka to a customer were treated as a joke.[29] Restaurants themselves profited by maximizing the sale of alcohol, which required no kitchen labour to produce and not very much to clean up. Waiters especially liked the easy way that serving alcohol boosted the size of the bills and the percentage added for service, and they treated teetotallers with hostility.[30]

The drive for progressive trade and cultured service attempted to replace this reputation with the idea of the restaurant as a destination for leisure and entertainment, a place to celebrate important events in one's life and career, an opportunity to enjoy Soviet luxe. One Korolev, a representative from the Hotel Moskva's restaurant, emphasized in 1968 the special role of Moscow restaurants: not a place where people come simply to eat something quickly and then leave, but a cosy, welcoming space organized for the relaxation of its patrons. It should have a pleasing interior, and its

[24] Confirmed by personal account from a Russian language teacher in Moscow in 1973.

[25] TsAGM, f. 2 (Moscow City Committee of the Trade Union of Trade and Cooperative Employees), op. 2, d. 626, ll. 10–11.

[26] A. Rubinov, 'Siadem za stol!' *Literaturnaia gazeta*, 23 August 1967, p. 13; Ark. Minchikovskii, 'Vser′ez o restoranakh. V chas sukhogo zakona', *Literaturnaia gazeta*, 25 January 1967, p. 13.

[27] *Krokodil′*, 5 February 1966, p. 2.

[28] Georgia National Archive, f. 2006 (Republic Ministry of Trade), d. 1632, l. 6; d. 2459, l. 108; A. Volkov, E. Egorov, A. Lasin, 'Za sobstvennuiu produktsiiu –v dva raza bol′she. Novoe v oplate truda ofitsiantov', *Obshchestvennoe pitanie*, 11, 1962, pp. 55–56.

[29] TsAGM, f. 2, op. 2, d. 626, ll. 51, 63.

[30] *Krokodil′*, 20 May 1957, p. 14.

serving staff should be smartly dressed and courteous.[31] Restaurants offered a space for civic and private banquets to observe birthdays or weddings. Moscow's Budapesht restaurant reported that in the fourth quarter of 1962 alone it had arranged over one hundred banquets, including twenty-three weddings.[32] *Obshchestvennoe pitanie* regularly provided advice to waiters and restaurant managers on methods of staffing and serving the banquet table.[33] Restaurants organized special events to make their customers feel more welcome, including thematic balls, special tastings of international foods, 'days of the hunter and fisherman' and special vegetarian days. The workers at the Hammer and Sickle Factory had forged a special relationship with the restaurant at the Ukraina Hotel, coming on Sundays with their families to sample highlights of Ukrainian cuisine.[34] Restaurants increasingly sought to create their own unique brands, and chefs were encouraged to develop their own house specialties. 'We want every restaurant to be celebrated for its own distinctive dishes', insisted I. D. Shevelev, the head of Moscow's public catering administration in 1968.[35] In the 1960s, the restaurant, with all of its extensive service staff, had become a legitimate scene of Soviet public life.

In theory, Soviet restaurants would be accessible to all strata of Soviet society, as the Ukraina's outreach to Hammer and Sickle Factory workers attests. In practice, restaurants remained the privilege of Soviet officialdom, foreign delegations, foreign tourists, Western graduate students with foreign currency stipends, and those earning money in the black or grey markets.[36] Ordinary working people and students visited restaurants rarely if at all: once in five years, averred a correspondent to *Literaturnaia gazeta* in 1969.[37] 'People with modest budgets rarely go to restaurants — they're

[31] The director of the fictional restaurant Oduvanshik gives a pep talk to her staff emphasizing precisely these qualities in the film, *Daite zhalobnuiu knigu*.

[32] TsAGM, f. 224, op. 1, d. 246, l. 21.

[33] Examples can be found in N. Nadezhdin, V. Krasil'nikov and N. Krasil'nikov, 'Restorany i obsluzhivanie. Obsluzhivanie banketov', *Obshchestvennoe pitanie*, 9, 1966, pp. 58–61; N. Nadezhdin, V. Krasil'nikov and N. Krasil'nikov, 'Svadebnyi banket', *Obshchestvennoe pitanie*, 6, 1971, pp. 62–63.

[34] TsAGM, f. 224, op. 1, d. 272, l. 21.

[35] TsAGM, f. 224, op. 1, d. 286 (Stenogramma sobranie aktiva tresta ot 2 Feb 1 1968 'Itogi raboti predpriatii tresta za 1967 g.'), l. 55.

[36] This generalization is supported by Soviet feature films from the period such as *Daite zhalobnuiu knigu*, in which the patrons include public catering officials and journalists.

[37] Anatolii Zakharovich Rubinov Papers, 1968–1996. European Division, Library of Congress, Washington, DC, Box 3, Folder 6, Letter 41611/25 (K.A.M., a machine builder from Gor'kii).

expensive', wrote another correspondent to that paper. A family of three or four might go out for a celebration, or to meet friends from the front.[38] Thus, a restaurant evening was almost always a special occasion.[39] In the course of this research, I asked a number of Russian academics about their restaurant experiences in the 1960s, the years of their student days. None of them could afford such a luxury, they told me. Moreover, asserted one Muscovite in a letter to *Literaturnaia gazeta* in 1969, workers did not go to restaurants and didn't need to: they should be reserved for tourists as a mechanism to extract foreign currency.[40]

The Soviet waiter was the final point of contact in the long supply/service chain that began with the state farm (or alcohol factory) and ended at the table. Behind the scenes, the restaurant director organized the entire operation of the enterprise, from planning to purchasing to the kitchen to accounting to service. In the kitchen, the cooks were asked to produce tasty dishes according to plan and from often uncertain supplies. Their creativity was celebrated in the pages of *Obshchestvennoe pitanie*, but their low level of skill was also held up for criticism in closed-door meetings and in the pages of *Krokodil′*. Directors also came under attack for their inattention and low skills.[41]

In this article, I am concerned with the front of the house, the 'hall', the public face of the restaurant staffed by the maître d'hotel and the waiters. Waiters comprised the largest number of service staff in Soviet restaurants. According to the two Soviet censuses of 1959 and 1970, the number of waiters across the Soviet Union grew from 184,000 in 1959 to 204,000 in 1970, an increase of only 11 per cent. In the Russian Federation, the number of waiters did not grow at all.[42] The overwhelming proportion were women: 98 per cent in 1959, and 96 per cent in 1970.[43] Waitresses were especially prominent in the less prestigious public catering enterprises: in stolovaias (when they were not self-service), bufets, cafés and snack bars. In my own experience in the 1970s, I encountered waitresses in the upscale Professors' dining room at Moscow State University and in cafés attached to the Praga and Natsional′ restaurants, but in those and other restaurants' main halls, the waitering staff was male.

[38] Rubinov Papers, Box 3 Folder 6C, Letter 41622/25 (A. D., Moscow).

[39] Rubinov Papers, Box 3, Folder 5, Letter 41645/25 (S. I. L., Lviv).

[40] Rubinov Papers, Box 4, Folder 7, Letter 113/25 (Pensioner V. V. M., Moscow).

[41] TsAGM, f. 224, op. 1, d. 107; d. 108; d. 286. In 1958, only half of Moscow's restaurant directors had completed grade school. (d. 108, l. 32).

[42] *Itogi vsesoiuznoi perepisi naseleniia 1970 goda*, Moscow, 1972–74, vol. 6, tab. 2, p. 19; tab. 3, p. 29.

[43] Ibid., vol. 6, tab. 18, p. 166.

Between 1959 and 1970, the number of cooks and auxiliary personnel about doubled: public catering expanded, but waiter service did not.[44] In Moscow, arguably the showplace of Soviet dining culture, males were more predominant in the trade. The Moscow restaurant trust in 1958 employed 5,661 women (68.2 per cent) and 2,640 men (31.8 per cent) in its establishments. Most had at least three years of experience, and 30 per cent had been at their jobs more than ten years.[45] Waitering here was a profession for a lifetime, not a casual stopgap on the way to another career. As far as I can tell, there was no separate staff to clear tables. This was the job of the waiter, and one of the symbols of bad restaurant service was tables that remained uncleared for successive seatings of customers.[46] In addition to these servers, restaurants also employed cashiers, who not only handled the customers' payments brought to them by waiters, but also rang up each individual order to the kitchen and billed the responsible waiter. At the end of each day, they verified the total cash received from each waiter.[47] Bufet servers provided the same service for alcohol and cold drinks: waiters 'purchased' these items in order to serve them at the table. These transactions gave cashiers significant informal power in the restaurant economy.

The role of the maître d' was changing in 1960s Moscow. In many establishments, his job was to oversee the functioning of the dining room, serving as the director's deputy and remaining aloof from the customers. But in more progressive restaurants such as the Praga, the maítre d' was taking a more active role in serving: these maître d's greeted guests and showed them to their table, gave skilled consultation in choosing food and drink, assisted the waiter and handled the bill at the end of the meal.[48] At the start of 1958, the ratio of waiters to maître d's was twenty-three to one.[49] Cashiers and most wait staff were female, and the maître d's seemed almost exclusively to be male.

Waitering was hard work. According to a *Komsomol'skaia pravda* account in 1968, foreign specialists claimed that it was the second most difficult profession, after mining. Waiters made repeated trips to and from the kitchen, carrying heavy trays of dishes each way. The news article estimated that a waiter walked forty kilometres per daily shift, carrying

44 Ibid., vol. 6, tab. 2, p. 19.

45 TsAGM, f. 224, op. 1, d. 108, l. 32.

46 *Daite zhalobnuiu knigu* provides a vivid example, as the protagonist and his friends sit waiting to order amidst a stack of dirty dishes.

47 TsAGM, f. 224, op. 1, d. 231, l. 19.

48 TsAGM, f. 224, op. 1, d. 231, l. 4.

49 TsAGM, f. 224, op. 1, d. 163, l. 10.

two-and-a-half tons a day. By comparison, the average postal route was a mere sixteen kilometres. The waiter's work day lasted from noon until one in the morning, with a two-hour break between the noon rush and the evening meal.[50] By the time they finished cleaning up after the evening shift, public transport had stopped running and they either had to walk home or pool for taxis.[51] And the job entailed more than taking orders and serving. As a Riga waiter noted in another journal article, the waiter must also arrange his assigned tables, making sure they didn't wobble, ensure that the place settings were in order and confirm that fresh flowers were displayed. He had to look after his own appearance, knowing every day he must look ready for a holiday stroll. A waiter should be always prepared with her pencil in hand, never in her pocket or under her arm, equipped with matches and bottle opener, and an extra order book in her pocket. Even more important, a waiter had to understand the needs of her guests, to be able to advise them on the menu, and to assess their mood in order to make them feel welcome and at ease. She should pay special attention to regular customers, to the elderly, invalids, and to VIPS. [52]

Yet the Soviet waiter or waitress did not receive the respect that a coal miner or even a postman could expect. A *Komsomol′skaia pravda* correspondent decided to go under cover in 1968, learning a few tricks of the waiter's trade at Moscow's elite Aragvi restaurant and then job-shadowing a veteran Leningrad waiter as he did his work. 'Each one of us, dear reader, agrees that the occupation of waiter is not what people dream about even when they are in school', he wrote:

> So much has already been written about the family 'tragedies' when the daughter goes to work behind a shop counter, when the son enrols in cooking school [...]. But if a guy goes to be a waiter — that's even worse.[53]

One year later, a writer in *Literaturnaia gazeta* concurred that restaurants in the Soviet Union had long been viewed as unsavoury places, but while

[50] Ignatenko, 'Ofitsiant', *Komsomol′skaia pravda*, 14 November 1968, pp. 2, 4.

[51] GARF, f. 5452, op. 37, d. 955, ll. 180–85.

[52] Leonidov, 'Chelovek i professiia'; N. Tsyplenkov, 'Gde nachinaetsia vzaimnaia vezhlivost′?', *Obshchestvennoe pitanie*, 7, 1969, pp. 56–57; N. Nadezhdin, V. Krasil′nikov and N. Krasil′nikov, 'Pravila i tekhnika raboty ofitsiantov', *Obshchestvennoe pitanie*, 3, 1973, pp. 60–61.

[53] Ignatenko, 'Ofitsiant', *Komsomol′skaia pravda*, p. 2. On the role of the Aragvi and Georgian cuisine in Soviet dining, see Erik R. Scott, 'Edible Ethnicity', in Scott, *Familiar Strangers: The Georgian Diaspora and the Evolution of Soviet Empire*, Oxford and New York, 2016, pp. 87–122.

that reputation had finally been overcome, negative attitudes towards wait people had not. 'And that's why there is a severe shortage of cadres in the service sector.'[54]

Part of the stigma came from the Soviet ambivalence towards restaurants as pleasure zones, as I have already mentioned. Part of the stigma came from the conviction that producers of material things were more valuable to society than providers of services, as I have written elsewhere.[55] But waiters themselves contributed to this image through their own behaviours. As the stories that began this article attest, Soviet restaurant service was notoriously slow. 'Waiters have developed the idea that restaurants are meant for rest', said one Moscow public catering official in 1968. A recent check had revealed that customers in the Praga restaurant had waited thirty minutes for a waiter to appear, and in the Sovetskii, it took customers one hour and twenty minutes to be served, when the restaurant was only 20 per cent full.[56] At the Slavianskii Bazaar, only tables of four were served promptly; couples had to wait to be teamed up, and even then, it took forty minutes for a waiter to take their order. And the waiter himself was dressed so slovenly he should not have been permitted to serve, alleged the customers.[57] A Russian trade official recalled a case in which a waiter at the Ural restaurant spilled a plate of salad onto the floor, and merely scooped it up and served it to the patron.[58] Rudeness and drunkenness among wait staff were commonly noted at regular meetings of the restaurant administration.[59]

The dishonesty of many waiters (and their managers) also contributed to the negative image of the trade. A waitress at the Sovetskii restaurant was caught substituting inferior cognac, serving only two portions of meat instead of three, and omitting the crab from the Stolichnyi Salad.[60] Cheating on the bill was common.[61] One experienced restaurant patron wrote to the editors of *Literaturnaia gazeta* that he had spent his entire

[54] Liubov′ Iunina, 'Kak li strashny chaevye?..,' *Literaturnaia gazeta*, 12 February 1969, pp. 10–11.

[55] Koenker, 'Smile behind the Sales Counter'; and Diane P. Koenker and Benjamin Bamberger, 'Tips, Bonuses, and Bribes: The Immoral Economy of Service Work in the Soviet 1960s', *Russian Review*, 79, 2, April 2020, pp. 246–68.

[56] TsAGM, f. 224, op. 1, d. 287, ll. 53–54.

[57] TsAGM, f. 224, op. 1, d. 286, l. 50.

[58] TsAGM, f. 224, op. 1, d. 108, l. 85. At the same restaurant, customers complained of splinters and hair pins in their food.

[59] TsAGM, f. 224, op 1, d. 108, ll. 108, 93; d. 272, ll. 26–27; TsAGM, f. 2, op. 2, d. 626, ll. 16–17.

[60] TsAGM, f. 224, op. 1, d. 272, l. 26.

[61] TsAGM, f. 224, op. 1, d. 286, l. 31. More examples can be found in TsAGM, f. 2, op. 2, d. 626, ll. 18–21.

life eating at restaurants, and he insisted that waiters would almost always cheat their customers, giving you 150 grams of vodka instead of the 200 you paid for, or 'accidentally' charging a higher price for a menu item than what had been posted.[62]

Soviet customers wanted better treatment, food and service, and they knew they were entitled to register their dissatisfaction in the obligatory complaint book.[63] Every enterprise was required to maintain such a book and to provide it when requested. Trade officials were supposed to regularly review these books and use their contents to evaluate performance, to shame, and to suggest improvements. Some establishments went to great lengths to prevent their customers from accessing these books;[64] others simply ignored them. The complaint book motif was so standard that *Krokodil′* could generate a laugh when the book was used to provide something positive: a customer at an outdoor café demanded the complaint book from a terrified waiter, but then used it to shade his table from the sun.[65] When restaurant officials reported on conditions in their sector, their accounts were based largely on reviews of these collections of complaints.[66] The head of the Moscow restaurant trust in 1958, for example, noted that 136 complaints about bad service had been logged, compared to sixty-nine in 1957, and the director of one restaurant had to be reprimanded for withholding the book from his customers.[67] Another admitted the number of complaints would have tripled had the complaint book been more readily accessible.[68] A Leningrad restaurant official ten years later noted all the positive improvements that had occurred in their network, but acknowledged that the restaurant Moskva had received forty-five complaints in the previous year, a sign they were still not performing well enough.[69]

It is reasonable to assume that Moscow and Leningrad were most amply endowed with restaurant places and skilled restaurant staff, but in fact, it was public catering in the Baltic republics that offered the most successful examples of service and dining innovation. In early 1969, a

[62] Rubinov Papers, Box 5, Folder 8, Letter 1497/25 (A. G. M.).

[63] *Krokodil′*, 5, 1972, p. 14.

[64] *Krokodil′*, 15 May 1969, p. 13.

[65] *Krokodil′*, 19 July 1971, p. 8.

[66] See also, Marjorie L. Hilton, 'The Customer Is Always Wrong: Consumer Complaint in Late NEP-era Russia', in Hilton, *Selling to the Masses: Retailing in Russia, 1880–1930*, Pittsburgh, PA, 2012, pp. 231–63.

[67] TsAGM, f. 224, op. 1, d. 108, ll. 19–20.

[68] TsAGM, f. 224, op. 1, d. 107, l. 63.

[69] TsAGM, f. 224, op. 1, d. 286, l. 37.

delegation from the Ministry of Trade of the Republic of Georgia (a region known for its culture of hospitality) visited Moscow, Leningrad, Tallinn and Riga. They were especially taken with the high level of public catering in Tallinn, which included many specialized cafés and restaurants, often located in atmospheric vaulted cellars, such as the Hungarian-style Café Solnek. Tallinn's eating places catered to a segmented clientele, rather than for the Soviet everyman: the variety restaurant Aurora worked from 9 pm to 3 am, with a floor show at 10.30 pm; a pastry café attracted mostly men. In the Gulf of Finland, the city had outfitted a sailing ship as a floating restaurant, open from 5 pm to 3 am, which had recouped its 30,000 ruble investment in only six months. They noted approvingly that all the restaurants in Riga and Tallinn featured their own distinctive décor, dinner plates inscribed with the name of the restaurant, and uniforms unique to each establishment. (The Tbilisi delegation recommended that the Georgian Ministry of Trade also acquire a sailing boat to convert into a restaurant, and to open in Tbilisi subterranean restaurants outfitted to represent Georgia's distinctive regions.)[70] A feature in *Obshchestvennoe pitanie* celebrated the exemplary work of young Riga waiter Karl Bilders, acknowledging the renowned tradition of service in the Baltic cities. Without fuss, Bilders noted the mood of his customers, tactfully suggested dishes to order and how to combine elements from the menu. He took care with his appearance. In his previous job at the Riga airport restaurant, he served many transit passengers, and determined to give each of them a good impression of the city through the quality of his service.[71] A young Leningrad waiter enthused about his exchange visit to Riga, noting the way in which Riga waiters challenged one another to improve their culture of service and admiring the tastefully decorated Riga restaurants. Like the Georgian delegation, he vowed to apply these lessons to his own workplace back home.[72] But both in the Soviet capital and in most of its provincial cities, poor service and monotonous menus remained the norm.

Economic reform: Motivating the Soviet waiter

Complaints, journalism, popular film and self-assessments provided ample evidence of the problems in restaurant service. Comparisons with dining culture abroad or in the Baltics revealed alternative models.[73] Finding

[70] Georgia National Archive, f. 2006, d. 2407 ('Otchety o rezul'tatakh komandirovkakh dlia izucheniia peredovogo opyta organizatsii torgovli v g. Moskvy, Leningrada, 8/V/1968 po 9/II/1969'), ll. 20–23, 30.

[71] Leonidov, 'Chelovek i professiia', pp. 12–14.

[72] GARF, f. 5452, op. 37, d. 1513, ll. 180–81.

[73] See Koenker, 'Taste of Others'.

a solution was a constant preoccupation of officials. Did the answer lie in better education and training, in organization, or in economics and incentives? Throughout the 1960s, planners and specialists explored techniques for improved management practices. They turned increasingly to mechanisms of market research in order more efficiently to match supply with demand. Architects and economists lent their expertise to advising on how optimally to build and organize restaurant dining.

Of course, the overriding economic fact of Soviet life was that *everything* was in short supply, not only good service. Restaurant managers complained constantly about their inability to source the ingredients they needed for dishes on their menus. At the Belorusskii Railway Station restaurant, the head chef Rybkin bemoaned in 1961 the disappearance of many cuts of meat: he had worked there eleven years, he used to have chops, and now he did not; he listed many items on the menu, but few could be served because there was no entrecote, filet or onglet of beef.[74] Again in 1967, chef Aristov from Moscow's Sovetskii restaurant recited a litany of shortages: his restaurant couldn't get tomatoes and cucumbers even when they were plentiful in stores; in a country of forests and steppe, there was no game for his kitchen; during the winter only root vegetables were available, even though traders were bringing fresh greens from the south to local markets. The only spices he could secure were bay leaves, pepper, salt, cinnamon, and the occasional clove. But to make popular Georgian dishes, he moaned, he needed cilantro, plums and spices that could not be found.[75]

Supplies that restaurants and stolovaias could obtain were often of poor quality. Stolovaia cooks complained they were cut off from top quality ingredients and had to settle for second and third grade items that not even food stores could sell.[76] The Sovetskii restaurant chef Kozyrev complained in 1958 that he couldn't obtain greens for his kitchen, and the 'suckling pigs' they received were big enough to ride on.[77] Nine guests from India reported they had got food poisoning at the Ukraina restaurant in 1958.[78]

Or instead of serving their customers, restaurants were incentivised to take the food products they received and sell them directly on the street. The manager of Magnitogorsk Stolovaia Number Six took the beef stewing meat he had bought for a ruble a kilo and asked a kitchen worker to sell

[74] TsAGM, f. 2, op. 2, d. 626, ll. 47–48.
[75] TsAGM, f. 224, op. 1, d. 277, ll. 40–44.
[76] GARF, f. 5452, op. 37, d. 651, ll. 35–36.
[77] TsAGM, f. 224, op. 1, d. 107, l. 27.
[78] TsAGM, f. 224, op. 1, d. 107, l. 62.

it on the street at a 10 per cent markup. She was also 'not shy' and sold it for one ruble fifty kopecks.[79] Both enterprise and seller profited from this arrangement, but the stolovaia patron went without meat. In Moscow, workers at the Moskva restaurant set up a stall and sold black caviar to passers-by, netting 40,000 rubles for the restaurant. The plan requirements did not distinguish between food sold inside the restaurant or on the street. It was common, said a Ministry of Trade official, that 'goods of high demand are sold on the right and on the left'.[80] Food sold on the street contributed to the restaurant's bottom line, but it also meant there was less in the kitchen to serve the seated customers.

The shortages extended to dishes, utensils, and technology. One waiter complained of the motley assortment of unmatched serving platters, and a cook about the dismal quality of chef's knives. In 1958, he said, 'Pretty soon Soviet people will be flying to the moon, and we still haven't solved the problem of knives'.[81] A restaurant official from Uzbekistan lamented in 1968, they lived in the atomic age, they flew to the moon and around the earth, but they couldn't even produce an ice-making machine. The Uzbek national dish *lagman* was notoriously labour-intensive, and he rejoiced when he was able to purchase an Italian pasta machine at a Sokol′niki trade fair, but after only a few uses it broke down. Why couldn't Soviet science make a pasta machine, he wondered.[82]

Regardless of the supply problem in the 1960s, restaurant officials thought they could motivate their waitering staff to provide cultured and timely service. As always in the Soviet sphere of work, socialist incentives — exhortation and emulation — played a role in encouraging performance, although it is hard to gauge their effectiveness. Posters hung behind the scenes encouraged wait staff to help others do their jobs: 'Waiter! Your comrade has a large number of guests. Help him quickly serve them.'[83] Special days honouring various specialties, such as 'day of the maître d'' and 'day of the pastry cook', cast celebratory attention on exemplary performers and served to instruct others in how better to perform their jobs.[84] Schools of Communist labour also mobilized collective energy that shared techniques and etiquette of serving patrons,

[79] E. Kolkov, 'Rabotat′ po starinke nel′zia', *Obshchestvennoe pitanie*, 7, 1963, p. 43
[80] TsAGM, f. 224, op. 1, d. 107, ll. 40–41.
[81] TsAGM, f. 224, op. 1, d. 107, l. 26; GARF, f. 5452, op. 37, d. 71, l. 89.
[82] TsAGM, f. 224, op. 1, d. 286, l. 19.
[83] *Obshchestvennoe pitanie*, 11, 1960, p. 37.
[84] TsAGM, f. 224, op. 1, d. 272, l. 20; d. 286, l. 16.

teaching newcomers how to set their tables and serve banquets.[85] Socialist emulation campaigns pitted individual work places against one another in pledges to improve performance but also to share experience and learn from one another, as with the Leningrad visitor to Riga noted above. Slogans such as 'Raise the culture of service every day in every workplace' also served an exhortatory function.[86] Production conferences brought together management and labour to discuss problems and collaborate in their solutions.[87] But these practices, part of the Soviet repertoire of non-pecuniary incentives since the 1920s, seem to be more notable for their absence in the 1960s than their effectiveness.[88]

Another mechanism for motivating and stimulating waiters was proper training. At the beginning of the 1960s, a six-month course for waiters was standard but widely considered to be inadequate, and officials recommended establishing one- or two-year courses, following the examples of other socialist countries.[89] In 1962, only eighteen thousand students a year graduated from Soviet 'trade-culinary schools', out of seventy thousand annual recruits to the sector.[90] And not all of these courses offered training for waiters.[91] Even a year-long course failed to prepare waiters adequately, said a restaurant manager in 1968. Up to 70 per cent of such graduates lacked the necessary skills or knowledge to provide proper service.[92] More effective was to use experienced waiters and waitresses — the 'golden fund' — to tutor new wait staff under their direct supervision.[93] But this was slow and expensive in terms of labour time. Increasingly, restaurants turned to evening schools to provide formal training — in foreign languages and other skills — for their staff. One

[85] TsAGM, f. 224, op. 1, d. 286, l. 16.

[86] GARF, f. 5452, op. 37, d. 1332, ll. 67–68; TsAGM, f. 224, op. 1, d. 108, l. 37; f. 2, op. 2, d. 626, ll. 35, 82. But socialist competition was unpopular. TsAGM, f. 224, op. 1, d. 272, l. 31; d. 286, l. 29.

[87] TsAGM, f. 2, op. 2, d. 626, l. 25.

[88] The trade union chief Shalaurova noted as much in her speech to the VII congress in February 1972. GARF, f. 5452, op. 37, d. 1513, ll. 104–05.

[89] GARF, f. 5452, op 37, d. 955, l. 8; TsAGM, f. 224, op. 1, d. 277, ll. 8-9; TsAGM, f. 2, op. 2, d. 626, l. 94; *Obshchestvennoe pitanie*, 5, 1969, p. 62.

[90] 'Podbor, rasstanovka i vospitanie kadrov reshaiut uspekh dela. Vserossiiskoe soveshchanie rabotnikov torgovli i obshchestvennogo pitaniia', *Obshchestvennoe pitanie*, 6, 1962, p. 14.

[91] Georgia National Archive, f. 2006, d. 1421, lists the training objectives for cooks and for sales clerks only.

[92] TsAGM, f. 224, op. 1, d. 287, l. 10.

[93] TsAGM, f. 2, op. 2, d. 626, l. 94; 'Podbor, rasstanovka…', *Obshchestvennoe pitanie*, 6, 1962, p. 14; A. Michurin, 'Dorogoi tvorcheskikh poiskov', *Obshchestvennoe pitanie*, 5, 1969, p. 29.

Leningrad waiter described a 'school of young waiters' in his restaurant that held twice-monthly classes demonstrating new approaches to service.[94]

The Soviet socialist economy never abandoned its commitment to material incentives, despite the well-known joke 'They pretend to pay us, and we pretend to work'. By the 1960s, there was little challenge to the primacy of material incentives as the best way to motivate good work. Rather than debate whether money stimulated workers to provide good service, officials discussed the best methods of monetary compensation. Soviet waiters received a base salary whose level depended on their skill grade and experience. Notably, their wages were among the lowest in the USSR in the 1950s, and in order to improve service in public catering, in 1959 the government decreed raises of up to 40 per cent for cooks and waiters.[95] At the exemplary Sovetskii restaurant, for example, a waiter's pay rose from 60 rubles a month in 1959 to 92 in 1961. The average pay of waiters at the Praga in 1961 ranged from 85 to 89 rubles, depending on the month. Maître d's there earned 100 rubles.[96] But away from the capital's elite restaurants, waiters — almost all of them women — earned closer to 30 to 40 rubles a month.[97] Attempts to improve the economic lot of waiters and cooks continued into the 1960s. By 1970, the average worker in public catering and trade earned 95 rubles. (A skilled coal miner made 133.)[98] The outstanding Leningrad waiter Rudol′f Egorov, subject of a *Komsomol′skaia pravda* profile in 1968, earned 90 rubles for his work as a fifth rank waiter, and he also often took home a monthly bonus of 20 rubles.[99] (I will return to Egorov.)

From this salary, waiters were expected to pay for summer and winter uniforms, and pay could be docked for breakage of dishes, damaged tablecloths and napkins, and customers who left without paying. New uniforms cost 170–80 rubles, more than two months' pay. Even when management subsidized the purchase of uniforms, they had to be tailor-made at prices the subsidy did not cover.[100] A 1963 exposé in *Izvestiia*

[94] GARF, f. 5452, op. 37, d. 1513, ll. 133, 138, 179.

[95] GARF, f. 5452, op. 37, d. 258, l. 52. See Kristy Ironside, 'Income Redistribution without "Leveling"', in Ironside, *A Full Value Ruble: The Promise of Prosperity in the Postwar Soviet Union*, Cambridge, MA, 2021, pp. 54–88. This raise was part of a general programme to level up the least-well-remunerated workers in the Soviet economy, most of them employed in service.

[96] TsAGM, f. 224, op. 1, d. 231, ll. 5–7.

[97] TsAGM, f. 2, op. 2, d. 626, l. 51.

[98] GARF, f. 5452, op. 27, d. 1513, ll. 332–33.

[99] Ignatenko, 'Ofitsiant', *Komsomol′skaia pravda*, 14 November 1968, p. 4.

[100] TsAGM, f. 2, op. 2, d. 626, ll. 41, 44, 51, 52, 65, 69, 92, 98.

alleged that in addition to paying for breakage, waiters had to pay bribes up and down the internal chain of command, from the cashier to clear their accounts in a timely way, to the head waiter according to 'the unwritten rule'.[101] Workers in public catering also pointed out that compared to industrial workers, they received far fewer non-pecuniary benefits such as vouchers to rest homes and sanatoria, and nursery and summer camp places for their children. As one waitress pointed out at a 1961 meeting of Moscow waiters, despite women being the majority of the sector, they were not provided with nurseries and pioneer camps for their children. And she complained further, 'We never receive vouchers for sanatoria. Are we somehow different from everybody else?'[102]

Could all of these problems be solved by simply raising wages and providing sufficient housing, childcare and rest home spaces? The level of wages in public catering increased throughout the 1960s, but complaints about quality and service did not disappear. Soviet planners and restaurant officials also discussed and experimented with new forms of pay and new systems of service. Above all, they grappled with the question of whether and how to reward good service without the odious bourgeois practice of tipping.

The basic form of payment for waiters was an amount based on the sum of the bill — a service charge, with adjustments for experience and level of skill.[103] In Kyiv, one reported practice was to pay waiters a given rate per 100 rubles of receipts, with bonuses for the overfulfillment of planned receipts depending on the level of skill.[104] In some places, waiters received a supplemental bonus if they could use a foreign language.[105] The customer did not see the service charge, rather it was built into the price of the meal. Such a system of remuneration encouraged waiters to sell high-priced items such as caviar and alcohol, and to ignore modest-looking customers. So the public catering administration continually attempted to adjust the

[101] E. Garina, 'Budte khoziaevami', *Izvestiia*, 2 August 1963, p. 3. In tsarist times, new hires and subordinates were expected to treat their supervisor with a round of drinks, *magarych* (maybe). See Laura L. Phillips, *Bolsheviks and the Bottle: Drink and Worker Culture in St. Petersburg, 1900–1930*, DeKalb, IL, 2000. The practice was condemned by the Soviet regime, but it continued.

[102] TsAGM, f. 2, op. 2, d. 626, ll. 99, 101; f. 224, op. 1, d. 107, ll. 28, 47; d. 277 (1967), ll. 20, 33, 67; d. 108, l. 47 (1958); GARF, f. 5452, op. 37, d. 955, ll. 184–85 (1967). The union claimed to have solved the day care problem by 1967, asserting that only 300 of 3,000 families remained on a waiting list for places. GARF, f. 5452, op. 37, d. 955, l. 107.

[103] As in TsAGM, f. 2, op. 2, d. 626, l. 12 (1961).

[104] *Obshchestvennoe pitanie*, 6, 1973, p. 61.

[105] TsAGM, f. 224, op. 1, d. 108, l. 35.

percentages and the indicators in order to maximize revenue, minimize labour costs, and still keep the complaint book idle.[106] The economic reforms of the mid 1960s aimed to simplify the planning indicators and to encourage enterprises to make their own management decisions. Thus, restaurants were measured by only two things: the sale of their own product (as opposed to something purchased from a third party — alcohol) and 'profitability' — a rough bottom line. Waiters would earn a higher percentage of the revenue for selling house-made production than for alcohol.[107] They were encouraged to contribute to 'cost-consciousness' by reducing waste and becoming more efficient: profits would be returned to the firm in the form of social spending on housing and childcare.

Other restaurants experimented with paying waiters through a service charge added directly to the bill and clearly visible to the customer. The new Rossiia and Arbat restaurants in Moscow introduced this reform in late 1968 as a way to eliminate tipping and encourage good service. The bill clearly indicated that 5 per cent had been added 'to the waiter for service'. And waiters knew that they would lose that increment if a complaint was filed. As a result, wrote the directors of the two restaurants, take-home pay grew significantly, labour turnover was reduced and service had been improved.[108] A visiting delegation from Georgia commented approvingly on this experiment, noting that the extra charge for service had added 80 to 100 rubles to a waiter's monthly pay, which could now total 200 rubles. (An exclamation point appears in the document next to this number. Remember a coal miner earned around 130 rubles.)[109] In a variant at the Kyiv restaurant Dinamo, patrons paid 4 per cent extra for service, and they were told the sum that would be shared among all of the serving personnel at the restaurant, from cooks to dishwashers to coatroom attendants. The number of tables assigned to each waiter was reduced from twelve to ten, and as a result, service had improved, the restaurant served more meals, and waiters' wages had risen 29 per cent.[110]

Some restaurants sought to improve service and interest waiters more in their work through structural reform inspired by professional visits

[106] TsAGM, f. 224, op. 1, d. 108 (1958), l. 58.

[107] TsAGM, f. 224, op. 1, d. 277 (1966), l. 6. But such a system had already been implemented in Leningrad in 1962. Volkov et al., 'Za sobstvennuiu produktsiiu', *Obshchestvennoe pitanie*, 11, 1962, p. 55, and in Moscow by 1961 (TsAGM, f. 2, op. 2, d. 626, l. 57).

[108] 'Ofitsiantu za obsluzhivanie', *Vecherniaia Moskva*, 27 February 1969.

[109] Georgia National Archive, f. 2006, d. 2407, ll. 5–6.

[110] A. Vetrova and V. Ospishchev, '4% ot summy scheta: chto eto dalo', *Obshchestvennoe pitanie*, 6, 1973, p. 61.

to restaurants in socialist Europe. Instead of waiters serving only their individual set of tables, they worked as teams of three or four, either dividing the roles of order taker and server, or making sure that one team member was always in the dining room to attend to the needs of their patrons.[111] Other restaurants experimented with assigning the bill-paying function to the maître d', freeing the waiter to focus on service and eliminating the temptation to pocket the change either as a tip or illegally.[112]

Tipping in the Soviet Union was officially proscribed as a demeaning holdover from capitalist times, which placed the server in an inferior position to the guest. It was characterized as an infection, an insult, and a source of shame both for the recipient and the tipper. It led to favouritism in restaurants, encouraging waiters to treat big tippers with extra care and to ignore customers who clung to the Soviet anti-tipping morality. Some Soviet waiters defended the practice as a necessity to supplement their low wages, and some customers suggested that tips might be seen as a kind of personal bonus, a recognition of overfulfilling the plan at the point of service. Other waiters proudly refused to accept gratuities as unbecoming to a Soviet person.[113] Restaurant officials hoped that instituting clear service charges would wean customers away from the practice of tipping and make the reward for good service transparent, rational and still financially meaningful.[114]

By the second half of the 1960s, alongside the economic reforms that sought to incentivise good service, there came to be promoted a new, professional standard of restaurant service. The waiter's job was not merely to transmit the customer's desire to and from the kitchen, but to shape the customer's total experience. The waiter now aspired to be a psychologist who could assess the customer's mood and adjust their interaction accordingly. The exemplary Leningrad waiter Rudol′f Egorov explained that his job entailed more than 'serving and feeding'. The 'Egorov method' involved making the customer feel comfortable, as if she were at home. He could produce a smile by telling his customer, 'I've brought you the left

[111] TsAGM, f. 2, op. 2, d. 626, l. 93; d. 224, op. 1, d. 108, l. 54; f. 224, op. 1, d. 231, l. 48 (1962).

[112] TsAGM, f. 224, op. 1, d. 231, ll. 4, 48.

[113] Koenker and Bamberger, 'Tips, Bonuses, and Bribes'. The article is based on a series of letters sparked by the 1969 article in *Literaturnaia gazeta*: Liubov′ Iunina, 'Tak li strashny chaevye?...', 12 February 1969, pp. 10–11. The letters are held in the Rubinov Papers.

[114] TsAGM, f. 224, op. 1, d. 108 (1958), ll. 57–58. Words of Miroliubova, director of restaurant Severnyi in Moscow.

chicken leg, it's fattier than the right'; he studied the mood of each customer and treated them accordingly: the shy ones with care, the rude ones with reserve, the insulted with tact. He would sometimes advise on the choice of a meal. And as an involuntary witness to intimate conversations, he took care to be discrete.[115] Tarasov, a waiter at Moscow's Volga restaurant, emphasized that the essence of cultured service was to love and respect the customer's psychology:

> Our job isn't only to give out the food and drink that the customer orders, no, that's not all. It's important to create conditions of warmth and hospitality in order to enable positive impressions. We want the people who come to our restaurant to be pleased and not annoyed.[116]

A Frunze waiter, S. A. A., echoed this philosophy in his letter to the editors of *Literaturnaia gazeta*: 'An experienced waiter has to be both psychologist and artist, able to figure out the mood and desires of the patron.'[117]

Such aspirations had been expressed since the 1930s as part of the Soviet drive for 'cultured service'.[118] But they received new affirmation through the concrete experiences of Soviet travellers abroad, who encountered standards of service that were totally different from expectations at home. Waiters in Hungary drew frequent praise for their professional treatment of their customers. As one traveller wrote to *Literaturnaia gazeta*, Hungarian waiters' 'professional experience teaches them to be attentive, nicely dressed, and psychological. They deal politely with people who are new to the restaurant experience. They can recognize the difference in behaviour between a married couple and a couple who are not married'.[119] Another Budapest visitor testified to the high level of service in its restaurants:

> You're struck by the affability of the waiters, their attention and interest in their customers. When he comes to take your order, he always greets you first, and when he presents the bill, he wishes you well and invites you to come back again.[120]

115 Ignatenko, 'Ofitsiant', *Komsomol'skaia pravda*, 14 November 1968.

116 TsAGM, f. 224, op. 1, d. 287 (1968), ll. 27–29 (l. 29). This is essentially the pep-talk given to the assembled waitresses in *Daite zhalobnuiu knigu*.

117 Rubinov Papers, Box 3, Folder 6, Letter 680/25.

118 Amy E. Randall, *The Soviet Dream World of Retail Trade and Consumption in the 1930s*, Basingstoke, 2008; Hessler, *Social History of Soviet Trade*.

119 Rubinov Papers, Box 3, Folder 6, Letter 300/25.

120 'V restoranakh Budapeshta', *Obshchestvennoe pitanie*, 4, 1959, p. 61.

A Moscow restaurant official noted that foreign restaurants everywhere — but not in Moscow — strove to create a good mood, from the glass of water (and hot towels in Japan) served while the customer studied the menu, to their knowledge of the menu items, to their impeccable uniforms.[121] In one Yugoslav restaurant, said another traveller in his account in the industry journal, you didn't see waiters hanging around a table or 'propping up the wall'; they were few but they were always at your service.[122]

Soviet officials and customers apparently knew what good service looked like. What about the waiters? How did they understand the challenges or attractions of their work? As always with histories of working people, sources from those observing and criticizing waiters are easier to come by than sources generated by the actors on the restaurant floor. The trade journal *Obshchestvennoe pitanie* published many articles giving advice to waiters, sometimes written by waiters themselves, such as features by three veteran waiters describing how properly to set the restaurant table or how to create a good mood for the customers.[123] Other testimonials that appeared in *Obshchestvennoe pitanie* may be presumed to reflect an editorial agenda but they can also offer insight into waiters' own experience. The stenographic reports of trade union meetings reveal more open and frank discussion, although here too the recorded words of union delegates were spoken in aid of particular agendas and by chosen and approved representatives rather than the rank-and-file.

In March 1961, A. N. Ershov, the head of Moscow's public catering administration, addressed a meeting of waiters to discuss the dismal state of service in the trade. At the moment of the launch of an ambitious new party programme, Ershov outlined a history of bad service and bad attitudes and concluded:

> Restaurant workers do not appreciate the fact that in our conditions, a restaurant is not a place for getting customers drunk, for burning through life, and gluttony. It's a place for cultured leisure, gatherings, and gaiety.[124]

In response, waiters talked about customers who ruined tablecloths with their cigarettes or who bolted without paying, about dealing with

[121] TsAGM, f. 224, op. 1, d. 287, ll. 41–42. The commentator was A. N. Ershov, who would lambast the 1961 meeting of Moscow waiters for their shortcomings (see below).

[122] M. Pol´skii, 'Iz Iugoslavskikh vpechatlenii', *Obshchestvennoe pitanie*, 12, 1966, p. 57. See Koenker, 'Taste of Others'.

[123] For example, Nadezhdin, Krasil´nikov and Krasil´nikov, 'Restorany i obsluzhivanie'; Nadezhdin, Krasil´nikov and Krasil´nikov, 'Pravila i tekhnika raboty ofitsiantov'.

[124] TsGAM, f. 2, op. 2, d. 626, ll. 26–27.

inadequate food supplies. They spoke about customers who refused to accept the 100 gram limit on vodka sales and then wrote a complaint about the server. 'You spin like a fox in front of them, and then they go and write a complaint', reported waitress Vybornova.[125] All the boss saw was the written complaint, not the pressure from the customer that the waitress break the rules.

Above all, these waiters emphasized the fact of their low pay. If some of them cheated the customer, it was because they needed to make ends meet. If their service was substandard, it was because they had to cover four tables instead of three in order to survive. 'We're given three or four tables, and we run, excuse me, like donkeys.'[126] They compared their miserly pay with the handsome salaries of their bosses, and noted how the pay mechanisms perpetuated their poverty. Rates were higher for serving dishes à la carte, but these could not be ordered before 5 pm. Working mothers were more likely to be assigned to the day shift, missing out on the more lucrative evening service. Paid on a percentage of sales, most of this went to pay for uniforms and broken dishes, leaving little pay to take home. If pay was higher, there would be fewer violations, said waiter Loginov from the Moskva restaurant.[127]

Women spoke of their particular grievances in addition to low pay: inadequate childcare and housing. Waitress Rybakova from the Luzhniki restaurant 'Olimpiada' described the worries of the wait staff there, almost exclusively women. 'Why has none of the speakers said anything about the sore point of kindergartens and pioneer camps? Almost all women have children, but there is no provision of camps and nurseries'. The summer months, when work at the restaurant was at its peak, were especially hard on these women, who worried about their children left to the whims of fate. 'If a waiter comes to work nervous because she has nowhere to leave her children, she will relate badly to the customers. She thinks constantly about home and worries what's happening there'.[128] Other industries provided housing for their workers, but not trade and public catering. Gruzhevskaia, a waitress at the Sofia restaurant, lamented that although she had been born and raised in Moscow and had worked at the restaurant for ten years, she lived in a cellar, 'and I can't get out of it'.[129] Rybakova challenged her fellow waitresses to speak up about the lack of housing, but

[125] TsGAM, f. 2, op. 2, d. 626, l. 51.
[126] TsGAM, f. 2, op. 2, d. 626, l. 50.
[127] TsGAM, f. 2, op. 2, d. 626, ll. 109, 54, 69, 98.
[128] TsGAM, f. 2, op. 2, d. 626, l. 100.
[129] TsGAM, f. 2, op. 2, d. 626, l. 109.

Beliakova, from the Peking restaurant, noted that they were unable to find redress for their poor conditions. They gave up their health for their work, but got no thanks, only complaints:

> When we speak to someone with any kind of question, we're answered with 'a chicken is not a bird, a woman is not a person'. Why make such a comparison? Everyone knows that there are many women leaders in our country.[130]

We see here, even allowing for the filter of trade union discourse, a profession with substandard wages and working conditions, which encouraged some waiters to cut corners and cheat the customers. It was also a profession dominated by women, whose double shift of home and wage work was never properly appreciated, let alone compensated.

If we fast forward to 1970, we find that the published testimonials of wait staff had taken on a new tone. During the 1960s, pay had been raised, and economic reforms had aimed to make the industry more productive, more efficient and better remunerated. Catering officials sought to counter the prevailing negative attitudes toward workers in the service sector with a new campaign to elevate their profile. Three waiters writing for *Obshchestvennoe pitanie* emphasized that the qualities required for good service — politeness, attentiveness, anticipation — were not just desirable, but necessary, just as a musician needed a developed ear and a sharpshooter needed good eyesight.[131] Waitress-in-training Nadezhda Vetrova wrote in 1973 about why she chose this career:

> In my view, above all a waiter should be attentive to people. I believe that our basic, chief task is to give joy to people. And they will always respond with the same. When I enrolled in the school for maître' d's and waiters, I had to cope with a lot of opposition from my relatives and from my friends. Only now I understand that they spoke like that because they didn't know the wonderful feeling you get when your guest leaves the restaurant in a good mood, when they say to you as they depart, 'Thank you so much'.[132]

Waitering was now offered to the public as a calling, an honourable occupation no less important than any other.[133] And yet the public

[130] TsGAM, f. 2, op. 2, d. 626, l. 98.
[131] Nadezhdin, Krasil′nikov and Krasil′nikov, 'Pravila i tekhnika raboty ofitsiantov'.
[132] Iu. Mumrikov, 'Shkola gostepriimstva', *Obshchestvennoe pitanie*, 4, 1973, p. 30.
[133] Another example is the Leningrad waiter V. P. Vaver, who came to waitering after an

remained unpersuaded and waiters continued to resent their low status and low pay, as letters to the newspaper *Literaturnaia gazeta* in 1969 revealed. Discussing whether tips should be permitted, waiters acknowledged the new language about the role of wait staff in creating pleasant conditions for the diners. Both L. G. from Donetsk and A. S. A. from Frunze wrote that the press had been writing frequently about service and the work of waiters as being second in difficulty only to miners, but they insisted that it was difficult to live on wages of 60–80 rubles a month, standard in the sector. A. S. A. added that in addition to low pay, he didn't know a single waiter who had received an apartment, not to mention a discounted voucher to a health resort. Acknowledging the role of waiter as master psychologist, he asserted that the lack of compensation was the main reason for poor service.[134]

Conclusion: The revenge of the Soviet waiter

At the start of the 1960s, Soviet officials decided that Communists deserved a greater variety of opportunities for dining out, and they decreed a massive expansion of eating places of all sorts.[135] By the end of the decade, that expansion had been realized, attracting more customers than ever before. A great deal of the expansion was meant to take place in large and self-service stolovaias, applying technology and economies of scale. The number of waiters barely increased between 1959 and 1970. In this sphere of mass public catering, the Soviet waiter was meant to disappear, to be replaced by cafeteria steam tables, stolovaia trays and vending machines. But the expansion was also aimed to include the restaurant experience and to elevate it to a pleasurable entitlement of the Soviet public, providing them with a comfortable and cossetted night out with family or friends, with ample good food and entertainment, allowing them to return home in a sunny mood and proud of the socialist system that provided this privilege.

Experienced diners read these signals, and they now demanded the level of service that many had first encountered abroad. First-timers needed service that included the attentive guidance of their waiter through

initial career as a metalsmith, confessing in 1972 that he was attracted by the high spiritual human qualities of the role. GARF, f. 5452, op. 37, d. 1513, l. 178.

134 Rubinov Papers, Box A, Folder 7, Letter 935/25 (L. G.); Box 3, Folder 6A, Letter 680/25 (A. S. A.).

135 'In the Party and Central Committee and the USSR Council of Ministers: On further developing and improving public catering', *Current Digest of the Soviet Press*, 11, 9, 1959, pp. 44–45 (orig. *Pravda* and *Izvestiia*, 28 February 1959).

their dining experience. The expansion required reforms to improve the material incentives for conscientious and caring service, the creation of a modern class of psychologically savvy waiters and waitresses proud of their work and of their role in providing cultured leisure for their customers. But the examples given above, the satirical cartoons in *Krokodil′* and my own and others' experience suggested that for every Rudol′f Egorov, there were hundreds of other waiters and waitresses who had failed to be motivated by the regime's efforts to instil a new style of service in Soviet restaurants. On 19 July 1977, the Central Committee of the Communist Party and Council of Ministers of the USSR issued yet another decree on the development of trade and public catering. 'The quality of service does not correspond to the growing demands of the population', it admitted, not for the first time. It called on all state agencies to attract more and better-educated cadres to the service sector and to instil in them a high level of dedication to their jobs. But the bulk of the decree focused on producing more and better *things*: more meat and vegetables coming from collective farms, more semi-prepared foods to improve the quality and variety of public catering meals and more automobiles to move the raw materials from one place to another.[136]

Was the continuing disappearance of Soviet waiters simply the product of the shortage economy or did it also reflect the continuing aversion of the Soviet public towards service workers? Somehow, Soviet economic planners never figured out how to recognize and reward the value added by service. Waiters in their turn read these signals and exercised the monopoly power they possessed in the restaurant hall. Resisting the generally low level of remuneration attached to this work, the waiters disappeared and took their own leisure time when and where they felt like it, regardless of the complaint book or their 'socialist obligations'. As the waiter said in 1961, 'If you raise our pay, there will be fewer violations'. In 1984, *New York Times* correspondent John Burns wrote: 'Faced with inadequate supplies, low salaries, and endless lines of customers, many Russians in customer-service jobs lapse into an indifference bordering on contempt.'[137] And this attitude carried over into post-Soviet times, as with the young McDonalds trainee who asked his supervisor: 'Why do we have to be so nice to the

[136] *Pravda*, 19 July 1977, pp. 1–2. See also the *New York Times* article on the decree, Malcolm W. Brown, 'Soviet Asks New Consumer Era: Better Goods and Polite Service', 20 July 1977, p. 2. Brown reads a plea for 'dedication' in the decree as 'courtesy', but I believe the difference is significant.

[137] John F. Burns, 'In Russia, Many Are Customers, Few Are Served', *New York Times*, 25 February 1984, section 1, p. 2.

customers? After all, WE have the hamburgers, and they don't!'[138] As long as waiters or shop clerks had control over the goods that customers wanted, they knew they could complete their shifts without psychology, smiles, or care for the customer. And it seems that none of the economic reforms designed to incentivise courtesy or service made much of a dent in this culture.

Soviet restaurant managers had many tools to try to incentivise attentive service, including wage reform and service charges, training, public recognition and professional pride. But while they had many carrots, they possessed few sticks to discipline unwilling waiters, not to mention the ultimate punishment of dismissal. Not only was it extremely difficult to fire a bad worker in the Soviet economy, there were already too few waiters to staff the expanding restaurant sector. A bad waiter was more productive than no waiter at all. Nor were restaurant managers under much pressure to provide their customers with the level of service that officials and *Krokodil′* demanded: there were simply too many potential customers hoping to enjoy a leisurely meal chasing after too few places. There were no restaurant reviewers or guidebooks to advise customers on how to choose their dining out destination; the Soviet public did not have much choice. Waiters may have been looked down upon by those whom they served, but they had the hamburgers their customers wanted. Waiters used their power over the menu, the order, and the delivery of food to exact their revenge on those who went to restaurants. This everyday resistance was a logical outcome of the unequal power differential endemic to the economy of shortages. Waiters were in short supply too.

The disappearing waiter represents the continuing ambivalence of Soviet socialism about service work more generally. Many of the letters responding to *Literaturka's* tipping article made explicitly negative comparisons between the 'genuine' producers of *material value* and the providers of service. Only industrial workers contributed real value to the country, wrote one correspondent, because they manufactured material things.[139] Factory work is hard, wrote a Riga engineer. How can this compare to restaurant staff who carry their trays past tables and dance floors. 'Excuse my harshness, but such a comparison insults the dignity of a working person.'[140] For such citizens, maybe the Soviet waiter was *meant* to disappear, to be replaced by self-service cafeterias and take-away

[138] Peter Frase, 'In Defense of Soviet Waiters', *Jacobin*, 2, 2013 <https://jacobin.com/2013/02/soviet-waiters-emotional-labor-customer-service> [accessed 10 April 2023].

[139] Rubinov Papers, Box 4, Folder 7, Letter 2997.

[140] Rubinov Papers, Box 5, folder 7, Letter 2490/25.

kitchens that would issue meals to be consumed at home. In this vision of socialism, there was no room for restaurant meals and the people who served them.

As long as the majority of the population treated service providers with scorn, perhaps it was difficult for the regime to justify investments that would improve the material position of waiters. As long as the material position of waiters was too low to motivate good service, they would continue to work as they had always done, on their own terms, hanging out in the kitchen instead of attending to their customers, cheating on the bill and short-pouring the vodka, without a smile, please or thank you.

REVIEW ARTICLE

Textology versus Textual Criticism: Donald Ostrowski and Attributing Texts to Ivan IV and Andrei Kurbskii

CHARLES J. HALPERIN

THE texts attributed to Prince Andrei Kurbskii, notably his correspondence with Ivan IV and his *History of the Grand Prince of Moscow*, and to Ivan himself, first and foremost letters responding to Kurbskii, have long been central to historical analyses of Ivan's rule and reign, providing unequalled evidence of Ivan's political ideology in particular. Karamzin's conceptualization of the two periods of Ivan's reign, the 'good' Ivan of the reforms (1547–64) and the 'bad' Ivan's reign of terror, the *oprichnina* (1565–72), which dominated late imperial Russian historiography, derived heavily from Kurbskii's *History*. Kliuchevskii's vivid portrait of Ivan's personality relied heavily upon Ivan's letters to Kurbskii for its evidence. If these literary works were not authored by Kurbskii and Ivan, then much traditional scholarship on Ivan's reign (1533–84) would have to be fundamentally reconsidered.

Therefore it was no surprise that Edward L. Keenan, Jr.'s 1971 monograph impugning the authenticity of these works initiated a lively and at times heated scholarly discussion that continued for over twenty-five years.[1] The two sides did not reach agreement, but a majority of scholars in Muscovite history and literature concluded that Keenan 'had not proved his case'.[2]

Charles J. Halperin is a Research Associate in the Russian and East European Institute, Indiana University.

[1] Charles J. Halperin: 'A Heretical View of Sixteenth-Century Muscovy: Edward L. Keenan, *The Kurbskii-Groznyi Apocrypha*', *Jahrbücher für Geschichte Osteuropas*, 22, 1974, pp. 161–86; 'Keenan's Heresy Revisited', ibid., 28, 1980, pp. 481–99; and 'Edward Keenan and the Kurbskii-Groznyi Correspondence in Hindsight', ibid., 46, 1998, pp. 376–403.

[2] In *The 'Secret of Secrets': The East Slavic Version. Introduction, Text, Annotated*

After a hiatus in which proponents and opponents of authenticity did not produce any new evidence or arguments, since 2006 Donald Ostrowski, among others,[3] has revived the discussion and sought to develop Keenan's argument. In 2006 Ostrowski published an article that reconceptualized the reception of Keenan's conclusions on the attribution and dating of texts about Rus'-Tatar and Muscovite-Kazan' relations as well as texts attributed to Ivan and Kurbskii, and in 2015 he published a second article on attributions of texts only to Kurbskii. That article became a chapter in his 2020 monograph proposing the creation of a new field of attribution studies. This review article will analyse Ostrowski's conclusions, which, as far as I know, have not previously elicited any substantial response.[4]

This review article will present a fairly detailed précis followed by a point-by-point refutation of each of Ostrowski's articles. This structure is necessary because, first, without such a summary, it would be difficult for a reader to comprehend the often technical evidence adduced in the critique and, second, a running analysis of Ostrowski's articles alongside a summary of their contents would leave most readers confused as to Ostrowski's reasoning. I will also try to provide sufficient background so the reader can appreciate the significance of each piece of evidence without having to reread Ostrowski's publications.

Textual critical analysis: Exposition

In '"Closed Circles": Edward L. Keenan's Early Textual Work and the Semiotics of Response',[5] Ostrowski asserted that in the field in general and in responses to Keenan's work in particular, '[p]reference is frequently

Translation and Slavic Index, eds William F. Ryan and Moshe Taube, London, 2019, p. 61 n. 5, Ryan and Taube erroneously wrote that the majority view is the 'general consensus'. There is no consensus. Cornelia Soldat, 'Die gerechte Herrscher, das "Heilige Volk" und die Spielart des Dissenses in der Moskauer Rus' im 16. und 17. Jahrhundert', in *Gerechtigkeit und gerechte Herrschaft von 15. biz zum 17. Jahrhundert. Beiträger zur historischen Gerechtigkeit*, ed. Stefan Plaggenborg, Berlin, 2019, p. 118, concluded that the 'prevailing opinion' on the dating of Ivan's and Kurbskii's works is incorrect, which concedes that scholars who agree with Keenan constitute a minority in the field.

[3] Including Brian Boeck, 'Miscellanea Attributed to Kurbskii: The 17th Century in Russia Was More Creative Than We Like to Admit', *Kritika: Explorations in Russian and Eurasian History*, 13, 4, 2023, pp. 955–63, and Cornelia Soldat, 'Novgorod Counter Histories around 1700: The Story about Ivan the Terrible's Raid of Novgorod Reconsidered', *Russian History*, 48, 3–4, 2022, pp. 231–86.

[4] Konstantin Erusalimskii, *Na sluzhbe korolia i Rechi pospolitoi*, Moscow, 2018, p. 645, n. 2186, cites both articles, but only contests points of detail without engaging Ostrowski's thesis.

[5] Donald Ostrowski, '"Closed Circles": Edward L. Keenan's Early Textual Work and the Semiotics of Response', *Canadian Slavonic Papers*, 48, 2006, pp. 247–68.

given [...] to arguments in a different register [than Keenan's] — to semiotic description and content interpretation over internal text-structural analysis — and even within the same register, to an appeal to textological over textual critical principles'.[6] By 'semiotic' arguments Ostrowski means analyses of the significance or outward meaning of content and its relationship to other outward meanings in other texts, rather than Keenan's internal textual structural analysis.[7] Ostrowski defines the difference between textological and textual critical analysis in terms of tendencies: textology tends to favour longer (*lectio potior*), fuller readings over shorter, elliptical ones (*lectio brevior*), and smoother readings (*lectio facilior*) over rougher (*lectio difficilio*), whereas the opposite tendency can be found in textual criticism. The goal of textology is to restore the perfect linguistic and grammatical archetype, whereas textual criticism accepts mistakes in the original. Textology prefers manuscripts found in or near Moscow, but textual criticism prefers exocentric manuscripts.[8]

Ostrowski illustrates what he considers the weaknesses of Keenan's responders by quoting Isabel de Madariaga's declaration[9] as 'characteristic of this general tendency' of the field,[10] and goes on to generalize that a 'widespread assumption among scholars [...] seems to be that the semiotic, outward testimony is to be preferred to the results of the structural, internal analysis'. Ostrowski claims that he had identified this 'assumption' in the responses to Keenan before he read de Madariaga's monograph and was not singling her out on this score. He cites Nikolai Andreyev's comment that 'the multitude of stemmata in the book [*The Kurbskii-Groznyi Apocrypha*] prove nothing except the extent of the author's industry and imagination'.[11] Ostrowski declares that '[t]hose who have responded to

[6] Ibid., p. 247 (from Ostrowski's 'Abstract').

[7] Ostrowski's use of the word 'semiotic' is not always apposite. As the reader of this review article for the *Slavonic and East European Review* pointed out, sometimes he means semantics, not semiotics. Perforce I will follow Ostrowski's usage.

[8] Ibid., p. 250 n. 9. Ostrowski later reconsidered his choice of terminology and decided to abandon the term 'textology' because it has a broader meaning than the characteristics he identified it with. However, he remains committed to the methodological contrast between what he called 'textology' and textual criticism. See Donald Ostrowski, 'The *Povest′ vremennykh let* (*PVL*): Ends and Means', *Russian Linguistics*, 46, 2022, p. 12. I will continue to use the term 'textology' here because it appears in the publications under discussion.

[9] 'I am not qualified in linguistic and textual analysis. But as a practising historian I cannot accept the validity of Keenan's theories on historical grounds.' Isabel de Madariaga, *Ivan the Terrible: First Tsar of Russia*, New Haven, CT, 2005, p. xvi.

[10] Ostrowski, '"Closed Circles"', p. 248.

[11] Ibid., p. 249. Stemmata are charts that illustrate the relationships among the manuscripts and versions of a text to each other and to other texts.

Keenan's challenges at the level of structural analysis of the text have done so in two ways — textology and textual criticism — so that diametrically opposed conclusions have been reached about the relationship of texts'.[12] Ostrowski then proceeds to analyse the responses to Keenan's conclusions individually.

Keenan applied his mode of analysis to two texts not tied to Ivan or Kurbskii: the narrative *Kazan′ History* (*Kazanskaia istoriia*), the first recension[13] of which is often dated to the 1560s,[14] and the documentary charter (*iarlik*) of Ahmed-Khan supposedly from 1480.[15] In both cases Keenan redated the texts to the seventeenth century and assigned authorship to bureaucrats. Ostrowski notes that L. A. Dubrovina agreed with Keenan's revision of the sequence of recensions of the *Kazan′ History* but not on his redating. Several leading Soviet literary specialists (*literaturovedy*) (Dmitrii Likhachev, Iakov Lur′e) and historians (Ruslan Skrynnikov) accepted Keenan's textual critical conclusion that Ahmed-Khan's charter was not authentic.

Ostrowski's analysis of the debate over Kurbskii's *First Letter to Ivan* is the longest segment of the article.[16] Ostrowski adumbrates Keenan's elaborate analysis of the structure of Kurbskii's *First Letter to Ivan* as not just the product of textual borrowing but of constructing a subtle mosaic intertwining citations from its multiple sources. He writes: 'The general responses to Keenan's textual critical arguments has been to reject them on non-textual grounds, although there have been significant attempts to address the textual critical argument.' However, '[a]ttempts to deal with the mosaic argument at the textual level have been unsuccessful'.[17]

[12] Ibid., p. 250.

[13] In correspondence Ostrowski provided this definition of the difference between 'recension' and 'redaction': 'A "redaction" is a more or less systematic effort by a redactor to modify a text in a specific pattern. A "recension" refers to a group of manuscript copies that share certain characteristics, not necessarily the result of a conscious effort on the part of the redactor or editor.' Ostrowski did not intend the terms to be perceived as synonyms. Unfortunately the distinction he draws between them is not readily apparent in his publications.

[14] Ostrowski, '"Closed Circles"', pp. 250–52. Ostrowski takes issue with Jaroslaw Pelenski's remarks impugning the infallibility of textual critical arguments for textual borrowing (ibid., p. 251), but the responses to Keenan's arguments on Kurbskii's *First Letter to Ivan* and Ivan's *First Letter to Kurbskii*, let alone Ostrowski's and David H. Das's judgments of Keenan's conclusions of the relationship between Kurbskii's *History* and Lyzlov's *Scythian History* (see below), unambiguously attest to the fallacy of thinking that textual critical analysis is *ipso facto* incontestable: textual critical critics sometimes disagree with each other.

[15] Ibid., pp. 252–54.

[16] Ibid., pp, 254–63.

[17] Ibid., p. 256.

'Both Fennell and Zimin did reputable textual critical work of their own, but here [discussing Kurbskii's *First Letter to Ivan*] they seemed to have resorted to arguments based on "textology" rather than textual criticism.'[18] Concerning the relationship of Kurbskii's *First Letter to Ivan* to one of its sources, Ostrowski writes:

> Fennell is correct that in *textology* the more intelligible reading is taken as primary but in *textual criticism* the reverse is the default case. [...] The thinking among textual critics is that a subsequent writer is more likely to have smoothed out and made more understandable a rough passage than to have intentionally made an intelligible reading less intelligible.

Ostrowski then acknowledges that to textual critical critics the rough reading might be secondary if it is a copyist's error or a misunderstanding.[19] Keenan's argument relied upon the relationship between Kurbskii's' *First Letter to Ivan* from 1564 and Isaiah of Kam'ianets-Podil'sk's *Complaint*, written after 1564; Keenan claimed that Kurbskii borrowed from Isaiah, so the *First Letter to Ivan* could not be authentic. Skrynnikov contested that assertion by redating Isaiah's *Complaint* to before 1564 and arguing that Kurbskii in Lithuania in 1564 had access to it. Ostrowski expresses doubts concerning Kurbskii's ability in exile to gain access to Isaiah's text written in prison in Vologda, as proposed by Skrynnikov, but ultimately opines that speculation on issues of access cannot be tested, whereas 'hypotheses concerning the relationship of textual passages can be tested and thereby corroborated or refuted, but only if there is agreement on the textual principles to be used'.[20] If textual critical analysis establishes that Kurbskii's *First Letter to Ivan* was not written until after 1581, then a 1581 Muscovite diplomatic document mention of a 'rude' letter from Kurbskii to Ivan cannot pertain to the text we now call Kurbskii's *First Letter to Ivan*. This would also apply to another allusion to such a 'rude' letter in Nyenstädt's *Livonian Chronicle*, which Keenan dismissed for the very same reason.[21]

Ostrowski's briefer discussion of Kurbskii's *History*[22] declares that Keenan allowed for the possibility that it shared a common source with Lyzlov's *Scythian History* even though Keenan argued that Lyzlov was a

[18] Ibid., p. 259.
[19] Ibid., p. 261. Ostrowski's emphasis.
[20] Ibid., p. 263.
[21] Ibid., pp. 262–63.
[22] Ibid., pp. 264–66.

source of Kurbskii. The traditional view is that Lyzlov read Kurbskii; the earliest manuscript of Kurbskii's *History* predates Lyzlov's publication. David Das concluded that Keenan was on the right path in doubting the authenticity of Kurbskii's *History* but raised the possibility that Kurbskii and Lyzlov derived from a third source. Ostrowski faults Keenan for not showing through textual critical analysis the improbability that Lyzlov read Kurbskii. According to Das, Lyzlov contains the fuller, smoother text, so it was secondary. Ostrowski concludes:

> In this case, then, the textual critical analysis and other fontological evidence do seem to coincide. Even though a textual critical analysis confirms the traditional relationship of [Kurbskii's *History*] to [Lyzlov's *Scythian History*], that does not, however, necessarily corroborate the traditional dating or attribution of [Kurbskii's *History*] to Andrei Kurbskii.[23]

Ostrowski concludes *inter alia* that 'Keenan's application of textual criticism, nevertheless, is not some kind of linguistic legerdemain that can be used to prove any point one wishes'.[24] Summarizing the four case studies he has presented, Ostrowski finds the results 'mixed':

> In the case of the *Kazanskaia istoriia* and the *Iarlyk of Ahmed-Khan*, Keenan's structural (text-critical and redaction) analyses of the texts have not been responded to on a structural level, only on a semiotic one. His recension analysis of *Kazanskaia istoriia* has received acceptance, but his redating of the time of its composition has not even received a semiotic response. In the case of [Kurbskii's *First Letter to Ivan*] Keenan's structural analyses have received both semiotic and structural responses but those responding at the structural level have tended to use either textological principles or faulty text-critical arguments. [...] Finally, Keenan's analysis of the relationship of [Kurbskii's *History*] to [Lyzlov's *Scythian History*] has also been responded to on both semiotic and structural levels [by A. I. Gladkii and Das]. [...] Those comparisons point strongly [in the opposite direction of Keenan's conclusion]. To date, however, Keenan's redating of various versions of [Kurbskii's *History*] has not been responded to at any level.[25]

[23] Ibid., p. 266.
[24] Ibid., p. 267.
[25] Ibid., pp. 267–68. Keenan argued that the so-called 'Compilative Redaction', traditionally considered late and derivative, was actually the primary redaction, and that the 'Expanded Redaction', considered primary in traditional scholarship, was actually late. Boeck agrees with this schema; see below.

Textual critical analysis: Critique

Ostrowski unambiguously argues that Keenan's responders disagreed with him because they utilized a faulty methodology. In contrast to Keenan's valid textual critical methodology, the responders either used the invalid textological methodology or relied on non-textual semiotic evidence. Ostrowski intends to reconceptualize the disagreement between Keenan and his responders as methodological, a disagreement in which Keenan holds the methodological high ground.

I find Ostrowski's analysis inconsistent and unconvincing. He makes uncorroborated assertions about the responders; he elides evidence that contradicts his binary conception of the field, especially Keenan's reliance on semiotic argumentation; when responders do utilize textual critical methodology Ostrowski dismisses them as wrong, which is a substantive, not a methodological disagreement; and he relies upon subjective or one-sided judgments to prejudice the case against the responders.

Ostrowski does not define the 'field' his generalization encompasses. Because he developed his theories in the process of studying the Kyivan *Tale of Bygone Years*, I infer that he does not mean 'Muscovite history'. Although his abstract refers to 'historians', in the body of the article he refers to 'scholars' and discusses publications by Slavicists/philologists, so we may further infer that his generalizations are not confined to historians. He engages works by Russian and European authors, so the field encompasses international scholarship. I would tentatively conclude that the field is Early East Slavic Studies. In this field he finds that 'preference' is 'frequently' given to textological over textual critical studies. I have no idea whether this observation is valid. I would not even attempt to estimate what percentage of scholars in Early East Slavic Studies use textological versus textual critical studies in their research. Ostrowski confines his conclusion to a 'frequent' 'preference', which is almost redundant. If the 'preference' were not 'frequent', it would not be much of a 'preference'.

Ostrowski cites de Madariaga's judgment as 'characteristic of the general tendency' of the field, what 'seems to be' 'the widespread assumption' that semiotic evidence outweighs structural analysis. If Ostrowski is judging the field on the basis of the responders to Keenan's early publications, then the disparity in the form of those responses, from short book reviews to mini-monographs, severely inhibits extracting any meaningful generalization about these scholars' methodological 'preferences'. I would not attempt to classify all responders according to Ostrowski's dichotomy. Many (?), most (?) responders did not provide material upon which one could assign them to either 'tendency'. Perhaps for this reason Ostrowski's carefully qualifies his assertion ('seems to be'). Ostrowski did not name names except for de Madariaga, accurately described as a specialist in eighteenth-century Russian history who wrote a book about sixteenth-century Muscovite history, and this author. If some responders used semiotic interpretation to the detriment of even textological, let alone textual critical, analysis, that does not and cannot invalidate utilization by other responders of either textual methodology, and without considerable corroboration should not be used to stereotype all responses. Moreover, all the scholars named by Ostrowski as concurring with Keenan's textual critical analysis of Ahmed-Khan's charter disagreed with Keenan's ostensibly textual critical conclusions about the texts attributed to Ivan and Kurbskii, so that somehow their aversion to textual critical analysis was only selective. Somehow they 'preferred' textological methodology only when they disagreed with Keenan.

After the textual, even textual critical publications of John Fennell, Aleksandr Zimin, Skrynnikov and Harvey Goldblatt on Kurbskii's *First Letter to Ivan* had appeared, it would have been redundant for responders to Keenan who agreed with them to regurgitate their arguments. Their silence of convenience does not permit Ostrowski to characterize their methodological 'preferences'.

I interpret Andreyev's comment differently than Ostrowski. Andreyev did not reject all stemmata, just Keenan's. Only analysis of all of Andreyev's publication could demonstrate that he was opposed to the methodology of drawing stemmata. But even from Ostrowski's exposition if Andreyev denied the utility of stemmata in textual studies in general he was not speaking for all responders, because Ostrowski discusses stemmata by Fennell, Zimin and Skrynnikov, which are decidedly not based on semiotic evidence.

In that vein I cannot think of anyone responding to Keenan who expressed Ostrowski's third 'principle' of the 'tendency' of textology, to privilege central manuscripts over 'provincial' ones. As far as I recall, no author I have ever read did so. Of course authors do express preferences for some manuscripts over others, but not on the basis of archival geography.

Turning to Ostrowski's four case studies, Ostrowskii faults Dubrovina for accepting Keenan's recension schema of the *Kazan′ History* but not dealing with his new dating of the text. Keenan's analysis of the recension is the only textual critical segment of his discussion. Keenan's new dating derives exclusively from semiotic argument, from content and genre.

Ostrowski thus criticizes Dubrovina for not engaging in semiotic analysis, which hardly conforms to his overall schema of responders to Keenan as in general neglecting textual critical analysis for semiotic.

Ostrowski's analysis of Keenan's view of the *Kazan′ History* illustrates a broader feature of his article: its relative neglect of the extent to which Keenan's study of these texts was semiotic in argumentation.[26] This does not invalidate Ostrowski's point that Keenan privileged structural over semiotic evidence, but it does call into question whether the responders, particularly in textological and textual critical studies, paid more attention to semiotic matters than Keenan did.

Keenan's analysis of the *Iarlyk of Ahmed-Khan* was textual critical in its comparison of that text to other Rus' versions of Tatar diplomatic language and charters. However, having established that the text was not what it purported to be, Keenan then turned to semiotic analysis, again of content and genre, to date it and assign authorship to bureaucrats. Those Russian scholars who rejected Keenan's conclusion on the authenticity of the text included a specialist on Mongol charters who has written extensively on the form of Mongol documentation, A. P. Grigor′ev. He argues that Ahmed-Khan's charter was based upon an authentic original. I do not know if that argument constitutes privileging content over form in Ostrowski's judgment. Indeed, I do not know if such an argument is semiotic in Ostrowski's definition. The Soviet literary specialists (*literaturovedy*) (Likhachev, Lur′e) and historians (Skrynnikov) who accepted Keenan's conclusion that Ahmed-Khan's charter was not authentic cannot be accused of privileging semiotic over textual critical analysis.

Herein lies a major interpretive issue. Ostrowski describes 'tendencies' in textual study. The same scholar can adhere to one tendency in studying one text and the other tendency in studying another text. How Ostrowski categorizes their 'preference' would seem to be quantitative. Someone who favours rougher readings most but not all of the time is a textual critic, but someone who favours smoother readings most but not all of the time is a textologist. Ostrowski provides no indication that he has performed a quantitative analysis of all textual judgments by any of the scholars he ascribes to either textology or textual criticism. Obviously these scholars

[26] Whether Keenan remained faithful to Ostrowski's textual criticism methodology in his subsequent research on *The Lay of the Host of Igor′*, the *Tale of Petr and Fevroniia*, the *Vremennik* attributed to Ivan Timofeev, and other texts, fell outside the scope of Ostrowski's article. Ostrowski did comment that it was premature to judge Keenan's analysis of the *Lay of the Host of Igor′* but that Olga Strakhov's responses, which disputed Keenan's conclusions, qualified as textual critical studies (ibid., p. 247 n. 1).

did not think of the two options as mutually exclusive, but judged individual instances on a case-by-case basis, tendency or no. Ostrowski comments in passing that even when textologists agreed with Keenan's textual critical analysis, they did so for semiotic reasons. I do not know how to extract that conclusion from direct statements by Dubrovina on the *Kazan′ History* or Likhachev and Lur′e on the *iarlyk* that they found Keenan's conclusions convincing. If someone agreed with Keenan's textual criticism then there was no need for them to do further textual critical analysis; what remains would be to assess the consequences of that agreement for semiotic history. It might be more productive to conceive of textology and textual criticism as Weberian ideal types, neither of which exists in reality in a pure form. No one is a 'pure' textologist or textual critic.

These conundrums come out clearest in Ostrowski's discussion of Keenan's view of Kurbskii's *First Letter to Ivan*. That the 'general response' has been to reject Keenan's argument on semiotic grounds is simply not corroborated by any concrete analysis, just a blanket reference to my trilogy of articles without identifying who subscribes to what opinion. He concedes that there have been 'significant attempts' to engage Keenan's textual critical arguments but in dealing with Keenan's mosaic argument they have been 'unsuccessful' or 'faulty'. Here Ostrowski adduces Fennell's explicit expression of a preference for a smoother over a rougher reading, the only such case he cites. Ostrowski does not attempt to show that Fennell (or Zimin) 'tended' to prefer to the smoother reading. Ostrowski does not examine Fennell's text of Kurbskii's *First Letter to Ivan* to substantiate his assigning Fennell to the textology school. Ostrowski's article does not deal with Ivan's *First Letter to Kurbskii*, but it would take a similar quantitative study of the publication of that text in Soviet scholarship to demonstrate that its editors 'tended' to prefer the smoother reading. I cannot make sense of Ostrowski's scepticism that scribes '*intentionally* [my emphasis] made an intelligible reading less intelligible'. If this is Ostrowski's opinion, not Fennell's, not that of the textology, it seems counter-intuitive. No one has ever argued that copyists *deliberately* mutilated a text. Ostrowski acknowledges that to textual critics the rough reading might be secondary, if it is a copyist's error or a misunderstanding, in other words *unintentional*. Ostrowski seems to be saying that secondary rough readings may be intentional or unintentional. Every text Keenan analyses survives only in copies. Choosing between a rough and a smooth reading means comparing what two copyists wrote in order to decide whether a copyist *unintentionally* made a mistake.

According to Ostrowski, Fennell and Zimin had previously done good textual critical analysis, but when dealing with Kurbskii's *First Letter to Ivan* 'they seem to have resorted' to textology. 'Seem to have resorted'? Doesn't Ostrowski know if they did or did not shift preferences from one to the other? If the textology versus textual criticism contrast is legitimate, then why does Ostrowski need to use such ambiguous language? Either they are textologists or they are textual critics. If they do not exhibit unambiguous 'tendencies', then how can they be categorized methodologically? If Ostrowski cannot tell whether their articles on Kurbskii's *First Letter to Ivan* are textological or textual critical, then his conceptual dualism is guilty of reifying and exaggerating the methodological contrast he postulates.

Keenan asserted and Ostrowski agrees that the mosaic argument enhances the credibility of Keenan's conclusion concerning the direction of textual influence between what he thinks were the sources of Kurbskii's *First Letter to Ivan* and that letter. I once thought so but no longer. If anyone can prove on textual critical grounds that any text Keenan claimed was incorporated into his mosaic was not primary, then the entire mosaic edifice collapses. Such a development cannot prove the authenticity of the text, but it would disprove Keenan's mosaic theory. Of course, as Ostrowski does not hide, Keenan's mosaic theory was a moving target. Keenan subtracted and added texts to his list of sources of Kurbskii's *First Letter to Ivan*, so it becomes a matter of which of its incarnations Keenan ultimately endorsed.

The first of three responses to Keenan that Ostrowski fails to cite illustrates the difficulty of evaluating Keenan's conclusions. Ostrowski does not cite his own article, arguably the most overlooked contribution to the discussion of Kurbskii's *First Letter to Ivan*, an analysis, written presumably from a textual critical point of view, of the relationship of the manuscripts of Kurbskii's *First Letter to Ivan* that included new manuscripts discovered after Keenan published his monograph.[27] Ostrowski does not address the question of whether his stemma disputed any textual lines of influence among the older manuscripts in Keenan's stemma. A preliminary attempt to research that issue, obstructed by the fact the Keenan and Ostrowski used different abbreviations for the older

[27] Donald Ostrowski, 'A Stemma for the First Letter of A. M. Kurbsky', *Oxford Slavonic Papers*, 23, 1990, pp. 1–12. Aleksandr Il′ich Filiushkin, *Andrei Mikhailovich Kurbskii. Prosopograficheskoe issledovanie i germenevticheskii kommentarii k poslaniiami Andreia Kurbskogo Ivanu Groznomu*, St Petersburg, 2007, and Erusalimskii, *Na sluzhbe korolia i Rechi pospolitoi*, did not cite this article.

manuscripts, suggests that Ostrowski had somewhat revised Keenan's conclusions. Ostrowski includes in his schema at least one source, Isaiah's *Lament*, found in Keenan's mosaic in the monograph but later excised. Whether Ostrowski disagrees with that excision, while remaining in favour of the mosaic principle, remains unclear.

Second, considering the significance Ostrowski assigned to the mosaic issue, it was careless of him not to cite Goldblatt's article criticizing precisely that textual construction, even if Ostrowski obviously thought it 'unsuccessful'. Goldblatt disputes whether Keenan had accurately delineated the seams between the sources employed in constructing in Kurbskii's *First Letter to Ivan*.[28] Goldblatt's analysis is at least structural and perhaps even in Ostrowski's formulation textual critical. Ostrowski did not see fit to correct this bibliographic omission, which was brought to his attention, in his second article, which compounded his carelessness.

Third, for whatever reason, Ostrowski failed to cite two articles, presumably textual critical, by Thomas Owen, which support Keenan but amplified the mosaic.[29] I do not know if Keenan accepted Owen's emendation of the mosaic's structure.

Ostrowski's opaque presentation of the historiography of Keenan's analysis of the provenance of Kurbskii's *History* differs from how I would interpret what Keenan and Das write. On the basis of textual criticism (and acknowledging the fact that manuscripts of Kurbskii's *History* predate publication of Lyzlov's *Scythian History*), Keenan argued that there is no question but that Kurbskii's *History* was based upon Lyzlov's *Scythian History*. On the basis of textual criticism, Das (and Gladkii) argue that Lyzlov's *Scythian History* was based upon Kurbskii's *History*, although it is possible they had a common source. Ostrowski tries to confine his usually trenchant comments to agreeing with Keenan that Kurbskii did not compose the *History*, but he does not describe Keenan's textual critical analysis of the text as 'faulty', a word he readily applies to textual critical studies by responders who disagreed with Keenan. He also avoids the implication of this conundrum of Keenan and his supporters

[28] Harvey Goldblatt, 'Formal Structure and Textual Identity: The Case of Prince Andrei M. Kurbskii's First Letter to Tsar Ivan IV Groznyi', *Russian History / Histoire russe*, 14, 1987, pp. 155–78. Ostrowski rejects Goldblatt's arguments, he explained in an email, in part because they derive from Goldblatt's isocolic theory of Rus' literature, which Ostrowski finds unconvincing. I believe that Goldblatt's analysis of Keenan's mosaic can be evaluated independently of Goldblatt's isocolic principle.

[29] Halperin, 'Edward Keenan and the Kurbskii-Groznyi Correspondence in Hindsight', p. 377 n. 9.

(Das's dissertation was directed by Waugh) for the scholarly superiority he attributes to textual criticism over textology. Das did not publish his dissertation and Keenan did not to my knowledge respond to Das. Keenan never published more than a long endnote on his analysis of the redactions of Kurbskii's *History*; a promised monograph on the subject never appeared. Responders do not deserve criticism for not responding to Keenan's incomplete argument.

Keenan's analyses of all compositions attributed to Kurbskii are, to cite Ostrowski's opinion in a later work, 'well-argued', but the arguments of responders who contest Keenan's conclusions are never assigned that virtue. Ostrowski declares that Keenan's responders did not engage Keenan's textual critical studies, but he then concedes that those responders did sometimes engage in textual critical studies. However, even when they used the same methodology as Keenan, Ostrowski finds their conclusions deficient. In these cases the difference between Keenan and the responders cannot be methodological. Apparently the responders cannot use textual critical methodology correctly unless Ostrowski agrees with their conclusions.

Ostrowski criticizes this writer for privileging semiotic over textual evidence because after describing Keenan's textual evidence as his strongest, I turned in my second article to the semiotic evidence of a reference to a rude letter of Kurbskii to Ivan found in the inventory of the tsar's archive.[30] I quote my first article:

> Let it be said here: the common-sensical principle of dating texts by textological[31] analysis of their sources is unassailable: no text can be older than its sources. If Keenan's textological triangle [just the relationship of Kurbskii's *First Letter to Ivan* to two works by Isaiah] is correct, then, to be blunt, from the point of view of doing no more than proving that the 'Correspondence' is a forgery [*sic*, apocryphal], the rest of the monograph is superfluous.[32]

If Keenan's textual critical analysis (to revert to Ostrowski's terminology) were correct, then of course contemporary references to a letter from Kurbskii to Ivan could not possibly refer to the text of Kurbskii's *First Letter to Ivan* we now have. However, Ostrowski overlooks that I found

[30] Ostrowski, '"Closed Circles"', p. 263.

[31] Here 'textological' does not refer to Ostrowski's narrower definition of 'textology' as opposed to 'textual criticism' but to all text structural analysis.

[32] Halperin, 'A Heretical View of Sixteenth-Century Muscovy', p. 166.

Fennell's and Zimin's textual critical refutation of Keenan's textual critical argument convincing. Therefore contemporary references to Kurbskii's letter could refer to the text we have. I discuss the reference in the tsar's archive inventory because Keenan made much of the unreliability of a similar reference in a much less reliable source, Nyenstädt (discussed above), and failed to mention the inventory of the tsar's archive, thus arbitrarily weakening the evidence he was refuting.

The amount of semiotic content in *The Kurbskii-Groznyi Apocrypha* should not be minimized. Even if convoy analysis counts as textual critical studies, the book's chapters on the Two Cultures (the monastic religious culture in Slavonic and the court a-religious culture in chancery Russian; as a member of the latter, Keenan insisted, Ivan could not possibly have written a letter invoking religion in Slavonic) and Semen Shakhovskoi's biography (Keenan proposed that Shakhovskoi wrote Kurbskii's *First Letter to Ivan*; more on profiling below) are not textual critical, but extra-textual, ergo semiotic. Ostrowski shares what I consider to be the accepted wisdom manifested by Keenan himself and to which the responders adhered, that 'higher' (semiotic) and 'lower' (textual) criticism both have a place in the scholarly analysis of texts. Keenan's semiotic arguments play a greater role in Ostrowski's second article, to which we now turn, than in his first, which qualifies Ostrowski's putative hostility to semiotic evidence when adduced by Keenan's responders in Ostrowski's first article.

Attribution: Exposition

In his second article Ostrowski addresses exactly what his title describes, 'Attributions to Andrei Kurbskii and Inferential (Bayesian) Probability'.[33] Consequently he discusses only texts attributed to Kurbskii. I confess that I have no idea what Bayesian inferential logic is; I will confine my comments to the conclusions Ostrowski purports to reach on its basis. Of course proponents and opponents of the authenticity of Kurbskii's *First Letter to Ivan*[34] do rate the significance of evidence differently, but this is hardly news. The shift in the point of contention from 'authenticity' to 'attribution' might be more apparent than real: if texts attributed to Kurbskii were not written by Kurbskii, then they cannot be authentic.

[33] Donald Ostrowski, 'Attributions to Andrei Kurbskii and Inferential (Bayesian) Probability', *Canadian-American Slavic Studies / Revue canadienne-américane d'études slaves*. 49, 2015, pp. 211–33.

[34] 'Keenan' and his 'responders' in Ostrowski, "'Closed Circle'" become 'opponents' and 'proponents' in Ostrowski, 'Attributions to Andrei Kurbskii'.

In his second article Ostrowski devotes the most space to Kurbskii's *History*.[35] He correctly calls attention to different responses by proponents and opponents to the 'apparent anachronisms, contradictions, and outright errors' found in the text, which no one denies. To opponents, such anomalies are indicative that Kurbskii did not write the text; to proponents, they demonstrate that the extant versions have been adulterated.[36]

In connection with the literary history or redactions of Kurbskii's *History*, Ostrowski writes:

> A tendency of Russian 'textology' has been to accept the longest readings in and the fullest version of a text as primary [...], although this practice is contrary to the principle of textual criticism that the shorter reading tends to be primary. To be sure, texts can be and are shortened intentionally and unintentionally (especially through parablepsis) but the general tendency is for texts to be intentionally expanded as scribes seek to explain unclear passages and add related material.[37]

In this passage Ostrowski revises his definition of the distinction between 'textology' and 'textual criticism'. Here he refers to shorter versus longer readings, not rougher versus smoother readings, and he expands the scope of the distinction to shorter versus fuller 'versions' (redactions).

Ostrowski cites Boeck's observation that Kurbskii's *History* does not refer to Kurbskii's well-documented tenure in Volhynia after his defection. Ostrowski writes: 'One might expect something more specific than a general castigation of courtier behavior [...] from someone who had been living there for at minimum almost ten years.' Ostrowski notes that Kurbskii refers to the Muscovite language as 'their', implying that his audience knew Slavonic but not Russian, because the text was written in Muscovite Slavonic 'presumably for an elite Russian audience in emigration'.[38] Specialists disagree on whether the use of Polish words in the text represents genuine Polish linguistic influence on Kurbskii and whether such usage is 'consistent with the author's being someone other than Kurbskii, but trying to make it appear as though an émigré like Kurbskii wrote it'. To be sure, proponents and opponents agree that the macaronic language of the *History* requires further study.[39]

[35] Ostrowski, 'Attributions to Andrei Kurbskii', pp. 215–25.
[36] Ibid., p. 216.
[37] Ibid., p. 217.
[38] Ibid., p. 221.
[39] Ibid., p. 222.

The 'general castigation' to which Ostrowski refers is the well-known passage in which Kurbskii decries the moral turpitude, cowardice and selfishness of the members of the Polish court, which Kurbskii's *History* describes as 'here', giving the impression that he was in Poland-Lithuania and that his intended audience, per Ostrowski, consisted of Polish and Lithuanian readers. '[Y]et, the author, Ostrowski declares, makes disparaging remarks about those same supposed readers.'[40]

In discussing historical errors in the *History* such as confusion in Muscovite court ranks, Ostrowski concedes that Kurbskii might have suffered from faulty memory.[41] Concerning Kurbskii's declaration that he could not sign his name *po ruski*, which he takes to mean in the Cyrillic alphabet, Ostrowski cites Boeck's scepticism that Kurbskii was engaged in a 'legal ploy' because in the *History* Kurbskii 'spoke against the "perversion of judicial proceedings" and praised "impartial justice"'. However, Ostrowski adds that if Kurbskii did write the *History* then judicial prevarication is more likely. Still, Kurbskii's declaration of his inability to write Cyrillic lowers the probability that he wrote any of the works attributed to him, all of which were written in Cyrillic. Proponents need to explain Kurbskii's self-declared ignorance of the Cyrillic alphabet.[42] Ostrowski also admits that Kubskii's 'rudimentary' signature in the Latin alphabet might be the result not of his recent and inadequate acquisition of literacy in that language but that 'his years as a warrior may have made his fingers clumsy with a pen,[43] which resulted in script that appears unsteady', or he may have been ill.[44]

The appellation 'History' (*istoriia*) applied to the text also merits comment. Ostrowski notes that the word is not applied to narratives in Muscovite literature until the late seventeenth century. In the sixteenth century the more common term was *povest´* (tale). Slavist Dietrich Freydank proposed that in Kurbskii's case the title carried its Latin meaning, an account of contemporary events, rather than its Greek meaning, an account of past events, but Ostrowski writes that '(s)uch an understanding of *istoriia* would fit the intellectual context either of sixteenth-century Poland or of late seventeenth-century Russia'.[45]

[40] Ibid., p. 223.
[41] Ibid., pp. 223–24.
[42] Ibid., p. 232.
[43] I assume literary licence here on Ostrowski's part. If Kurbskii wrote anything, it would have been with a quill.
[44] Ibid., p. 231.
[45] Ibid., pp. 224, 224 n. 47 (quotation).

Turning to Kurbskii's *First Letter to Ivan*,[46] Ostrowski observes that Keenan attributed it to Semen Shakhovskoi on the basis of similarity of personal information and literary style.[47]

Ostrowski then turns to the manuscript of the Kurbskii's *First Letter to Ivan* watermarked by Boris Morozov. According to Morozov the watermarks on the folios with Kurbskii's *First Letter* are too unclear to date, but the watermarks on the quires with those folios date to 1594–95. Proponents cite this manuscript to reject Shakhovskoi's authorship of *Kurbskii's First Letter to Ivan*. Ostrowski points out that the watermarks which Morozov dated to the 1590s are 'similar' to watermarks from the 1610s or 1620s. Morozov prudently called for more research on the miscellany, which opponents of authenticity took as a cue to dismiss the evidence altogether.[48]

In recapitulating the textual connection between Kurbskii's *First Letter to Ivan* and Isaiah's *Complaint* Ostrowski refers to Isaiah's imprisonment in Vologda or Rostov. Ostrowski dwells again on the problem of how Kurbskii or Isaiah gained access to a text written by the other, but adds an *obiter dictum*: access is not a problem for Keenan because 'there are any number of possible ways for him [Shakhovskoi] to have gained access to a copy of a letter written sixty years later'.[49]

Although Ostrowski again omits reference to the inventory of the tsar's archive among sources that attest to a 'rude' letter from Kurbskii to Ivan, here he does concede that similar references increase the probability that Kurbskii wrote his *First Letter to Ivan*, which opponents need to explain.[50] Ostrowski discusses the attribution of the *History of the Eighth Council* (the ecclesiastical Council of Florence-Ferrara) to Kurbskii.[51] Concerning the thirteen letters supposedly written by Kurbskii in Poland-Lithuania Ostrowski concludes that their style, 'a combination of plain Slavonic and Ruthenian *prosta mova* [simple speech] and subject matter', differs markedly from the style and subject matter of the letters to Ivan.[52]

Ostrowski even-handedly identifies inadequately explained anomalies in the arguments of both opponents and proponents. His overall conclusion must be applauded: 'No one point of contention decides the case definitively

46 Ibid., pp. 225–27.
47 Ibid., p. 225.
48 Ibid., pp. 225–26.
49 Ibid., p. 227.
50 Ibid., p. 232.
51 Ibid., pp. 228–30.
52 Ibid., p. 218.

in favour of the sceptics or proponents', who should view each other as co-investigators, not opponents.[53]

Attribution: Critique

As far as 'expectations' are concerned about whether Kurbskii would criticize gentry in Poland-Lithuania when he was exile there, such 'expectations' exist in the eye of the beholder. What we might 'expect' to find in a *History* written by Kurbskii depends very much upon the unresolved issue of the text's intended audience. For an émigré like Kurbskii to be ambivalent, even to contradict himself, about his status, about what language is spoken 'here', meaning in Lithuania, versus 'their' language, meaning Russian, spoken 'there', in Russia, is hardly peculiar. The émigré mentality is frequently ambivalent.[54] Kurbskii's inconsistent use of 'grand prince' or 'tsar', even 'our tsar',[55] can be explained by that ambivalence. Ostrowski questions whether Kurbskii intended Poles and Lithuanians as his audience because he insults them. Choice of language alone provides the best reason to question the notion of Poles and polonized Lithuanians as the intended sixteenth-century audience of the text. A text directed at Polish and polonized Lithuanian aristocrats and gentry had to be written in Polish or Latin.[56] Unless Kurbskii intended his *History* to be translated into one of those languages, he cannot possibly have had such an audience in mind, so we can rule out the supposed contradiction between Kurbskii's purpose and his criticism of locals. Ostrowski suggests that Kurbskii supposedly intended the work for an 'elite Russian audience in emigration'. He does not reference Keenan's concept of the Two Cultures, to which he otherwise adheres. According to that theory sixteenth-century lay elite Russians, including émigrés like Kurbskii, did not know Slavonic. Because proponents date the *History* mostly to the 1570s or later, Kurbskii's Muscovite Slavonic would have been intelligible to the Ruthenian nobility of Volhynia and elsewhere in the Polish-Lithuanian Commonwealth after the 1569 Union of Lublin. Church Slavonic was sufficiently comprehensible on both sides of the Polish-Lithuanian/Muscovite border for religious literature to travel in both directions. Kurbskii could have intended the

[53] Ibid., p. 232.

[54] Inge Auerbach, 'Identity in Exile: Andrei Mikhailovich Kurbskii and National Consciousness in the Sixteenth Century', in *Culture and Identity in Muscovy, 1539–1584*, eds A. M. Kleimola and G. D. Lenhoff, Moscow, 1997, pp. 11–25.

[55] Ostrowski, 'Attributions to Andrei Kurbskii', pp. 224–25.

[56] Erusalimskii, *Na sluzhbe korolia i Rechi pospolitoi*, pp. 373, 507 proposes that Kurbskii intended his *History* for Lithuanian and Ruthenian szlachta, but in any case readers who could read *po-ruski* (here: Ruthenian).

History for both Ruthenians and fellow Muscovite émigrés. Following Keenan, Ostrowski, I infer, believes that late seventeenth-century lay elite Muscovites, who by then knew Slavonic, constituted the readership of Kurbskii's *History*, but Ostrowski does not develop that argument, which might have been off-topic.[57] Ostrowski raises the prospect of a Polish-Lithuanian readership only to refute it; his presentation could have been clearer.

Although Ostrowski subscribes to the view that the Polonisms in the text derived from an attempt to make it appear that an émigré wrote the *History* in the sixteenth century, he argues that the émigré Kurbskii could *not* have experienced Polish linguistic influence. In other words, in trying to make the text appear authentic the falsifier, familiar with Polish linguistic influence in Muscovy in the second half of the seventeenth century, actually provides evidence contradicting its authenticity.

Kurbskii's reliance on rumours coming out of Muscovy also created errors. Kurbskii admitted that sometimes his information might be unreliable.

Although, as we shall see, Ostrowski rates profile studies of potential authors very highly in determining attribution, he does not always take into account all elements of Kurbskii's authorial profile in assessing the probability of his authoring the *History*. The ample documentation of Kurbskii's life in Lithuania demonstrates incontestably that Kurbskii was a liar, hypocrite and criminal. The likelihood that for whatever unknown reason Kurbskii lied when he denied that he could write Cyrillic is of a very high order of probability. Proponents therefore already have an explanation of Kurbskii's declaration.

Whether Kurbskii could have called his work a 'history', according to Ostrowski, depends upon whether Kurbskii could have been influenced by Polish culture sufficiently to transport the word into Slavonic. Kurbskii claims in the *History* to have been a student of Maksim Grek, which some proponents take seriously, but may be self-serving, but no one studying the question has ever drawn a connection between Kurbskii's use of the word *istoriia* in his title and the appearance of the word *istoriia* in Slavonic in works of Maksim Grek. To be sure Maksim Grek never titled any of his works an *istoriia* because he did not write 'histories'.[58]

[57] Ostrowski mentions Boeck's theory that the oldest version of Kurbskii's *History* was actually a separate text, the 'Tale of Persecutions', written in Muscovy in the 1590s (ibid., p. 219). If so, then the audience of the text might still have been 'elite Muscovites', but a century earlier than Ostrowski proposes.

[58] *Sochineniia prepodobnogo Maksima Greka*, 3 v., Kazan', 1859, v. 1. pp. 413 [of *istoriekh* is a plural], 525; v. 2, pp. 306; vol. 3, p. 279.

Ostrowski's invocation of manuscripts from the 1620s and 1630s with watermarks 'similar' to those in the Morozov manuscript is not decisive. Daniel Waugh is an opponent. He supplied the manuscript descriptions for Keenan's monograph.[59] In 2014 he wrote about Morozov's argument: 'My impression of the evidence [...] supports Morozov's assertions about the early date of the manuscript in question.' 'The surrounding paper and the handwriting argue for a date at the end of the sixteenth century.' However, he concluded, the manuscript does not prove Keenan wrong about the authenticity of the text. Filigranology cannot prove or disprove authenticity.[60] Although everyone seems to agree that the Morozov manuscript watermarks require further study, no one seems to have done any. Consequently Morozov's dating has not been refuted. Ostrowski admitted to me in a private communication that he did have access to Waugh's article when he wrote his 2015 article but that he did not 'want to attempt to impugn Waugh's argument'. That a scribe or copyist in the 1620s or 1630s just happened to have enough 1590s paper lying around 'in the storeroom' to fit Kurbskii's *First Letter to Ivan* on it is painfully convenient, but in any case not a textual critical consideration.

Speculation over how Isaiah or Kurbskii could have acquired access to the other's texts is moot. If Isaiah used Kurbskii, then Isaiah had access to Kurbskii. If 'Kurbskii' used Isaiah, then 'Kurbskii' had access to Isaiah.[61]

Ostrowski argues that it is less probable that the same author, writing to different recipients about different themes, could muster different literary styles, than that different styles and subject matter derive from different authors.[62] To verify this assumption one would need works of different genres whose attribution to the same author is not contested. Obviously the texts attributed to Ivan the Terrible do not qualify. I wonder if the *Istiny pokazanie k vosprosivshim o novom uchenii* (Demonstration of Truth to Those who Asked about the New Teaching), an anti-heretical polemic, and letters of condolence and complaint authored by the monk Zinovii Otenskii might provide relevant evidence. It is premature to invoke Ostrowski's

[59] Edward L. Keenan, *The Kurbskii-Groznyi Apocrypha: The Seventeenth-Century Origin of the 'Correspondence' Attributed to Prince A. M. Kurbskii and Tsar Ivan IV*. With an appendix by Daniel C. Waugh, Cambridge, MA, 1971.

[60] Daniel C. Waugh, 'The Enthusiasms of Youth and Where They Led: A Memoir, Part 2', *Quaestio Rossica*, 3, 2014, p. 23.

[61] See Erusalimskii, *Na sluzhbe korolia i Rechi pospolitoi*, pp. 359–60 on the probability of textual borrowing in either direction. Cf. ibid., pp. 629, 638–53 on Kurbskii's *First Letter to Ivan*.

[62] Ibid., p. 661 averred that Ostrowski's contrasts require further substantiation.

speculative argument to minimize the likelihood that Kurbskii composed heterogeneous texts until someone has provided corroboration.

Erusalimskii, who does not doubt the authenticity of Kurbskii's *History* or his letters to Ivan the Terrible, includes the *History of the Eighth Council* among the works whose attribution to Kurbskii he considers doubtful,[63] suggesting that the division between proponents and opponents of Kurbskii's authorship is neither straightforward nor absolute.

In his second article Ostrowski provides a more balanced evaluation of references to Kurbskii's *First Epistle to Ivan* in contemporary documents than in his earlier article. It is also the first time to my knowledge that any opponent has done more than dismiss them out-of-hand on the spurious grounds that we do not know if they denote the extant text we know as Kurbskii's *First Epistle to Ivan*. This one-sided argument from silence fails to take into account that we do not know that these passages do *not* denote the extant text we know as Kurbskii's *First Epistle to Ivan*.

Juxtaposing Ostrowski's two articles leads to an interesting contrast. In '"Closed Circles": Edward L. Keenan's Early Textual Work and the Semiotics of Response' Ostrowski accorded higher probative power to textual critical analysis over textological analysis, and to all forms of textual study over 'semiotic' analysis of content, style and context. In 'Attributions to Andrei Kurbskii and Inferential (Bayesian) Probability', although Ostrowski occasionally alludes to textual critical studies, the evidence and arguments adduced overwhelmingly belong to the sphere of the 'semiotic'. Degrees of probability do apply somewhat to which direction of access and textual borrowing is more likely, but the degrees of probability derive mostly from context, not textual critical analysis. Ostrowski shows more respect for semiotic analysis in his second article than he did in the first.

Post-script: Attribution in world history

Ostrowski's *Who Wrote That? Authorship and Controversies from Moses to Sholokhov*[64] began as a comparison of the attribution questions attached only to Shakespeare and Kurbskii. As the concept of the book evolved, the material on those two authors was reduced to chapter length for each and seven other cases were added. This is truly a work of world history. Five of the nine cases come from what might loosely be called 'Western civilization': two on ancient history, one on the Old Testament, 'Did Moses write the

[63] Ibid., p. 625.

[64] Donald Ostrowski, *Who Wrote That? Authorship and Controversies from Moses to Sholokhov*, Ithaca, NY, 2020.

Pentateuch?' and one on the New Testament, 'Who wrote the Secret Gospel of Mark?', one on medieval history, 'Did Abelard and Eloise write the letters attributed to them?', one on Renaissance history, 'Who wrote Shakespeare?', and one on the Enlightenment, 'How inauthentic was James Macpherson's translation of Ossian?'. One article comes from (ancient) Chinese history, 'Who wrote the Analects?' attributed to Confucius, and another from medieval Islamic history, 'Who wrote the *Compendium of Chronicles* (*Jami al-tawarik*) attributed to Rashid al-Din?', and two from Russian history, one early modern, 'Who wrote the works attributed to Prince Andrei Kurbskii?' and one modern, 'Did Mikhail Sholokhov write The Quiet Don?'.[65] Ostrowski makes a convincing case that the same kinds of evidence and arguments appear in all cases, which does not mean that the same kinds of evidence and arguments appear in all chapters. Ostrowski is forthright about admitting that he has his own opinion in many if not all of these cases, but largely succeeds in presenting the evidence objectively and fairly, regardless of his preferences. He does allow himself to point out 'fallacious arguments, faulty use of evidence, and lack of evidence'.[66] I note in passing that the advent of printing seems to have made no difference in creating indisputable evidence of attribution, a surprising conclusion at least to me and one to which Ostrowski pays no attention.

For lack of sufficient expertise I will not discuss eight of the nine chapters, but I will note some of his comments in those chapters that are relevant to discussing his chapter on Kurbskii. Ostrowski writes: 'A basic principle of textual criticism is that the earliest manuscripts do not necessarily contain the best readings.'[67] I am positive that this principle also applies to 'textology' in Ostrowski's terms as well as to 'textual criticism'. He declares that all authors make mistakes, so mistakes, inconsistencies and anachronisms do not prove that a text was not written by the person to whom it is attributed, a dictum that he does not always apply to Kurbskii's *History*. Ostrowski also insists that it is not necessary to provide a motive to prove a forgery,[68] but I would add: it certainly helps.

Chapter seven, 'Who wrote the works attributed to Prince Andrei Kurbskii?',[69] basically reprints 'Attributions to Andrei Kurbskii and

[65] On Sholokhov Ostrowski consulted Boeck (Ostrowski, *Who Wrote That?*, p. ix) and quotes Brian Boeck, *Stalin's Scribe: Literature, Ambition and Survival. The Life of Mikhail Sholokhov*, New York, 2019.

[66] Ostrowski, *Who Wrote That?*, p. 3.

[67] Ibid., p. 83.

[68] Ibid, p. 124.

[69] Ibid., pp. 160–89.

Inferential (Bayesian) Probability'. On the very first page of this chapter Ostrowski calls into question the quality of the criticism of Keenan's conclusions by describing Keenan's monograph as a 'carefully researched, well-argued treatise', previously quoted above, without paying a similar tribute to anything written that was critical of it.[70] He also notes that when he published that book Keenan had few defenders.[71]

Ostrowski calls attention to the efficacy of profiling for attribution, not just of who wrote 'Kurbskii', but also who wrote 'Shakespeare', whether Rashid ad-Din wrote the letters attributed to him, and whether Sholokhov wrote *The Quiet Don*.[72] Ostrowski notes that Kurbskii engaged in correspondence, especially about literary matters, and owned books,[73] but, as mentioned above, he still contests the attribution of the Lithuanian letters to him and how Kurbskii used those books. Ostrowski concludes the chapter on Kurbskii by reverting to the key conclusion of '"Closed Circles": Edward L. Keenan's Early Textual Work and the Semiotics of Response', now applied to all the cases discussed in *Who Wrote That* but especially to Shakespeare: 'The general tendency in the scholarship has been to respond to textual critical and linguistic arguments and evidence with arguments and evidence that are in a different register, that is, of a non-textual critical or non-linguistic variety.'[74]

Ostrowski's chapter on Kurbskii ably illustrates that his mode of analysis of attribution concerning Kurbskii is applicable on a world stage, but here, as close reading of his conclusion surprisingly shows, he seemingly discards the distinction between textology and textual criticism as if they constituted a unified methodology in contrast to 'non-textual' and 'non-linguistic' arguments. Of course, even in his first article Ostrowski does not deny that textology is textual analysis, not semiotic analysis.[75] Concerning Keenan's conclusion on attributing works to Kurbskii, because there is no way to judge the opinions of scholars who have not commented on the work in print, estimating how many or how few specialists agreed with Keenan when he first published is impossible. It is true that few colleagues defended Keenan in print at the time, but later that number grew sufficiently to dominate the agenda of the field to the point that disagreeing with Keenan could be treated by some as a scholarly

[70] Ibid., p. 160.
[71] Ibid., p. 162.
[72] Ibid., p. 122.
[73] Ibid., pp. 182–89 (p. 187).
[74] Ibid., p. 189.
[75] Ostrowski, '"Closed Circles"', p. 234.

weakness. Currently, as mentioned above, it is legitimate to state that a majority of scholars in the field do not agree with Keenan.

Conclusion

This review article sincerely affirms that there is no doubt of the good intentions motivating Ostrowski's publication of the two articles and monograph discussed here. His conclusions deserve broader discussion.

In '"Closed Circles": Edward L. Keenan's Early Textual Work and the Semiotics of Response' Ostrowski sought to attribute the disconnect between Keenan's conclusions and the responses of those scholars who contested them to different methodological tendencies. Keenan relied upon internal textual critical analysis, but his responders primarily on external semiotic evidence, on textological rather than textual critical studies and on faulty textual critical arguments. However Keenan used semiotic data more than Ostrowski credits, and Ostrowski fudges the dichotomy between textology and text-criticism by admitting that the same scholars at different times used different methodologies and that in specific cases adherents of either 'tendency' could reach the same conclusion. His identification of scholars as belonging to one or the other 'tendency' of textual analysis or of favouring semiotic evidence over textual evidence from either 'tendency' does not rest upon a quantitative or qualitative examination of all contributions to the discourse on the texts in question. Moreover he discredits the opponents' use of critical textual arguments by labelling them 'faulty' when they reach conclusions he finds unconvincing, which substitutes his own substantive judgment for methodological criteria. He prejudices the case by one-sidedly praising Keenan's research. The distinction between what Ostrowski calls textology and textual criticism is real, even if the categories are only Weberian ideal types, and may in some cases be significant, but that distinction does not rationalize the disagreements over Keenan's argument concerning the authenticity of the texts attributed to Kurbskii and Ivan. The most significant responses took the form of textual critical attempts to refute Keenan's textual critical conclusions and cannot be dismissed on methodological grounds because of 'guilt by association' with responses that invoked semiotic over textual argument. The very methodological heterogeneity of responders to Keenan's conclusions belies any attempt to attribute the disagreement to methodological incompatibility.

In 'Attributions to Andrei Kurbskii and Inferential (Bayesian) Probability' Ostrowski applied Bayesian theory to explore the different responses to the authority of evidence of the proponents and opponents of the authenticity of Kurbskii's works. The two 'camps' differed significantly in the significance they assigned to evidence. However in this article Ostrowski adduces overwhelmingly external, 'semiotic' evidence and arguments by both sides despite his insistence in his first article that such evidence and arguments possess less probative value than textual critical (or even 'textological') analysis. Ostrowski's objectivity and fairness induce him here to treat one type of evidence, contemporary references to a rude Kurbskii letter to Ivan, more seriously than any other opponent has done.

In *Who Wrote That? Authorship and Controversies from Moses to Sholokhov*, Ostrowski succeeds in placing the Kurbskii attribution polemics within the context of world history historiography. He shows that the types of evidence and arguments applied to the writings attributed to Kurbskii parallel in many ways those in other attribution discussions. The scope of this book dramatically attests to the value of seeing themes in Russian history within a world-historical framework.

Ostrowski's goal in all three cases is to raise the quality of the discussion of authenticity and attribution issues related to Ivan IV and Kurbskii by assisting the participating scholars on each side to have a better appreciation of the point of view of their counterparts. Adherents of neither side have the right to claim a monopoly of scholarly rectitude and read adherents of the other side out of the historical profession. Unfortunately Ostrowski's presentation at times privileges Keenan's views, which does not contribute to that goal. Nevertheless this is a vast improvement over the worst polemics during the 1970s which cast the debate as a battle between Russophobes and Great-Russian chauvinists. Ostrowski does not expect legitimate scholarly differences of opinion to be resolved and a consensus to emerge, but we can all hope that his publications will have a beneficial impact upon the discussion. This article shares that intent.

Reviews

Offord, Derek. *Ayn Rand and the Russian Intelligentsia: The Origins of an Icon of the American Right*. Russian Shorts. Bloomsbury Academic, New York, London and Dublin, 2022. xiv + 130 pp. Notes. Selected bibliography. Index. £45.00; £12.99; £11.69 (e-book).

Derek Offord, Emeritus Professor and Senior Research Fellow at the University of Bristol, specializes in pre-revolutionary Russian history, thought, literature and language. In addition to numerous publications on these topics, he has written two widely used books on the modern Russian Language — *Modern Russian: An Advanced Grammar Course* (1993) and *Using Russian: A Guide to Contemporary Usage* (1996) — co-edited *A History of Russian Thought* published by Cambridge University Press (2010), and co-authored the monograph *The French Language in Russia: A Social, Political, Cultural, and Literary History* (Amsterdam, 2018), which won the Marc Raeff Book Prize and the R. Gapper Book Prize.

His most recent work is published in the Bloomsbury Academic series Russian Shorts, which aims to present with each title 'a side of Russian history and culture that has not been well-understood', and covers a broad range of topics from the Russian Civil War to Russian internet memes. In a compact one-hundred-and-something page format, uniform to the series, Offord convincingly and eruditely demonstrates the decisive influence of the nineteenth- and early twentieth-century Russian intellectual legacy on the literary style, philosophical emphases and ideological positions of Ayn Rand (1905–1982), the influential and controversial American writer and philosopher.

Rand was born Alisa Zinovievna Rosenbaum to a secular Jewish family in St Petersburg. After the October Revolution, the Communists destroyed her father's business and confiscated the family's property. The impoverished Rosenbaums fled to Crimea, hoping for the success of the White Army, and returned after its final defeat. Despite living in meagre conditions and being briefly expelled from the university for her bourgeois background, Alisa completed her degree in history in 1924 and a year later emigrated to the USA, where she began to pursue a screenwriting career in California, already using her pen name, Ayn Rand.

Rand gained prominence as a writer in the early 1940s, mainly through the astounding commercial success of her novel, *The Fountainhead* (1943). Through the story of Howard Roark (partly modelled on the American architect Frank Lloyd Wright), she developed her trademark formula of a highly creative, entrepreneurial hero with stark individualistic ideals, fighting against the burdens of a collectivist society obstructing his visionary goals and parasitizing his exceptional achievements. Rand cemented her fame in the

1950s with the release of her last novel, *Atlas Shrugged* (1957), which built upon the 'individual vs. collective' theme of *The Fountainhead* but added to it a grim dystopian vision of an authoritarian collectivist society, already explored in her novella *The Anthem* (1938), and even a romantic depiction of revolutionary action leading to the establishment of an anti-collectivist utopia.

The booming popularity of her fiction propelled Rand to become an influential, albeit divisive figure in American libertarian and conservative circles. While they shared her uncompromising rejection of socialism and passionate embrace of capitalism as the core American value, the other vital aspects of her world-view were — and, to a lesser degree, still are — antithetical to the mainstream currents of the American Right. She was a staunch atheist, a militant opponent of Christianity and all other religious, spiritual and metaphysical traditions, which she commonly labelled and attacked — in recognizable Marxist terminology — as 'mysticism'. Her system of thought, which she called Objectivism, was a blend of positivistic, rationalistic and materialistic ideas, and hailed selfishness as its main ethical virtue. Rand also expressed, as Offord notes, a 'scant respect for laws or regulations', an 'aversion to representative democracy' and a 'reverence for self-designated elites'.

How was this peculiar mix of seemingly heterogeneous positions, which fascinates and attracts her loyal admirers as a particularly daring, original, and at the same time authentically American world-view, constructed? Offord argues that it is a unique collage of ideas, values and habits which Rand selectively, and to a certain extent polemically, adopted from some of the most distinguishable trends among the Russian radical intelligentsia. In the central chapters of his book, Offord expertly guides the reader through the intellectual life of nineteenth- and early twentieth-century Russia, highlighting those figures, phenomena and controversies that he sees as the decisive building blocks of Rand's formation.

Besides the biographical observation that the suffering inflicted on her family by the Bolsheviks played a clear role in motivating her anti-Communist fervour, the topic of Rand's Russian roots may be less known (and perhaps genuinely of less interest) to her general readership. Nevertheless, since the mid 1990s, it has gradually gained the attention of scholars. 'Few of Rand's admirers and detractors were more than marginally aware of her Russian cultural background and its impact on her intellectual and literary development prior to the 1995 publication of Chris Matthew Sciabarra's ground-breaking *Ayn Rand: The Russian Radical*' (D. Barton Johnson, 'Strange Bedfellows: Ayn Rand and Vladimir Nabokov', *The Journal of Ayn Rand Studies*, 2, 1, 2000, p. 47). Sciabarra's book laid the foundations for the past two decades of lively scholarly debate on this topic, most of which saw the light of day in *The Journal of Ayn Rand Studies*, which he co-edits. While Sciabarra's intriguing central thesis — that the philosophical system of Rand's professor, Nikolai Losskii, one of the foremost Russian neo-idealists, significantly shaped her intellectual horizons (Offord mentions him only as a potential influence) — did not gain much traction outside of his own continued research, another comparison that he briefly examined in *The Russian Radical*, and which Johnson (and Offord) fully embraced, became the central topic of the debate: namely, a comparison between Rand's work and that of Nikolai Chernyshevskii.

Chernyshevskii's novel *What Is to Be Done?* (1863) — which has been, much like *Atlas Shrugged*, ever since its appearance derided by critics as one of the worst literary works of all time — was an immense inspiration for the Bolsheviks. According to Joseph Frank, 'no work in modern literature, with the possible exception of *Uncle Tom's Cabin*, can compete with *What Is to Be Done?* in its effect on human lives and its power to make history. For Chernyshevskii's novel, far more than Marx's *Capital*, supplied the emotional dynamic that eventually went to make the Russian Revolution' (*Through the Russian Prism: Essays on Literature and Culture*, Princeton, NJ, 1990, p. 187).

The novels of Chernyshevskii and Rand share strikingly similar plots, characters, literary styles and philosophical outlooks. Both authors propagate atheism, materialism and 'rational egoism', a morally reductive pursuit of self-interest, and weaponize didactical, one-dimensional narratives to convince their readers — as they both did, in the tens of millions — of the superiority of their politico-economic ideologies of choice. But these two radical ideologies — namely, utopian socialism and utopian capitalism — were through most of the twentieth century by and large perceived as opposite extremes of the modern ideological spectrum and at the same time — with a complex web of their less fanatical variations — as the main contestants in the Manichean battle for the future world order. How is it possible, then, that two of their most popular zealots shared such perplexing, mirror-image commonalities?

In explaining this phenomenon, Offord acknowledges what he sees as one of the rare creative aspects of Rand's appropriation of the Russian legacy. While Chernyshevskii's ethics put self-interest on the highest pedestal, one of the main objectives of *What is to be Done?* is 'to persuade readers that the personal interests they inevitably pursue are best served if they act in ways that benefit the larger community' (p. 61). In Offord's view, this speaks of an essential value that was in principle shared by Chernyshevskii and the most famous of his opponents, Dostoevskii, even though they drastically disagreed on why it was important and how it could be attained: 'At the very centre of their outlooks were ethical doctrines which seem at first sight to be diametrically opposed to one another but which in fact attach equal importance to harmonious human association' (p. 61). While Dostoevskii argued that one can only achieve this ideal through sincere adherence to Orthodox Christianity, Chernyshevskii's rational egoism was 'conceived as a species of altruism' for a 'post-Christian world' (p. 62). In Offord's interpretation, Rand detected and detested this supposedly common striving of Russian thought as its rotten core and adopted its radical inversion as her main principle. Within the explications of her ethical system, where any notion of 'common good' is renounced as 'utterly evil' (pp. 44–45), Rand 'deplores both the varieties of altruism, religious and secular (both a Dostoevskian and a Chernyshevskian variety, we could say), that she has identified' (p. 63).

Even though Offord's genealogy of Rand's hostility to altruism sounds plausible, at least as a psychological explanation, his watering-down of Chernyshevskii's egoism into a project of benevolent secular 'preservation of a sense of brotherhood' (p. 62) makes one raise an eyebrow. In the recently published *Nikolai Chernyshevskii and Ayn Rand: Russian Nihilism Travels to America* (London, 2021), the most in-depth comparative reading of Rand and Chernyshevskii thus far, Aaron Weinacht compellingly argues that the essence of Chernyshevskii's programme remains intact in its Randian variation. Their superficially antagonistic 'sociopolitical theses tend to function as different means to the same ends. Chernyshevskii's fictional heroes may admire the British socialist Robert Owen or the French socialist Charles Fourier; Rand's heroes resemble a hyper-capitalist product of a DNA cross between Henry Ford and Achilles. But, these political differences are symptomatic of different beliefs about what context is necessary for the achievement of the same end: realization of the full potential of the individual self, liberated from all possible constraints' (p. 32). Crucially, both writers 'envision the unfettered egoist individual reigning supreme in a utopian future' (p. 47).

Offord is no fan of Russian nihilism, but his questionable argument that Rand's Americanized adoption of its pioneering expositions 'reversed' their essential tendency may have played a role in the only glaring weakness of his book. While he defends the thesis — with similarities to Weinacht's monograph and Adam Weiner's study of the effects of Randianism on the 2008 financial collapse (*How Bad Writing Destroyed the World: Ayn Rand and the Literary Origins of the Financial Crisis*, London, 2016) — that some of the most destructive ideas of the Russian radical intelligentsia found fertile ground in the mainstream ideological currents of post-war America, he tries to convince his reader that this influence is safely isolated — and evenly distributed — at only one end of the political spectrum. This narrative ignores the fact that Rand's message was from the 1950s onwards vehemently criticized by numerous prominent representatives of American conservatism (these criticisms are meticulously chronicled in Jennifer Burns's biography of Rand — *The Goddess of the Market: Ayn Rand and the American Right*, Oxford, 2011 — which Offord frequently quotes) and fails to acknowledge that some of her most cherished ideals — and, indeed, those of the Russian radicals — found a much broader home in modern US society.

Offord's simplistic take on the American political arena, which represents only a minor part of this otherwise highly nuanced book, should not distract from its superb qualities. He draws telling connections between the Russian reception of Nietzsche and the *Übermensch* dimension of Rand's characters, and expands the topic of the earlier nihilist parallels to her work beyond the usual focus on Chernyshevskii, with an elegant explication of Dmitrii Pisarev's 'elitist' revolutionary thought, Nikolai Dobroliubov's utilitarian literary criticism, and the destructive 'future building' of Evgenii Bazarov, the proto-nihilist character of Turgenev's *Fathers and Sons*.

On the literary front, Offord also discusses the influences of the Socialist Realist novel, Russian dystopian fiction and Dostoevskii's novel of ideas. Even though '*Atlas Shrugged* may also be seen as a subversion of Socialist Realist prose', writes Offord, 'typical features of novels in the Socialist Realist canon are replicated in *The Fountainhead* and *Atlas Shrugged*' (pp. 56–57). In this regard, he gives special consideration to Rand's variations on the positive literary hero, 'epic struggles in which ideologically pure heroes triumph because of their determination in the face of apparently overwhelming odds', and the admiration of 'breakneck industrialization' (p. 58).

While Offord's hypothesis that Rand modelled her dystopian themes directly on Evgenii Zamiatin's genre-defining novel *We* (first published in 1924, in English translation) is a little more speculative — especially given the prominence of English dystopian fiction in the decades of Rand's literary creativity — he nonetheless exposes striking similarities. At the minimum, Zamiatin's tangible indirect influence on Rand — perhaps via his impact on Huxley, Orwell and other dystopian writers of the era — seems to be hardly deniable.

Last but not least, Offord persuasively argues, with due respect to the previously discussed influences, that it was in fact Dostoevskii who 'provided the most powerful and influential models for the sort of novel Rand wrote, in which characters are reifications of ideas and an apocalyptic struggle between good and evil is taking place' (p. 101). He also points the reader to 'irrefutable evidence of Rand's unacknowledged debt to Dostoevskii's Raskol′nikov for her classification of humankind and her characterization of her heroes' in *The Fountainhead* (p. 68) and the kinship of Ivan Karamazov's motto, 'everything is permitted', to the ethical dispositions in *Atlas Shrugged* (pp. 68–69). Dostoevskii's darkest characters, who excel at negating any moral obligations to their fellow human beings, are, as Offord concludes, from Rand's vantage point, 'heroic rule-breakers to be emulated rather than examples of monsters unleashed in a world without religious belief, as Dostoevsky had intended them to be' (p. 101).

Despite its short format, Offord's *Ayn Rand and the Russian Intelligentsia* delivers an impressively rich analysis and a comprehensive overview of the definitive, likely and potential Russian influences on Rand's *oeuvre*. It will undoubtedly serve as one of the essential references for future researchers of this topic.

University of Ljubljana MATIC KOCIJANČIČ

Tyerman, Edward. *Internationalist Aesthetics: China and Early Soviet Culture*. Columbia University Press, New York and Chichester, 2022. xi + 353 pp. Illustrations. Notes. Bibliography and sources. Index. $35.00: £28.00 (paperback).

THIS subtly nuanced study of the early stages of Sino-Soviet relations is even-handed in its description of Comintern's attempts to come to terms with its huge neighbour at a time when both countries were in a state of great political flux after centuries of imperialism, and their experiment to bring aesthetics into previously biased and clichéd conceptions; an attempt that seemed 'marked by the shadow of failure' (p. 35). Few, however, would disagree with Professor Tyerman that both the aspirations and failures of this project remain of interest today. This remarkable book, the first of its kind in English, is evidence of his belief.

The very full Introduction brings to the reader much of what comes in the following four chapters and epilogue. The book's basic concept is that 'internationalist aesthetics refers to a collective attempt to express and resolve the contradictions of internationalism through the production of culture' (p. 5). Here are also introduced two of the main Soviet Sinologists, A. Ivin (pen-name of Aleksei Alekseevich Ivanov, 1885–1942) and, most important, Sergei Mikhailovich Tret′iakov (1892–1937), who figures in every chapter of this book. It may be mentioned here that the comprehensive index is a great aid in following a fascinating and complex, thoroughly annotated text.

Chapter one, 'Sight, Sound and Similarity', describes the experiences of early Soviet writers visiting China as mediators between the countries, both through what they wrote and whom they met. The main elements are Tret′iakov's many newspaper articles, for which he had to rely on Chinese interpreters, and his onomatopoeic dramatic poem, *Roar, China!* Also considered in this chapter are Boris Pil′niak's 'Kitaiskaia povest′' and how this, together with the Russian writer's failed attempt at cinematic collaboration with left-leaning Chinese intellectuals, 'illustrate[s] the divergent understandings of nation and internationalism that circulated across the Sino-Soviet encounter' (p. 32).

Chapter two, 'Translating China Onstage: *Roar China!* and *The Red Poppy*', discusses, amongst other things, questions of translation: in Tret′iakov's drama for the Meierkhol′d Theatre the language switched between Chinese, Russian and Chinese Pidgin Russian, the effect being 'a performance that gestures toward the existence of a foreign social context, while simultaneously admitting that this foreign context is not fully present onstage' (p. 33). Glière's ballet, on the other hand, had a title that the Chinese associated not with international love but with the opium trade; two years later in Russia it was re-named 'The Red Flower'. Chapter three, 'Through an Internationalist Lens: China in Early Soviet Cinema', is concerned mainly with Tret′iakov, who had easily entered the lively Russian cinematic world, and his various collaborations with Eizenshtein. He apparently found the new medium capable of a closer mediation than the printed word. Although their joint trilogy 'Dzhungo' was never made, nonetheless several Soviet films about China are discussed, as well as the undoubted influence of Soviet experimental films on the Chinese cinema industry.

The last chapter, 'Confessions and Collaborations: Authority, Agency and Factographic Internationalism in *Den Shi-khua*', describes how Den (for convenience here) was a student of Tret′iakov in Beijing University, who when he came to Moscow renewed their acquaintance; after numerous meetings, the Russian started to write his student's life story for the July 1927 issue of *Novyi Lef*, changing his family name to Deng to protect his 'identity in Nationalist China newly hostile to the Soviet Union' (p. 187). The many episodes in this chapter and elsewhere are described exceptionally well, but there is no room to discuss or recount them in a review.

The Epilogue, subtitled 'International Literature, National Form and Missed Connections', begins with Oskar Tarkhanov's *Kitaiskie novelly* (1929), before turning to the various twists and turns in the two countries' political systems and beliefs. There are many ironies in this book, and Tyerman expresses one of them when he writes: 'The irony of history lies in the fact that Soviet cultural influence in China increased just as Soviet political influence declined' (p. 234). A visit by the famous actress of the Beijing Opera, Mei Lanfang, in 1935 created a sensation and many misunderstandings. The book ends on a realistic, though perhaps wistful note: 'Yet, once again, the mediation could not hold, leaving only traces of a socialist Eurasia that failed, ultimately, to connect' (p. 246).

Professor Tyerman's splendidly detailed and yet very readable study deserves the attention of Sinologists as well as Slavists. It should find a place in many libraries.

London ARNOLD MCMILLIN

de Oliveira, Cassio. *Writing Rogues: The Soviet Picaresque and Identity Formation, 1921–1938*. McGill-Queen's University Press, Montreal, QC and Kingston, ON, London and Chicago, IL, 2023. xiii + 290 pp. Illustrations. Notes. Bibliography. Index. $75.00: £55.00.

CASSIO DE OLIVEIRA's book is based on his Yale University doctoral dissertation, defended in 2014, and represents a detailed and vivid history of the Soviet picaresque from 1921 to 1938. The book's parts are structured chronologically and discuss the periods of the early 1920s, the NEP and the Stalinist 1930s. *Writing Rogues* presents a rich and original collection of texts representing the adventures of the Soviet rogue that includes such classics of this genre as Il′ia Erenburg's *Julio Jurenito* (1922) and *The Stormy Life of Lazik Roitshvanets* (1926), Babel′'s *Odessa Tales* (1926–33), as well as Il′ia Il′f and Evgenii Petrov's diptych about Ostap Bender (1928, 1931/33) and Aleksandr Kozachinskii's *The Green Cart* (1938). *Writing Rogues* significantly enriches the canon by treating as picaresque such less obvious texts as Shklovskii's *Sentimental Journey*, Ehrenburg's *The Grabber* (1927), Leonid Leonov's *The Thief* (1927), Veniamin Kaverin's *The End of the Gang* (1924), Veniamin Kataev's *The Embezzlers* (1926) and, most convincingly, Zoshchenko's 'Story of a Reforging' (1934), from the infamous volume, *Belomorsko-Baltiiskii kanal imeni Stalina*.

Having reviewed the prehistory of the genre, de Oliveira arrives at a somewhat narrow definition of the picaresque as a genre focused on the marginal protagonist with a broad 'tour d'horizon' who seeks his place in a changing reality (p. 27 and *passim*). This definition obfuscates many other distinctive features of the picaresque — first and foremost, its comedic component. Following de Oliveira's definition, one could qualify as picaresque Sholokhov's *And Quiet Flows the Don* or Gor′kii's *The Life of Klim Samgin*, for example, not to mention any adventure novel, like Kaverin's *Two Captains*. De Oliveira's research intuition is far more sensitive, however, and his book contains many brilliant ideas and observations. I am especially fond of the analysis of the (quasi)autobiographical picaresque narratives represented by Ehrenburg's *Julio Jurenito* and Sterne's *A Sentimental Journey*; or his discussion of the process, in the NEP-period novels, of 'the rogue becom[ing] an allegory for the persona of the writer, an expression of an author's aspirations and desires rather than an ostensible literal expression of who he really is' (p. 77); or the comparison between Hasek's Svejk and Ehrenburg's Lazik; or the conceptualization of the *Odessa Tales* through 'Benya as a character increasingly in control of time' (p. 99); or the interpretation of the finale of 'Story of a Reforging', in which an imprisoned Jewish rogue becomes the Stakhanovite, where de Oliveira detects 'a greater affinity of the picaresque with the mischievous concept of (re)qualification than with the ostensible reforging that authors and the secret police alike wished to see in their heroes' life trajectories' (pp. 174–75).

De Oliveira treats the Soviet rogue as the embodiment of an 'apparent contradistinction between a subversive, individualistic character and the collectivist impulse of the Soviet project' (p. 4). However, *Writing Rogues* is founded on the tacit implication that a collective identity is something that any character (or any person, for that matter) automatically strives to obtain, and that a Soviet novel without the glorification of the collective identity just cannot exist. The idea of resistance to collective identities seems to the author so hopelessly conservative that it does not receive any consideration. As a result, de Oliveira transforms picaro characters, who incessantly subvert Soviet models of community, into catalysts and even vehicles for new Soviet collective identities. To achieve this, he forgets that in all these texts, the picaro's attempts to lead any group — from Julio Jurenito's circle of disciples to Ostap Bender's little gangs — end with the leader's isolation and betrayal by his 'disciples'. The imagined community that these characters form mainly includes their readers — who also resisted collective identities and needed justification for their suppressed individualism.

De Oliveira argues that the Soviet picaro 'played a key role in mediating between the several dimensions of the Soviet collective identity, from the progressive policies of the Affirmative Action Empire to the relatively more conservative ideology of the 1930s' (p. 24), and 'served to emphasize a kind of supra-national collectivity, offering a counterbalance to ethnic particularism while depicting the multi-ethnic character of the Soviet Union' (p. 26). This *ustanovka* is very promising, but does it agree with the literary material? Nowhere is the dissonance between the researcher's *ustanovka* and the textual material as obvious as in de Oliveira's analysis of Il′f and Petrov's novels. In the beginning of Part Three, de Oliveira claims that *The Twelve Chairs* and *The Golden Calf* belong to a category of texts that 'depict a rogue whose life trajectory entails a measure of reconciliation with the society against which he rebels. The reforging (*perekovka*), becomes central to the picaresque and to Soviet society' (p. 129). Although Il′f and Petrov famously only claimed that they were going to write a novel about Ostap's reforging but never did, de Oliveira asserts that 'Ilf and Petrov's novels allegorize not the chaos of Stalin's reforms, but rather the kernel of stability that arises from these reforms' (p. 133), and that these novels depict its protagonist, Ostap Bender, as 'the perfect vehicle for the Soviet satirist's goal of disciplining and correcting social behaviors perceived as anti-Soviet' (p. 134). The later conclusion is based on Ostap's impersonations of Soviet police authorities, such as in his interrogations of the Herkules staff by which he accumulates *kompromat* against Koreiko. In these actions, de Oliveira sees Ostap's 'newfound loyalty to the workers' state' (p. 150) and his desire to join a *kollektiv*, which is also exemplified by the creation of the Horns and Hooves, which 'as soon as it is established, appears to be seamlessly integrated into the economy, receiving regular shipments of horns and hooves and summonses for its management to serve on various boards' (p. 153) The fact that Bender actively disregards horns, hooves and summons, and uses the organization exclusively as a front for his investigation of Koreiko's business activities, which he is conducting under the cover of Herkules, does not seem to concern the author of *Writing Rogues* in the least.

Throughout the monograph, and especially in its final part, de Oliveira argues that 'the picaresque as a whole, and the rogue in particular, are ultimately co-opted by the dominant ideology in a way that neutralizes whichever subversive power they possess' (p. 15). At the same time, in the book's finale, de Oliveira concludes that the Soviet interwar picaresque presented a challenge to the regime's power expressed through a demonstrated 'affinity between state sovereignty and acts of roguery' (as per Derrida, p. 189). Had the dominant ideology neutralized the subversive power of the picaresque, or, conversely, absorbed it and turned the picaro's deception, cynicism and famed instability into its own methods of power, repression and control? This is the main question that *Writing Rogues* raises, a question which could probably be best addressed in a sequel, focusing perhaps on such important picaresque works as Voinovich's *Life and Adventures of Ivan Chonkin*, the multiple novels by Iuz Aleshkovskii and Vasilii Aksenov, and many other popular texts and films of the 1960s to 1980s. De Oliveira has laid a solid foundation for such an exploration. His book will also be very useful in both undergraduate and graduate classes in the history of Soviet literature and culture, and inspire interesting discussions. Lucidly written and well researched, *Writing Rogues* highlights previously unnoticed aspects of the classic texts of the Soviet era.

Columbia University Mark Lipovetsky

Finnin, Rory. *Blood of Others: Stalin's Crimean Atrocity and the Poetics of Solidarity*. University of Toronto Press, Toronto, ON, Buffalo, NY and London, 2022, xii + 334 pp. Maps. Illustrations. Notes. Bibliography. Index. $80.00 (hardback & e-book).

This superb book is both innovative and traditionalist. Innovative, in that it places the unjustly neglected theme of Crimea and Crimean Tatars at the centre of a complex and fascinating study of connections and antagonisms between the cultures of Crimea itself, Ukraine, Russia and Turkey. Traditionalist, because it reaffirms with conviction, eloquence and force a proposition seldom articulated in a sceptical age: that literature and works of the imagination more generally can, and in special circumstances do, conceive, model and propel social and political change for the good.

The central theme of the book is the resonance in four of the cultures of the Black Sea littoral of one of the Soviet Union's genocidal acts: the deportation in 1944 of the Crimean Tatar people from their homeland and the attendant endeavour to extinguish Crimean Tatar identity. This theme also organizes the book's symmetrical tripartite structure, constituting as it does the main content of its second and longest part, 'Dispossession'. The first part of *Blood of Others*, 'Possession', scans the preceding cultural histories of Crimea and the Crimean Tatar presence there before and during the peninsula's incorporation into the Russian Empire and, thereafter, the USSR. The third part considers developments since 1989, when the self-repatriation of Crimean Tatars became possible. The title of this final part, 'Repossession', captures two processes opposite in cultural meaning and ethical justification: the return of many Crimean Tatars to their homeland, and the Russian Federation's illegal seizure of Crimea from Ukraine in 2014.

In each of the parts the evolution of four cultures' understandings and representations of Crimea and Crimean Tatars, as well as the ways in which these representations influenced each other, are illuminated by Finnin's close readings of works of poetry and literary prose, but also of film, drama, music and the visual arts. Since the focus of the study is the capacity of works of the imagination to influence the sentiments and ethical dispositions of their recipients, Finnin explicitly affords works of 'high' and popular culture equal attention. The analyses themselves bear witness to Finnin's rare and admirable erudition in languages and cultural traditions seldom studied together. Such breadth of expertise enables revealing comparisons and observations of intertextual connection. Thus, for example, Crimean Tatar poetry of the late nineteenth and early twentieth centuries by Hasan Çergeyev and Üsein Samil Toktargazy is considered alongside the Crimean-themed works of, respectively, the Ukrainian writers Lesia Ukraïnka and Mykhailo Kotsiubyns'kyi; the role of Crimean Tatar subject matter in advocacy for various forms of pan-Turkism is demonstrated in discussions of Ottoman and Turkish texts — Namık Kemal's novel *Cezmi* (1880) and Cengiz Dağcı's popular prose of the 1950s and 1960s. Not unexpectedly, Crimea as refracted through Russian culture in its colonial as well as oppositional variants looms large in the overall picture. Pushkin's poem, 'The Fountain of Bağçasaray', is examined as the most familiar and historically generative formulation of the idea of a Crimea alienated from its Crimean Tatar history and stripped down to its alluring landscape, a place open for imperial appropriation. At various points in the book Finnin observes intertextual — generally polemical — rejoinders to Pushkin's poem from each of the cultures under discussion. The unavoidable omnipresence of Pushkin in the book serves as a reminder of the aporia of scholarly engagement with cultural colonialism: even as one deconstructs the metropolitan text, one inevitably reinforces its visibility and canonicity.

A similarly poignant irony attends Finnin's leitmotivic invocation of the poet Boris Chichibabin and his poem, 'Crimean Strolls'. The book begins with an account of the poet's awe-inducing reading of the poem in Kharkiv in 1963. The poem not only named what was then unnameable — the Soviet crime of the deportation of the Crimean Tatars; it not only condemned the atrocity and expressed empathy with its victims; even more shockingly, it confessed to guilt on behalf, as Finnin puts it, 'of the Soviet "we", the civic collective that abets the state or, at best, stands aside as fellow citizens are slandered and dispossessed' (p. 118). The book's most detailed close reading is dedicated to this poem; it is the key exhibit that illustrates Finnin's discussion of literature's capacity to involve readers in the psychologically difficult, but ethically reparative process of agreeing to share in collective guilt. The very title, *Blood of Others*, is a quotation from 'Crimean Strolls'. The poem is an act of solidarity with Crimean Tatars by a poet who was born in Kremenchuk and lived in Kharkiv, both in Ukraine. Yet the poem, like the rest of Chichibabin's *oeuvre*, is in Russian, and no doubt the fact that 'Crimean Strolls' was in the language of empire enabled its condemnation of that very empire to resonate as no Crimean Tatar or Ukrainian text of equivalent content and aesthetic force could have done.

Finnin invites Karl Jaspers onto the pages of *Blood of Others* to help shape his discussion of guilt, as he does Wolfgang Iser when he reflects on the appellative capability of the literary text, or Edward Said and Frantz Fanon when the classics of postcolonial theory offer relevant insights or felicitous formulations. The coercive and discursive practices of colonialism are the stuff of every page of the book, yet Finnin is not beholden to the vocabulary of postcolonial studies. He does, however, introduce a conceptual distinction that is useful for comprehending the experience of dispossessed Crimean Tatars, but potentially of all subaltern communities that think of themselves as linked by a special bond to a territory they consider their own: 'place' and 'personality'. 'Place' Finnin defines as 'space endowed with affect and cast as a "center of felt value"' (the quoted phrase he attributes to the geographer Yi-Fu Tuan) (p. 27); 'personality' is the 'cultural colouring perceived to fix to a space, conducting "felt value"' (p. 28). In colonial discourse, Finnin observes, the tight bond of the two — of the 'native' and the seized colonial territory — is at first, paradoxically, emphatically asserted, but only as a prelude to that bond's destruction in the course of the imposition of the power of the new possessors. Discursive 'de-Tatarization', modelled as a process in Pushkin's 'Fountain', is already complete in the Crimean-themed works of Tolstoi and Chekhov, from which Crimean Tatars are entirely absent. Erasure of the bond between Crimean place and Tatar personality, Finnin observes, was an objective not only of Russian colonialism, the deportation of 1944, or the annexation of 2014, but of both Turkish and Crimean Tatar pan-Turkism. A yearning to restore that bond was shared by advocates of Crimean Tatar identity at the turn of the twentieth century, Crimean activists of Soviet *korenizatsiia* (nativization) in the 1920s, members of Crimean Tatar, Ukrainian and Russian dissident movements from the 1960s onward, and the descendants of expellees who returned to the peninsula in the 1990s. The chief virtue that Finnin sees reflected in the words and actions of these friends of the unity of place and personality is solidarity, which he defines as 'an active convergence of interests and fellow feeling between groups that bridges a distance. It is achieved, not given — a dynamic physics of human connection that can turn outsiders into insiders' (p. 20). Solidarity manifests itself, Finnin observes, especially profoundly between leading figures in the Crimean Tatar and Ukrainian national movements. Their affinity, which rests on the similar fates of their nations as objects of colonialism, moves Finnin to see them as 'bound [...] tightly in metaphorical relation' (p. 209). As Ukraine's most resonant contemporary author, Serhiy Zhadan puts it, 'The plight of Crimean Tatars is the plight of Ukrainians' (p. 236), or, as the Crimean Tatar singer Jamala even more succinctly states, 'Crimea is Ukraine' (p. 227).

In *Blood of Others* Rory Finnin has given us a book that tells us much that we should have known long ago, but did not, for the most part because of the efficiency of empire in amplifying its own narratives while suffocating those of its victims; a book that honours the courage of righteous speech and behaviour, calls perfidy and injustice by their proper names and itself thereby becomes a powerful moral statement. And it is a book whose eloquence is commensurate with its high purpose. It would be remiss of this reviewer to conclude without sharing at least a sample of Finnin's potent formulations: 'Crimea may have been anointed in neoclassical fashion as the new Greece, but it was consumed with Romantic ardour as the conquered land of the Crimean Tatars' (p. 27); 'After 1927, Stalin's geopolitical paranoia slowly perverted what had been a policy of ethnophilia into a program of ethnocide' (p. 76); and finally: 'In identifying as a member of the nation, in claiming proprietary access to its constellation of symbols, traditions, and achievements, the individual abnegates the stance of the moral individualist and takes on obligations arising from national identification — including those related to historical wrongs committed against Others' (p. 157).

School of Languages, Literatures, Cultures & Linguistics MARKO PAVLYSHYN
Monash University

Bullock, Philip Ross (ed.). *Rachmaninoff and His World*. University of Chicago Press, in collaboration with the Bard Music Festival, Chicago, IL and London, 2022. xxii + 355 pp. Illustrations. Music examples. Notes. Index. $105.00; $35.00; $34.99 (e-book).

EARLY in the Introduction to this well presented, enterprising and thought-provoking collection of essays the editor states one of the basic points of the 'Rakhmaninov question': 'despite — or perhaps because of his great popularity, Rachmaninoff has had perhaps more detractors than any other major composer' (p. vii). This theme recurs more than once later in the book, as does Stravinskii's caricature of him as 'a six-and-a half-foot scowl' (p. 22). But the collection as a whole presents a restrained aristocratic figure who was generous with money as well as judicious praise for contemporaries like Skriabin, with whom he has in earlier literature been unfavourably compared, often by the same critics who treat him as an epigone of Chaikovskii.

The collection is divided into three parts: 'Moscow and Modernity', 'Three Operas' and 'New Worlds'. The first begins with Peter Franklin's 'Reading the Popular Pessimist: Thought, Feeling and Dance in Rachmaninoff's Symphonic Narrative', which analyses, amongst other works, the First Symphony, presenting a picture of the composer as one who thought and experimented far more than criticism usually allowed. The second essay by Rebecca Mitchell, 'Sergei Rachmaninoff and Moscow Musical Life' introduces the young writer Marietta Shaginian (1888–1982) who became a friend of the composer, defending him vigorously against fashionable modernist critics; she also discusses in detail the various places where Rakhmaninov's early works were played. The third essay, 'Love Triumphant: Rachmaninoff's Eros, the Silver Age, and the Middlebrow' by Marina Frolova-Walker begins with a discussion of mass songs before turning to the composer's pioneering settings of verses by women poets. Shaginian's defence of Rakhmaninov against the many snide criticisms of him, curiously warns him about using middlebrow libretti, lest they weaken his music (p. 68), clearly forgetting Schubert's immortal songs. Dr Frolova-Walker offers a robust defence of the composer's work: 'we can accord Rachmaninoff's audiences of the past and present the respect they deserve and finally agree that their persistent love for this music is not a cause for sneering' (p. 77). The last essay in the first part is 'Rachmaninoff and the "Vocalise": Word and Music in the Russian Silver Age' by Philip Bullock, in which he speculates, with a wealth of detail on song writing in general, on why the composer added one of his most popular pieces to his Fourteen Romances op. 34.

The first of the three operas is treated very thoroughly by Emily Fry in 'Tchaikovsky's Echoes, Chaliapin's Sobs: *Aleko*, Rachmaninoff, and the Contemporary', mainly as the work of a composer whom many thought belonged to an earlier age. Caryl Emerson's short but magisterial essay

'Rachmaninoff's *Miserly Knight* (On Money, Honor, and the Means to Create' concentrates on the composer's use of various forms of leitmotifs, which led some contemporaries (Rimskii-Korsakov among them), to complain of the opera's lack of melody. Simon Morrison's 'Burning for You: Rachmaninoff's *Francesca da Rimini*' is valuable for its close attention to Dante's text for his 'anti-opera' (p. 160).

The third section of the book begins in lively fashion with Bullock's 'Rachmaninoff and the Celebrity Interview: A Selection of Documents from the American Press'. Steven Swayne's 'The Eighteenth Variation' outlines the history and form of *The Rhapsody on a Theme of Paganini*, one of the composer's most famous and (ab)used pieces. Christopher H. Gibbs's '"One of the Outstanding Musical Events of All Time": The Philadelphia Orchestra's 1939 Rachmaninoff Cycle' describes the composer's ecstatic reception on his first visit to America, and the strong impression made on him by the Philadelphian musicians. '"The Case of Rachmaninoff": The Music of a White Emigré in the USSR' by Marina Raku (translated by Jonathan Walker) describes the composer's lasting popularity in his homeland, despite a few critics calling him a figure of the past, and the famous boycott of his *The Bells* in 1931. The consistently anti-Soviet composer's music continued to be played, and was used in several Soviet films. This richly detailed book ends with a broad article by Leon Botstein, 'Aesthetic Ambition and Popular Taste: The Divergent Paths of Paderewski, Busoni and Rachmaninoff', contrasting the Russian's pessimism with the views of the other two virtuoso pianists. He concludes by referring to 'a magical glass dome of "incredible bliss" associated with longing and loss, one that shut out pain and tedium and offered solace, relief from sorrow, and a temporal hiatus between past, present and future' (p. 340).

The editor and contributor, Philip Ross Bullock, should be congratulated on producing a collection of articles that adds much detailed substance to the quotation above. It deserves a place in libraries everywhere and in the collections of those music lovers for whom 'romantic' is not a dirty word.

London ARNOLD MCMILLIN

Gordienko, Anastasia. *Outlaw Music in Russia: The Rise of an Unlikely Genre.* The University of Wisconsin Press, Madison, WI, 2023. xiii + 319 pp. Illustrations. Glossary. Notes. Bibliography. Index. $89.95.

AT the heart of Anastasia Gordienko's vivid and engrossing new study is the Russian *shanson* (not to be confused with the suaver French *chanson*), a contemporary musical and poetic genre that draws on various subgenres, extensively listed as including 'the *blatnaia pesnia*, prison songs, bard songs produced by so-called *blatnye* bards, romance songs (romansy), emigrants' songs (emigrantskie pesni), restaurant songs (restorannye pesni), street songs (ulichnye pesni), short humorous ditties (chastushki/kulplety), Gulag songs (pesni Gulaga), penal servitude songs (pesni katorga), slum songs (pesni trushchob), Odessa songs, romantic shansons, and others' (p. 5). Combining both historical narrative and close textual analysis, Gordienko traces how the *shanson* emerged from the underground culture of the late Soviet era (in particular, the guitar poetry that has been the subject of major English-language studies by G. S. Smith and Rachel Platonov), only to be co-opted by the modern Russian state, despite its fundamental associations with criminality. As Gordienko argues, 'the shanson, richly representative of the domain of "the alegal" (that is, the sphere with an implied or indirect connection to the illicit), mirrors the particular path of Russia's recent development and also its sense of national identity' (p. 14).

Before tackling such questions, Gordienko offers a historical precis of the emergence of songs on underworld themes, from a longstanding Russian empathy for criminals and rebels from the seventeenth century onwards, to the emergence of a distinct form of urban folklore in early twentieth-century Odesa that soon found its way into Soviet popular culture during the 1920s and New Economic Policy. Although the songs of this era and milieu were largely suppressed under Stalin, they went on to flourish in the prison camps, from where they came back into unofficial metropolitan Soviet culture during the Thaw. A source of inspiration to the bards (and an elicit source of countercultural delight to the children of many a party apparatchik), this repertoire retains a certain nostalgic allure on account of its melodramatic themes, a playful use of criminal *argot* and a raw, untrained performance style. Having established a historical genealogy of the *blatnaia pesnia*, Gordienko turns her attention to a more typological study of the themes and motifs of its contemporary progeny, the *shanson*. Many of these are predictably grizzly (gangster rivalry and gratuitous violence, offended masculinity and heroic codes of misplaced honour), although there are occasional lyric digressions (even if the *shanson*'s treatment of women is still largely patriarchal) and even moments of subversive humour and resistance (as in the queer shanson's playful reworking of the homophobic language of the GULag and gangland comradeship). There are even walk-on parts for a few female *chansonnières*, whose sultry glamour makes for a glittery contrast with the tattooed machismo of their male counterparts.

In keeping with previous studies, Gordienko tends to focus primarily on the texts of her chosen repertoire, although there are nods towards its performative contexts too. The sophistication of her methodology — which is as likely to refer to Adorno and Habermas as it is to historians and sociologists of Russia — is lightly worn and informed by some fifteen years of close-up anthropological observation working in the world of Russian and Ukrainian broadcasting. In her sixth chapter, 'The Shanson in Russia: From the Slums to the Kremlin', Gordienko turns to the collapse of state socialism, which transformed the genre in unexpected ways. Here, the author traces the *shanson*'s ability to evoke the uncertainty and instability of 'perestroika; privatization; the chaotic, lawless 1990s; two Chechen wars; several economic crises, the annexation of Crimea, the invasion of Ukraine; and bureaucracy and corruption taken to the state level' (p. 176). Yet Gordienko also makes a more powerful argument, noting that the *shanson* has become 'an institutional "soundtrack" for some Russian governmental events' (p. 153). As she argues: 'Originally subversive of the powerful and their institutions, the genre has now put itself at the service of traditional values (patriotism, Orthodoxy, and hero worship) and existing power structures (including corrupt authority). No longer opposing mainstream values, some shanson songs now express support for the Russian president and his administration' (p. 164).

Members of the artistic and intellectual elite in all countries are wont to exaggerate the supposed risks of popular culture, seeing it as a corrupting force on the morals of its allegedly impressionable audiences. As Gordienko demonstrates, however, the *shanson* has developed into one of the most potent means by which a very particular ideological discourse has penetrated Russian society at large and articulates a language of criminality whose consequences are all too clearly seen today. *Outlaw Music in Russia: The Rise of an Unlikely Genre* will certainly be of interest to scholars of literature, music and cultural studies. It should also be consulted by curious and receptive political scientists and analysts of contemporary Russia itself.

Wadham College, University of Oxford PHILIP ROSS BULLOCK

Daniel, Michelle S. *The DJ Who 'Brought Down' the USSR: The Life and Legacy of Seva Novgorodtsev.* Modern Biographies. Academic Studies Press, Boston, MA, 2023. 292 pp. Illustrations. Notes. Bibliography. Index. $149.00; $25.00.

SEVA NOVGORODTSEV (real name Vsevolod Borisovich Levenshtein, b. 1940 in Leningrad) is a retired radio presenter who worked at the BBC Russian Service between 1977 and 2015 and was awarded an MBE (2005) for his services. Trained in the USSR as a naval officer and English interpreter, in the mid 1960s Seva (as he is commonly known) became a professional jazz musician, playing saxophone in Iosif Vainshtein's orchestra and then briefly managing the Dobry molodtsy band, before emigrating to the West in 1975 and eventually settling in London.

At the BBC Russian Service, Seva anchored a regular shortwave programme about popular Anglophone rock music, airing a selection of soundtracks after listening to ten to fifteen albums per week. Owing to the dearth of information about such music in the USSR and despite the intermittent radio signal jamming, he gained a cult status among his audiences behind the Iron Curtain (present writer included). Daniel justifiably calls Seva 'a rock priest' (p. 224) and 'a fully embraced icon' (p. 239). Moreover, even though Seva's 'primary intention was to inform and entertain' (p. 141), his microphone apparently transformed rock tunes into a 'precursor to change in a totalitarian regime' (p. 77) at a time when music and politics were inseparable and an annotated hit parade could feel as significant as a current affairs programme. Daniel's monograph is the first book-length attempt in English to chart and explain Seva's remarkable impact in the context of the Cold War, involving the comparable experience and input of his colleagues and competitors on both sides of the Iron Curtain, including Willis Conover (a jazz presenter at the Voice of America radio station), Semen Yossman (aka Sam Jones, also of the BBC Russian Service) and Artemii Troitskii (who started his music journalist career in the Soviet youth journal, *Rovesnik*).

Daniel concentrates on the relationship between these journalists, who aimed to counter 'communist ideology with Western [and Westernized] music and culture' (p. x), on the one hand, and their listeners — mostly youngsters — on the other. Her sources comprise visuals, sound recordings, press cuttings and fan mail from various archives (some of them private), as well as secondary literature on the use of radio for propaganda purposes, at home and abroad, by both Communist and anti-Communist regimes ('soft power combatting soft power', as Daniel puts it; p. 105). Quotes from Seva's autobiography, *Saksofon pokhozh na integral* (Saxophones Resemble the Integral Sign, St Petersburg, 2011), taking his life journey up to the point of emigration, and the programme series, *Rok-posevy* (Planting Rocks, first published in two volumes in Russia in the 1990s), about such bands as Black Sabbath, Led Zeppelin and Deep Purple, provide the reader with samples of Seva's disarmingly informal storytelling style.

Seva accounted for his success as a radio DJ thus: 'I had been touring Russia with a band for twelve years before the emigration, so I understood the audience. [...] I saw enough of the hardships of young people in faraway towns, who felt absolutely miserable. [...] I tried to entertain them, [...] to show them that there is some other way of life... In general, I treated them like friends, and it was important for me that the programme was captivating and funny' (p. 95). As a result, for his estimated audience of twenty-five million, predominantly male, Seva became not only a go-to data supplier but a 'paternal role model' (p. 3), 'friend and mentor' (p. 10). One Soviet fan called him 'a longtime ray of light in the darkness of totalitarianism' (p. 195). Another went as far as to claim: 'My life has been consumed by love for Seva. He [...] shaped my language, my speech, my taste. I owe him a lot. [...] He is to me the Man from the Stars, although he is earthly' (pp. 217, 220). In 1988, a USSR-wide Seva fan club was established by a man from Karelia's Medvezh′iegorsk, of all places (which proves that Seva's appeal was wide indeed). Daniel mistakenly calls Medvezh′iegorsk a 'tiny northern village' (p. 194), while since 1938 it has actually been a town whose population by the 1980s amounted to 20,000. The fan club became known as NORIS, or Nezavisimyi ob″edinennyi rok-informatsionnyi sindikat (The Independent United Rock-Info Syndicate). Its membership peaked at about 3,000 (only 10 per cent of whom were female), and the club conducted opinion polls, published in-house bulletins and arranged rock concerts and personal meetings with Seva.

Yet did Seva's fans (whose number must have far exceeded those in NORIS) truly become, under his subtle influence, 'the community that did eventually overwhelm and force the Soviet system to change' (p. 274)? Can Seva therefore be credited with bringing the down USSR, as Daniel asserts? The book does not seem to present any incontrovertible evidence in support of its title, similar to a direct connection that exists, for instance, between the viral song, 'Rais Lebled', by the Tunisian rapper El Général (addressing the Tunisian President Ben Ali) and the Jasmine Revolution of 2010–11 (see Mike Thomson's article at <https://www.bbc.co.uk/news/world-africa-66221762>).

What is more, some of the fans' statements cited by Daniel appear to undermine her understanding of the role that Seva allegedly played in the USSR's demise. In late 1986, i.e. less than two years into Gorbachev's rule, a fan letter to Seva (one of those that made it to the addressee despite Soviet censorship) declared: 'your anecdotes and jokes are nothing compared to the materials that appear in our press every day' (p. 183). In other words, Seva's authority found itself in inverse relationship to society's openness. Another fan testifies: Seva 'showed us a way of life within the [Soviet] system without having to have something in common with it' (p. 262). If so, why bother dismantling the system at all?

The definite article in the book's title (*The DJ Who...*) is not corroborated by the book's content either. Take Willis Conover (1920–96), who played jazz records for some forty years on behalf of Voice of America. Daniel tends to tone down his influence by comparison with Seva's because Conover broadcast in English, and jazz is arguably a more elitist musical genre than rock (p. 115). Yet Conover's audience in his heyday outnumbered Seva's, reaching thirty million listeners, and spread throughout the entire Eastern bloc. Unsurprisingly, Conover has also been branded a person 'responsible for breaking up the Soviet Union' (see James Lester, 'Willis of Oz', *Central Europe Review*, 1, 5, 26 July 1999 <https://www.pecina.cz/files/www.ce-review.org/99/5/music5_lester.html>). Last but not least, one should not forget the internal Soviet influencer Artemii Troitskii (b. 1955), who in his own assessment complemented Seva's activities by adopting a somewhat different focus: 'I was for the weirdness in the underground and Seva was catering to the mainstream' (p. 130). Without diminishing their overall importance, it would probably be fair to say that no single radio DJ warrants the appellation of Communism's gravedigger.

UiT The Arctic University of Norway ANDREI ROGATCHEVSKI

Romaniello, Matthew P., Smith, Alison K. and Starks, Tricia (eds). *The Life Cycle of Russian Things: From Fish Guts to Fabergé, 1600–Present.* Bloomsbury Academic, London, New York and Dublin, 2022. xii + 248 pp. Maps. Illustrations. Notes. Select bibliography. Index. £85.00; £28.99; £26.09 (e-book).

THIS welcome contribution to the material history of the Russian space offers a provocative and useful guide for thinking about things and doing material history. The editors argue that material culture is an important way for situating Russia's place in the world, given Russia's location along multiple crossroads and with continent-spanning borders. A brief introduction explores the theoretical uses of material history, focusing on two key ways of approaching the topic. The editors trace ideas about commodities as the stuff of global development from Karl Marx to Immanuel Wallerstein, emphasizing the importance of networks and webs of exchange. They also acknowledge the cultural work done by things, following Thorstein Veblen and contemporary anthropologists. For them, material culture includes ideas about conspicuous consumption (sign value) as well as utility. It also includes the role played by commodities/objects/things/goods in defining a community or in understanding the relationship between a physical object and its user.

Some of the contributors wrestle with the paradox of explaining *things* by means of *language*. Others follow the reasoning of archaeologist Christopher Tilley, who insists on parity between language and material culture: 'to be human is to speak and to make and use things' (p. 121), as one of the authors puts it. Neither language nor material culture has primacy, and this leads several authors to emphasize the agency of things: apothecary ware had the property of interacting with ingredients to create something new. The Russian stove created the necessity for the use of samovars to boil water for tea. Cigarette cases cued cravings and induced nicotine use. Other contributors follow the prompt of the collection's title and focus on the life cycle of particular things, from idea to physical material, from product to object, from object to exhibit, and thence back to memory or idea.

The concept of life cycle or change structures the book's chapters, but individually the authors adopt varied methods and approaches. Some chapters embed a single thing in a dense web of theory, others narrate the thing's life cycle (including journeys and preservation), and still others concentrate on the meaning of a thing.

Part One looks at 'Transforming Things', beginning with Clare Griffin's provocative analysis of the use in early modern Russian medicine of apothecary ware, which could be prized for its capacity to transform medicine or to remain inert to chemical reaction. This is also an essay on the unknowability of things. Alison K. Smith explores the 'lime cycle' of building materials in eighteenth-century Gatchina, where locally sourced lime can serve as building stone but also as cement to hold bricks together and whitewash to decorate exteriors. Ann Komaromi examines the life cycle of samizdat texts and the ways in which Soviet conceptual artists transposed everyday materials from the late Soviet context to create new forms of meaning. In Part Two, 'Making Things', three chapters look at examples of Russian commodities through the lens of the material life cycle. Matthew P. Romaniello investigates Russia's early modern exports of fish guts, used both to make isinglass, a highly prized substance for the European brewing and wine-making market, and fish glue, an everyday product of no particular local distinction. He employs the concept of 'bioprospecting' to emphasize the commercial goals of producers of these things. Katherine Pickering Antonova offers the example of estate-produced textiles in 1830s Vladimir Province to meditate on production processes and the meanings of skill and craft, local and metropolitan. Charles Steinwedel moves from the place of production to the locus of administration in his chapter on state regulation of sugar production in early twentieth-century Russia. Here the thing — sugar — is an object of conflict, as the state sought to mediate between the revenue-maximizing interests of sugar beet growers and the welfare need to provide Russian society with cheap carbohydrates.

Part Three, 'Touching Things', turns to the interaction between objects and humans. Audra Yoder compares the place of the samovar as a household appliance in eighteenth-century Britain, where it fell from favour, and in Russia, where it became a national symbol. She points to the material reality of the Russian stove, which unlike the British fireplace pairs poorly with a tea kettle. Tricia Starks offers a richly illustrated discussion of the place of decorative cigarette cases, most notably those made by the House of Fabergé. These things had both use value — to hold cigarettes and to cue smokers' desire, and sign value — to signal the characteristics and wealth of their possessors. Brandon Schechter discusses the unique properties of the T-34 Tank in World War Two, as a manufactured object produced in great quantities with minimal skilled labour, as the locus of intense physical and emotional labour by soldiers and mechanics, and as symbols of wartime myths and imperialist oppression. Part Four, 'Preserving Things', considers the ephemerality of the material. Erika Monahan traces the journey across time and space of an early eighteenth-century manuscript map of Siberia drawn by Semen Remezov. Initially it served as a material way to fix knowledge about the imperial territory of Siberia, but it also reminds us of the mutability of knowing, as the intellectual apparatuses that made this artifact legible have receded over time. In a chapter by Marisa Karyl Franz, the threadbare coat of a Siberian shaman provides another example of movement and decay. Like the atlas of Siberia, this collector's object ended up in North America, and it serves as the focus of reflections on the in-betweenness of things, on collecting and classifying, and on the ethnographer's gaze. The final chapter by Ulrike Schmiegelt-Rietig also investigates the work of collection, here examining a German art protection unit in World War Two and its encounters with the salvaged icons of Novgorod. This essay on the destruction of war and the randomness of material preservation is a fitting conclusion to this exploration of the life cycle of things.

UCL SSEES DIANE P. KOENKER

LeDonne, John P. *Forging a Unitary State: Russia's Management of the Eurasian Space, 1650–1850*. University of Toronto Press, Toronto, ON, Buffalo, NY and London, 2020. xvii + 663 pp. Maps. Tables. Notes. Bibliography. Index. $166.00; $88.00 (paperback & e-book).

FEW historians have done more to help us understand the administrative structures and elite strategies of the Russian Empire than John LeDonne. In a series of weighty books — *Ruling Russia: Politics and Administration in the Age of Absolutism, 1762–1796* (Princeton, NJ, 1984), *Absolutism and Ruling Class: The Formation of the Russian Political Order, 1700–1825* (Oxford, 1991), *The Russian Empire and the World, 1700–1917: The Geopolitics of Expansion and Containment* (Oxford, 1996), and *The Grand Strategy of the Russian Empire, 1650–1831* (Oxford, 2004) — he has built up a composite and detailed account of how the Russian state expanded over time and how its administration, taxation and bureaucracy functioned, all underpinned by a careful attention to hard geographical constraints. This mammoth volume is a culmination of this life's work, and seeks to provide a comprehensive account of the integration of what LeDonne calls the western, southern and eastern theatres of expansion into the Russian 'core', from the mid seventeenth to the mid nineteenth century. While these terms are used as shorthand, LeDonne provides detailed explanations of what they mean in terms of both physical (watersheds, rivers, soil types) and political geography. The western theatre corresponds to Poland, Lithuania, the Baltic Provinces and Finland, the southern to Ukraine, the Black Sea Steppes and Crimea, and the Eastern to the Urals, Siberia and the Steppe frontier. All of these presented different challenges when it came to their integration with the Muscovite core of the Volga-Caspian basin — a complex process which unfolded in administrative, legal, economic and ecclesiastical terms — and, he argues, led to the creation of the 'unitary state' of the title.

LeDonne contrasts this term to the more familiar 'empire', which for him does not properly explain what those who controlled the Russian state were trying to achieve as it expanded — not simply the ad-hoc management of difference through existing elites, customs and practices across these vast territories, but an often ruthless elimination of local particularities and privileges in favour of a single unitary administrative and legal regime. Here he is setting himself against much recent Anglophone writing on the Russian empire, such as that of Jane Burbank, which has emphasized its legal pluralism and the local adaptations of its governance to the heterogeneity of its population. It is true that much of this scholarship focuses on the later imperial period, after the Great Reforms (which in many ways set metropolitan Russia apart from its borderlands once again) and further Russian expansion into the Caucasus, Central Asia and the Far East. LeDonne very deliberately excludes these latter regions, which proved unassimilable in cultural and administrative terms, and indeed he acknowledges that even within his chosen geography and chronology there were some groups — notably the Poles and Crimean Tatars — who proved resistant to co-optation and integration into the Russian core. Even on its own terms then, there are some clear limits to LeDonne's argument, which — partly because of his main source base, the *Polnoe Sobranie Zakonov Rossiiskoi Imperii* — frequently tells us more about the Russian state's goals than about what actually happened on the ground.

What LeDonne refers to as 'superstratification' — i.e. the assimilation of existing elites in newly-conquered areas to the all-Russian nobility — was of course the touchstone of Russian statecraft from the fall of Kazan′ in 1552 to the mid nineteenth century. It had some notable successes among the *sluzhilye* Tatars of the Volga, the Bashkirs, the Baltic Germans and later the Georgians. However in all these cases this rested on the acknowledgement and preservation of existing privileges and particularities, such as the practice of Islam among the Tatars and Bashkirs (and in the latter case strong noble land rights) and of Lutheranism and the particular privileges of the *Ritterschaft* in the Baltic region. The Russian state certainly sought to erode these over time, as LeDonne shows, but it had to proceed cautiously — attempts to interfere with Bashkir land rights provoked major uprisings in the 1660s and 1730s, while it was not until the very late imperial period that the 'Germanness' of the Baltic nobility really came under pressure from the centre, or that there was a determined attempt to suppress the separate constitutional arrangements of Finland — and both proved very destabilizing to the imperial structure. LeDonne recognizes this, writing (p. 296):

> Petersburg still had to deal with the intractable fact that the expansion of the core kept bringing into it people who were not Russian — even if conversion to Orthodoxy created the fiction that converts were supra-ethnic Russians — and could not erase the fact that some people were nomads, and thus had a different type of economy and different customs that translated into different legal systems. These could not be abolished outright without striking at the heart of an ethnic identity and creating major problems of internal security.

Perhaps most importantly, as LeDonne clearly explains, superstratification never worked on most of the Polish nobility, who had a rival imperial (or 'core') political project and high culture of their own. This had profound effects not just in later 'Congress Poland', but in most of Belorussia and Right-Bank Ukraine where the nobility was almost all Polish or Polonized. Special arrangements were also needed for nomadic groups such as the Nogais, and for the Crimean Tatars. When added to the acknowledged particularities of Russian rule in Caucasus and the Qazaq steppe, together with the later specialized military colonial regimes applied to Central Asia and the Far East, these exceptions are so important and so glaring that one does start to doubt the general rule that LeDonne is pressing for — the truth is that while a unitary state may have been the ideal, even within his chosen geography and chronology the reality on the ground fell well short of it more often than not.

Exploring these discrepancies in any kind of detail would have required a book twice as long as even this weighty tome, and would probably have been impractical, but I still felt LeDonne's argument would have benefited from deeper engagement with the specialist historiographies of some of these borderlands, and indeed with sources produced in them — looking inwards towards the imperial centre rather than always outwards as he does. To take an example which I know well, LeDonne's account (p. 428) of the supposed 'submission' of Abu'l-Khayr Khan of the Qazaq *kishi zhuz* (Junior Horde, not 'Western', as he describes it) in 1731 is greatly over-simplified. Abu'l-Khayr is not even named, nor is his key interlocutor on the Russian side, the *sluzhilye*

Tatar envoy Kutlu-Muhammad Tevkelev. LeDonne describes the former as 'pledging allegiance' to the Russian empress, when in fact it has long been recognized that Abu'l-Khayr sought a protective alliance, but certainly did not envisage a permanent cession of sovereignty, which would have made no sense in a nomadic context in any case. Abu'l-Khayr's principal goal in approaching the Russians was not the establishment of Orenburg as a bolt-hole to which he could escape if overthrown, but to make use of Russian power to secure his own authority over the unruly Qazaq Chinggisid elite and the hereditary succession of his offspring, something he made abundantly clear in his conversations with Tevkelev, which the latter recorded in detail for the College of Foreign Affairs. Within a decade of the Orenburg expedition Abu'l-Khayr would already have rejected Russian authority, as by and large did his successors until the early 1800s. While in a work of synthesis such as this LeDonne can perhaps be forgiven for not making use of the original of Tevkelev's account, whether from Soviet publications or the more recent, magnificent edition by the late Irina Erofeeva, it does seem baffling that he has not used Alan Bodger's well-known 1980 article on the topic in this journal, instead referring to two obsolete Russian histories of Bashkortostan (an entity which did not even exist at this date) and of the 1735 Orenburg expedition. The latter's leader, Ivan Kirillov, gets the detailed biography and analysis of personality Abu'l-Khayr is denied. LeDonne is generally an assiduous prosopographer of the agents of the Russian 'core', and also provides excellent biographical summaries of Polish magnates, Baltic nobles and Cossack *atamans*, but as he travels East his vision seems to blur.

Further evidence of this is that the Qazaq *orta zhuz* (Middle Horde) and its powerful Khan Ablai are barely mentioned, nor (p. 490) is one of the most significant of Mikhail Speranskii's Siberian reforms of 1822, the *Ustav ob upravlenii inorodtsev*, which first codified this elusive and enormously important category in Russian law, although there is an oblique reference (p. 505) to the 'regulations for the Siberian Kirgiz' which formed a part of it, which sought (not very successfully) to regulate nomadic nobility. The '*inorodtsy*' category, which was widely applied to Siberian peoples (and later to Muslims and Jews) further throws into doubt LeDonne's insistence on the forging of a unitary state — this was very much a category of exclusion from the civic and legal structures of the imperial metropole, and would later evolve into a full-blown colonial 'rule of difference' in Central Asia. The sense that LeDonne is less comfortable on Russia's Asian than her southern and western frontiers is reinforced by the use on the same page of both 'Gingissid' and 'Gengissid' in place of 'Chinggisid' (p. 5).

I have perhaps dwelt unfairly on the weaknesses of this book in my review, because they are not immediately obvious, while its strengths will I think be self-evident to any reader. In the epigraph, to which he returns at the very end of the work, LeDonne invokes an unknown eighteenth-century scholar who hoped that, while he could not complete the great task, the work of those who came after him would be rendered easier if he began it. This will certainly be the case — anyone wanting to know when and on what terms a territory was annexed, when a treaty was signed and what it contained, when law codes were introduced, superseded or adapted, who the leading political, military and ecclesiastical personalities were, what was traded and where, when institutions were founded and abolished, and indeed the basic geography of routes, rivers and soil across this vast crescent of territory over a 200-year period will be turning to LeDonne. I think it is also fair to say that few scholars are likely to read the book from beginning to end (it is heavy going). Its principal value will be as a reference work — a sort of concordance to the *Polnoe Sobranie Zakonov Rossiiskoi Imperii*, which LeDonne knows and can navigate better than any current historian, Anglophone or Russian. For these purposes the index is rather exiguous, and does not really match the scale and ambition of the work — however that problem can at least be solved by wordsearch in the book's electronic version.

New College, University of Oxford ALEXANDER MORRISON

Riegg, Stephen Badalyan. *Russia's Entangled Embrace: The Tsarist Empire and the Armenians, 1801–1914*. Cornell University Press, Ithaca, NY and London, 2020. xiv + 314 pp. Maps. Illustrations. Notes. Bibliography. Index. $45.95; $29.99 (e-book).

STEPHEN RIEGG begins his detailed re-assessment of Russian-Armenian relations in late imperial Russia by relating an account of when a young Armenian student at the 'prestigious Lazarev Institute of Oriental Languages in Moscow smothered his hated Latin teacher's chair with enough glue that the instructor, after sitting down, required a rescue from his colleagues' (p. 1). The student was Mikhail Loris-Melikov, who would later serve as an interior minister in the imperial regime of Alexander II. The Lazarev Institute, founded in 1815 by the Armenian Lazarev (Lazarian) family, would serve for decades as an 'intermediary between the autocracy and its minority subjects' (p. 1). From the increasing Russian expansion into the South Caucasus in the early 1800s to the First World War, the book's six chapters constitute, in chronological order, the experience of Eastern Armenians within the Russian Empire and the ways that Russian authorities encountered, perceived and accommodated, or cooperated, with Armenians. Mikhail Loris-Melikov's rise to the top of the

Russian government illustrates how Armenians might, and in many cases did, achieve success in the Russian Empire.

Riegg's study is also about the construction and operation of empire and the relationship of that empire to its subjects. It is an explicit effort, a point repeated throughout this volume by the author, to escape the still persistent binaries of success or subjugation. That these binaries have been long upended in the scholarship (see the evidence in his sources), undermines the innovativeness of the author's contentions. At first glance, his work is timely, coming as it does as the Russian-Armenian relationship (since the second Nagorno-Karabach war of 2020) is being re-assessed, at least on the Armenian side. To the author, far too many works portray Persian and Ottoman control over the Armenians as wholly oppressive. The Russian conquest of the Yerevan Khanate (much of modern Armenia) in 1828 was long seen as a deliverance of Armenian Christian brethren by their fellow Christians in Russia. Later, of course, more binaries would emerge when analysing the Armenian experience in the Soviet era. Were Armenians friends or foes of the Soviet experience? Were the Soviets friends or foes?

During much of the long nineteenth century, Eastern Armenians often worked with the Russians to 'colonize the South Caucasus' (p. 5); they were 'both agents and recipients of what the Romanovs portrayed as "European" imperialism. Some of the key protagonists were ethnic Armenian officers in the tsarist service who worked the state bureaucracy and commanded Russian troops, often against their own compatriots'. How were Eastern Armenians integrated? The tsars worked to co-opt the most important institutions within the Armenian diaspora, the merchantry and the clergy. They could therefore attempt to 'project diplomatic power from Constantinople to the Caspian Sea; to benefit economically from the transimperial trade networks of Armenian merchants', and ideally, 'to draw political advantage from the Armenian Church's extensive authority within far-flung Armenian communities' (p. 2). This Russian-Armenian association 'remained largely symbiotic until the clash of nationalism and empire-wide social instability jolted Russia's traditional nationalities policies' (p. 2). The emergence of Armenian nationalist groups in the late nineteenth century resulted in Russian efforts to curtail Armenian nationalism, and it also led to a Russian effort to curtail the power of Armenian merchants and the Armenian church.

The emergence of Armenian nationalism affecting Eastern Armenians, even though revolutionary groups such as the Hunchaks and Dashnaks were as yet marginal, presents a dramatic change to the narrative of 'symbiosis' that Riegg has presented to the reader. Before this, 'the Armenian diaspora, within and beyond the Romanov realm, sought security and prosperity, not a national state' (p. 122). Even the mid-nineteenth-century Armenian Catholicos in Ejmiatisn,

Nerses II, 'politically the most influential Armenian in that era, yearned to become the pope of the diaspora, not the president of the Armenian republic' (p. 122). Russians were ever more fearful in the South Caucasus of Armenian political pretensions. More than other national minorities, 'their economic standing and attendant social influence in the Caucasus and elsewhere, the domestic and foreign authority of their national church, and the diasporic distribution of Armenians throughout Eurasia, all affected tsarist officials' perception of Armenian political aims and abilities' (p. 157). Armenians, however useful in establishing the Russian presence in the South Caucasus in the past, might also emerge as a threat to Empire. Even given Russian worries, until the end of the nineteenth century, as Riegg demonstrates, 'most tsarist Armenians did not seek to fuse Western and Eastern Armenia into an independent nation-state' (p. 165).

In the decade or so before the 1905 revolution, the imperial authorities expanded Russification efforts among Armenians: 'Armenian students, teachers, priests, merchants, farmers, and refugees all found themselves on the receiving end of the state's redoubled effort to maintain the cohesion and vitality of the empire' (p. 197). The 'nadir' of Russian-Armenian relations came, as underlined by the author, when Alexander III's high commissioner in the Caucasus, Grigorii Golitysn (1896–1904), oversaw the confiscation of Armenian church properties. Golitsyn, who apparently 'scorned Armenians for what he viewed as their disproportionate political and economic sway in the region' (p. 206), was the victim of an attempted assassination by Armenian revolutionaries soon thereafter. Reforms enacted after 1905 restored a type of symbiosis to Russian-Armenian relations. This relationship would be severed by the genocide of 1915, the emergence of the Soviet Union, and Armenia's particular history within it.

As the author establishes in this monograph, 'no other country courted Eastern Armenians or offered them a better life than could imperial Russia' (p. 239). While Western Armenians faced destruction and dispersal, 'Eastern Armenians found the better life that their ancestors sought' (p. 244). Stephen Riegg's work is a strong, pioneering contribution to the study of the Armenian community in imperial Russia.

Department of History
Northern State University

STEVEN A. USITALO

Przebinda, Grzegorz. *From Chaadayev to Solovyov: Russian Modern Thinkers Between East and West.* Translated by Władysław Chłopicki. Eastern European Culture, Politics and Societies, 20. Peter Lang, Berlin, Bern, Brussels, New York, Oxford, Warsaw and Vienna, 2022. 479 pp. Notes. Selected bibliography. Index. £54.00 (hardbook & e-book).

GRZEGORZ PRZEBINDA's book discusses a group of nineteenth-century Russian thinkers who were preoccupied by the question of Russia's relationship to Europe. Some are typically understood as liberals or revolutionaries: Petr Chaadaev, Aleksandr Gertsen and Nikolai Chernyshevskii. Konstantin Leont′ev was a staunchly conservative, albeit idiosyncratic figure, while Fedor Dostoevskii and Vladimir Solov′ev are more difficult to categorize ideologically.

The chapters on Chaadaev discuss his *Philosophical Letters* (1829–36), the first of which notoriously lamented Russia's alienation from Europe. Przebinda convincingly argues that, rather than disowning the *First Philosophical Letter* in order to obtain leniency from the authorities, Chaadaev moved away from the anti-Russian views which it expressed, apparently in part due to his reading of Karamzin's *History of the Russian State* (1818–29). Przebinda's study would have been enhanced by some discussion of Ivan Gagarin, a pupil of Chaadaev who devoted more attention to the practical difficulties of reuniting the Orthodox and Catholic Churches.

In the chapter on Chernyshevskii, Przebinda interestingly argues that it is wrong to see him as an advocate of violent revolution, as did both Lenin and his conservative opponents. Rakhmetov, the main character of Chernyshevskii's novel *What Is To Be Done?* (1863), is implied to be a follower of the 'social evolutionist' Feuerbach (p. 145), not of contemporary revolutionaries. However, the chapters on Gertsen and Dostoevskii are poorly written and add little to our understanding of either of these men. The Gertsen chapter overlooks the contribution of Aileen Kelly's biography, *The Discovery of Chance* (Cambridge and London, 2016), which elucidates the influence of scientific concepts on Gertsen's political thought. The Dostoevskii chapter addresses Dostoevskii's complicated views about the relationship of religion and nationalism, but unclearly and in insufficient depth.

Likewise, the chapter on Leont′ev breaks relatively little new ground. Przebinda correctly observes that Leont′ev rejected nationalism in favour of monarchy, aristocracy and the international order established at the Congress of Vienna. He also notes that Leont′ev deferred to the institutional Church and the Church Fathers on dogmatic matters. Przebinda, here as elsewhere more judgemental than analytical, denounces Leont′ev's understanding of Christianity as 'inhuman' and 'degenerate' (p. 214). However, little effort is made to establish how familiar Leont′ev was with patristic writings or to identify the ways in which they shaped his religious thinking. This question is perhaps the biggest lacuna in the large quantity of Leont′ev scholarship which has appeared in the last three decades.

The most extensive chapters deal with Vladimir Solov′ev. Przebinda makes the interesting point that Solov′ev's treatise, *Byzantinism and Russia* (1896), can be read as a polemic against Leont′ev (p. 289). Whereas Leont′ev believed that Orthodox Byzantium had shaped and civilized Russia, Solov′ev argued that Russia would have collapsed had Peter I not repudiated 'the Byzantine distortion of the Christian idea — self-satisfied quietism' (p. 300). The discussion of Solov′ev's view of Patriarch Nikon, and how it differed from that of the British theologian William Palmer, is intriguing but underdeveloped. However, in many places, Przebinda's exposition of Solov′ev's ideas is confusing and hard to follow. Solov′ev's *Three Conversations, Including a Short Story of the Anti-Christ* (1899–1900) is paraphrased at great length with little attempt at analysis.

Throughout the book, barely any effort is made to draw comparisons between the thinkers under discussion, to explain why the author chose to include them, or to categorize them in accordance with a wider cultural pattern. In this regard, *From Chaadayev to Solovyov* cannot supersede Leonard Schapiro's classic, *Rationalism and Nationalism in Russian Nineteenth-Century Political Thought* (New Haven, CT and London, 1967). Furthermore, the book suffers from poor translation which at times makes the text difficult to understand.

Arkholme JAMES DAY

Gentes, Andrew A. *Russia's Sakhalin Penal Colony, 1849–1917: Imperialism and Exile*. Asia, Europe, and Global Connections: Culture, History, and Trans-Area Studies. Routledge, Abingdon and New York, 2021. xviii + 587 pp. Map. Illustrations. Tables. Charts. Glossaries. Chronology. Notes. Selected bibliography. Appendix. Index. £190.00; £36.99.

Iuvachev, Ivan P. *Eight Years on Sakhalin: A Political Prisoner's Memoir*. Edited and translated by Andre A. Gentes. Anthem Series on Russian, East European and Eurasian Studies. Anthem Press, London and New York, 2022. xxxix + 251 pp. Map. Illustrations. Glossary. Notes. Bibliography. £85.00; £40.00 (e-book): $140.00; $60.00 (e-book).

ANDREW GENTES has long been one of the leading scholars of imperial Russia's use of Siberian hard labour as the basis of its penal system. Within his *oeuvre*, numerous articles testify to a particular interest in Sakhalin Island's role as a penal colony in the nineteenth and early twentieth centuries. The latest fruits of that long engagement with the field are an extensive and impressive monograph and a translation of one of the most important memoirs by a former political convict on Sakhalin.

Although the focus on Sakhalin may appear quite narrow in both territorial and temporal terms, at least by comparison with the vast expanses of Siberian exile and *katorga* that Gentes's previous monographs covered, *Russia's Sakhalin Penal Colony, 1849–1917: Imperialism and Exile*, takes a deep dive to address everything from the minutiae of everyday life for convicts, settlers and officials, to the island's governance — or, frequently, lack thereof — both local and central. In doing so, Gentes shows how the island became not just a byword for the degrading treatment of prisoners, but emblematic of the tsarist government's moral and intellectual bankruptcy, and ultimately became a factor in the regime's demise.

As Gentes argues, from the moment Russia established a permanent presence on the island to its recapture by Japan towards the end of the Russo-Japanese war, Sakhalin encapsulated the intertwining of the imperial Russian government's colonizing aims with the development of its carceral system, and the alignment of the aims of the criminal justice system with those of capitalist development, through the exploitation of prisoners. The post-emancipation context of the establishment of Sakhalin's penal colony is important here. While the principle of convict labour had long been part of Russian penal policy, its implementation had been inconsistent. The idea that the peasantry needed to be controlled by another means following the end of serfdom became the imperative that entrenched the system, the criminalization of vagrancy to a significant extent neutralizing peasants' liberation from the land. As with the carceral colonization of swathes of Eastern Siberia more generally, the perception of Sakhalin as uninhabitable by 'civilized' Russians led the imperial government to embrace a penal policy of exporting the 'uncivilized' portion of its population. Thus Sakhalin was promoted as the solution to the penal problem not so much despite, but because of its manifest unsuitability in terms of climate, terrain and potential for agricultural exploitation. Its failure as a penal and settler colony was built in from the start, and Gentes catalogues in great detail the inhumane conditions and appalling abuses that ensued.

Underlying the move to place Sakhalin Island at the centre of penal policy was the tension between reformist and reactionary actors within the government, and respectively between the Ministry of Justice and the Ministry of Internal Affairs, the latter generally winning out to fully establish the tsarist regime as a police state rather than one governed by law. Alongside some eye-popping examples of corruption and graft, and of the brutal treatment of prisoners by officials, Gentes provides ample evidence of the willingness of administrators at both local and national levels to operate outside the law. The lack of oversight by officials, who exhibited astonishing ignorance of and lack of interest in conditions on the ground in Sakhalin, 'allowed the colony to function apart from the metropole as a hyper-reactionary outpost, where petty tyrants carved out fiefdoms of corruption and abuse and lived out fantasies of power', becoming 'a landscape that actualized tsarism's most reactionary tendencies while seeming to be hermetically protected against progressive reform' (p. 308). Among other results, this led to some of the features we more readily associate with the Stalinist Gulag already being well established in Sakhalin's carceral institutions, including the use of differential rations to punish labourers who failed to fulfil the norms, the practice of convicts becoming guards and less formal use of habitual criminals to control and abuse weaker prisoners, and even outbreaks of self-mutilation by convicts to avoid work and escape particularly hazardous situations.

Gentes should be commended particularly for the consistent attention he gives to the appalling situation of women and children on the island, as doubly deprived of agency. As Gentes shows, both female convicts and free women settlers, many of whom followed their convict husbands, were the victims of structural misogyny. Almost without exception, women were condemned to rape, sexual enslavement and endemic sexually transmitted diseases, because the authorities viewed them solely as vessels for achieving the russianization of the island. Children fared no better, the colony being little more than a school for criminality and sexual abuse.

While much of the monograph emphasizes the consequences of the failure of imperial policies and their implementation, Gentes's even-handed approach allows space for discussion of aspects of the penal and exile system that did, or could have been made to, work. Notably, despite the extremely poor record of ex-convicts remaining on the island after their period of exile expired, the evidence of Sakhalin convicts transported to the mainland to work on the Trans-Siberian railway indicates that exiles would have stayed on the island as settlers if they had the means of earning a living. However, negligence and poor planning on the part of the authorities prevented this happening in the majority of cases, with most settlers facing destitution, and unsurprisingly opting to escape this at the first available opportunity, legal or otherwise. Matters were hardly helped by the fact that in its persecution of vagrancy, the state was attempting to settle an inherently transient population — and one made more transient still by the very criminal justice system that supposedly aimed to reform it.

The monograph's focus is primarily on the peasant convicts who, as penal labourers and exile settlers, formed the vast majority of Sakhalin's population. As they left so few traces of their own, Gentes seeks peasants' voices and presence in other sources, and he makes excellent use of the memoirs of the much smaller number of political convicts sent to the island to achieve this.

As a result, the later lives on the island of *Narodnik* revolutionaries including Mikhail Trigoni, Ivan Manucharov (Ovanes Manuchariants), Liudmila Volkenshtein and Ivan Iuvachev, who were all previously imprisoned in the high security Shlissel′burg Fortress near St Petersburg, in conditions of strict solitary confinement, are brought to life.

Gentes's translation of Iuvachev's 1901 memoir, *Eight Years on Sakhalin*, joins his earlier publication of the first English versions of two notable works on the pre-revolutionary penal system, Petr Iakubovich's 1899 memoir, *In the World of Outcasts* (Anthem Press, 2015) and Vlas Doroshevich's sensationalist journalistic account of his trip to Sakhalin, originally published in 1903 (Anthem Press, 2009). Iuvachev, a naval officer and member of *The People's Will*, was convicted alongside Vera Figner, Liudmila Volkenshtein, Mikhail Ashenbrenner and others in 1884. His incarceration in Shlissel′burg Fortress led to a mental breakdown and he was transferred to Sakhalin's penal colony in 1887, one of the first political prisoners to be sent to the island.

The translator's Foreword to the Iuvachev text contextualizes the memoir effectively enough, yet suffers from a couple of odd omissions. While it notes the role of Sergei Degaev in Iuvachev's and his comrades' arrest in 1883, it fails to mention the surely relevant detail that Degaev was an Okhrana agent and provocateur. And in referring to Iuvachev's son's arrests in the 1930s, it does not indicate that Daniil Iuvachev is better known as the absurdist poet Daniil Kharms. It is also perhaps surprising that the translator is unaware of an earlier translation of one of Iuvachev's other works, the memoir-history *The Russian Bastille, or the Schluesselburg Fortress*, published in London in 1909, though admittedly, the quaint transliteration of the author's surname as 'Youvatshev' in that publication did not immediately compute for the present reviewer either. This last omission adds to the sense that the effect of Iuvachev's earlier imprisonment — and the religious conversion he experienced in Shlissel′burg Fortress — is somewhat underplayed here. Gentes describes the author's transformation into a useful, devout member of society from his earlier involvement in a terrorist organization as one of Sakhalin's rare success stories. Yet this change had already taken place before Iuvachev was transferred, as his Shlissel′burg memoir — and those of the fortress's other inmates — makes clear. *Eight Years on Sakhalin* is strong on detail on the island's governance, its flora and fauna, and many of its inhabitants, hence its abundant use in Gentes's monograph, but although there is discussion of the mental effects of isolation, the book as a whole does not impart a great sense of spiritual or moral transformation in its author.

The translation is nevertheless a valuable addition to the literature, supporting many of Gentes's arguments. In particular, Iuvachev's description of his work in surveying the coastline of the island confirms the penal settlement's role as a colonial enterprise, while the deep-rooted hostility of the local authorities towards their criminal charges clearly illustrates the underlying reasons for the colony's failure, as negligence, corruption and cruelty all undermine the supposed aims of settling the island, making it economically viable and reforming the convicts. Iuvachev's sympathy for the penal labourers and exile settlers he meets is notable, and enables various figures to emerge from the peasantry that is so seldom afforded its own voice. Likewise, albeit not entirely without racist overtones, Iuvachev's account of the Giliaks (Nivkhi) with whom he becomes acquainted on Sakhalin represents a remarkable source. It is a shame he did not record similar encounters with the Ainu or Oroki (Uilta), the other indigenous groups on the island.

Iuvachev's description of the officials on the island largely comes from the same perspective of sympathy, underpinned by a personal philosophy of compassion and a hesitation to judge others that was the outcome of his religious conversion. At times that leads the author to some jarring conclusions, as Gentes notes. Iuvachev may condemn the actions of the brutal prison warden Fedor Livin, but he effectively exonerates Tymovsk District Commander Arsenii Butakov of responsibility for the notorious Onor Affair, one of the worst incidents of the abuse of prisoners in the island's history. Personal sympathy may have played a role in Iuvachev's overly charitable assessment of Butakov, but the same cannot be said of Mikhail Mitsul, first agronomist and one of the early directors of *katorga* on Sakhalin, whose bizarre exaggeration of Sakhalin's potential for agricultural development played a disastrously influential role in the imperial government's decision-making, and who was guilty of large scale embezzlement of government funds intended for the island to boot. Mitsul died in 1883, four years before Iuvachev's arrival on Sakhalin, and certainly by the time Iuvachev wrote his memoir, the former's reputation was thoroughly compromised, as other sources attest.

Such incongruities in the original notwithstanding, this translation remains a powerful companion to Gentes's monograph. The latter is a masterly study that will be required reading not only for students of Sakhalin or of the Russian penal system, but also for those interested in Russian imperial governance more generally. As a study of the Russian state's colonial ambitions, and the brutality with which they have historically been implemented, it gains increased relevance in the context of Russia's full-scale war against Ukraine.

UCL SSEES SARAH J. YOUNG

Petri, Olga. *Places of Tenderness and Heat: The Queer Milieu of Fin-de-Siècle St. Petersburg.* Cornell University Press, Ithaca, NY and London, 2022. xx + 254 pp. Maps. Illustrations. Appendix. Notes. Bibliography. Index. $48.95; $31.99 (e-book).

In his 2001 book, *Homosexual Desire in Revolutionary Russia*, Dan Healey gave the first major scholarly account of the appearance of an urban homosexual subculture in imperial Russia, focusing on its capital St Petersburg. Two decades later, Olga Petri's *Places of Tenderness and Heat* examines the spatial patterns of that subculture in more detail.

As Petri puts it, the book scrutinizes 'the relationship between the bureaucratic management of space and queer spatial patterns' (p. 7). Exploring a variety of spatial management strategies from sanitary regulations to the landscaping of public gardens, Petri shows how urban planning shaped what she terms St Petersburg's 'queer milieu'. Her study divides into five chapters, moving from an overview of the city's 'queer milieu' from the perspective of the central government (chapter 1), to the realities of policing it (chapter 2), the risks and opportunities offered by queer street life (chapter 3), the uses and surveillance of bathhouses (chapter 4), and finally what Petri calls the 'emotional range' of queer spaces (chapter 5), looking at Mikhail Kuzmin's personal diary to provide emotional and experiential insight into a study that mainly discusses governmental sources.

The book offers several compelling conceptual frameworks for thinking about queerness in pre-revolutionary Russia, of which three, in particular, stand out. First, Petri shifts the focus away from imperial anti-sodomy laws, highlighting in their place the impact of seemingly mundane urban realities on the lived experiences of the capital's sexual minorities, something that has not been spotlighted thoroughly in previous research. Second, Petri sees queerness as co-existing with and within the normative. This allows her to find more ambiguities in what it meant to be queer — in spatial terms, at least — than one encounters in court cases revolving around sodomy, and to address what she calls 'the very ambiguity of sexual valences' (p. 18) head on. Third, harnessing her geographical expertise, Petri provides an innovative blueprint for queering the archive, illustrating how spatial awareness of the city's 'queer milieu' can equip researchers with new insight that could help them spot nods to queerness in archival sources that might otherwise go unnoticed.

However, approaching queerness as a spatial phenomenon turns out to be problematic, since Petri's mapping of St Petersburg's 'queer milieu' rests mainly on law enforcers' view of sexual minorities. In one example, Petri discusses an incident where a man named Johan went to the police to report that his flatmate, Dmitrii, was missing. She suggests that the two men were sexually connected on the basis of certain spatial cues. But this suggestion rests on assumptions about the meaning of those cues on the part of the authorities at the time. As such, using them to identify sexual minorities in the archive is, in effect, repurposing a historically punitive tool. Not only is this an issue worth acknowledging, but it seems pertinent to scrutinize the imperial mapping of queerness in more detail. In the end, Petri's evaluation of this episode seems insensitive: in her interpretation, the police officer declines to help Johan look for his lost lover out of homophobic prejudice, and yet Petri remarks that this episode shows how 'the late imperial capital married sexual opportunity and governmental surveillance in an uneasy, but arguably effective negotiation over the use of urban space' (p. 10). Elsewhere, approaching queerness as a spatial phenomenon seems to diminish the unique plight of sexual minorities, such as in the comparison that 'queer men, like all city dwellers, found challenges and opportunities in the rapid spatial, demographic, and technological transformations so characteristic of urban modernity' (p. 96).

The book engages in a sustained pattern of seeing — and arguably, objectifying — sexual minorities through the same lens as punitive Russian law enforcers. As a result, sometimes 'queer milieu' seems synonymous with 'deviant sexuality' and 'illicit sex', stigmatizing terms that appear throughout without scare quotes or interrogation. Discussing the importance of queer visibility, Petri remarks that 'visibility serves as an important role for any sexual minority and [...] this role was, perhaps, even more essential to the constitution of a queer milieu than any nascent or yet-to-be conceived political agenda: After all, visibility, even when partial and ambiguous, facilitates sex and communion' (p. 20). Here and elsewhere in *Places of Tenderness and Heat*, one gets the impression that the men who made up St Petersburg's 'queer milieu' were focused mainly on having (illicit) sex. This is certainly what law enforcers thought — unsurprisingly, since it is on this very idea that much homophobic stereotyping rests.

School of Modern Languages and Cultures NICK MAYHEW
University of Glasgow

Vaninskaya, Anna (ed.). *London Through Russian Eyes, 1896–1914: An Anthology of Foreign Correspondence.* Translated by Anna Vaninskaya and Maria Artomonova. London Record Society, 57. Boydell & Brewer, Woodbridge and Rochester, NY, 2023. xvii + 359 pp. Maps. Illustrations. Notes. Bibliography. Index. £60.00; £19.99 (e-book): $85.00; $24.95 (e-book).

THE study of Anglo-Russian cultural relations has become a buoyant field over the past twenty years or so, reflecting a burgeoning interest in transnational history that focuses on much more than questions of diplomacy and international relations. This new collection edited by Anna Vaninskaya provides readers with a rich set of readings that show how a number of Russian journalists and writers presented life in London to their readers back home. The book includes an excellent critical apparatus and a valuable introduction providing readers with important biographical information about the four journalists whose work features in the following pages: Isaak Shklovskii (better known by the pseudonym Dioneo); Kornei Chukovskii (later to become a prominent children's poet and literary critic in the USSR); Samuil Marshak; and Semion Rapoport. Their work appeared in many of the leading Russian journals of the day including *Russkoe bogatstvo* and *Vestnik Evropy* as well as leading newspapers like *Rech´*.

Most of the translations included here are of writings by Shklovskii and Chukovskii. Shklovskii was as Vaninskaya points out widely acknowledged in Russia as a leading expert on Britain. He lived in London for many years, and came to know the city well, but while he was deeply impressed by the Anglo-Saxon commitment to 'civil liberty' (p. 11), he was equally appalled by the poverty and jingoism that he considered a defining feature of London life. He was familiar with the numerous studies of the London poor that had been conducted by the likes of Charles Booth, and several of the pieces included here focus on the poverty and chaos found in areas like Whitechapel and Lambeth, as well as others that describe life in areas like Hammersmith where many better-paid skilled workers made their home. Shklovskii was a skilful writer who was adept at capturing the life of the streets in lively prose. He also on occasion made use of considerable poetic licence — inventing people and providing real characters with new names — to illuminate the trials faced by immigrant communities in London's East End. Other pieces by Shklovskii that appear here focus on subjects ranging from the celebration of Christmas in London through to the atmosphere of public life during a general election.

The pieces by Kornei Chukovskii have a rather different tone from those of Shklovskii, consisting of short pieces penned for the paper *Odesskie Novosti*. Chukovskii was less enamoured of London life than his compatriot, in part because he was himself desperately short of money, while he seems to have struggled to establish friendships both with the host community and members of the Russian émigré colony. He also had a difficult relationship with Shklovskii, regularly pointing out the errors in the older man's reports, suggesting that his accounts of life in London were often little more than fictions derived from books written by English authors about the life in the city. Chukovskii believed that the English were deeply philistine and materialistic, writing in a piece on 'Whitechapel' that Jewish immigrants from the Russian Empire had far more 'spiritual and intellectual interests' (p. 51) than the Londoners who swarmed through the streets around them. Chukovskii was only in Britain for a short period, and his views changed somewhat later in life, when he had become a well-known figure in Soviet literary life. As a young man, though, he had little good to say about a London where the streets were filled with detritus of 'human misery [...] clamorous, lurid and unashamed' (p. 54).

London Through Russian Eyes only contains brief examples of the work of Marshak and Rappoport, ranging from a piece about the behaviour of cinema audiences through to one describing the decline of a street in south-west London where houses once filled by middle-class residents had fallen into dilapidation to become the homes of prostitutes and petty criminals. Most of the articles included in the book are indeed focused on the 'lives of the streets' rather than vignettes of life in the wealthier areas of London. All four contributors whose work is included here were to a greater or lesser degree convinced that the kind of unfettered capitalism found in Britain condemned most of the population to poverty and insecurity. It might have indeed been helpful if Vaninskaya had done a little more in her introduction to set the attitudes so vividly outlined in *London Through Russian Eyes* within the wider development of Russian radical thought, including the development of a neo-populism that sought to identify ways in which the country could modernize and industrialize without the kind of urban poverty and squalor seen in Britain. That is nevertheless only a minor caveat. Vaninskaya has brought together a fascinating collection of sources that help to cast light on how London was constructed in the imagination of Russians in the decades before 1917. This meticulously edited book will be invaluable to students of Anglo-Russian relations as well as readers interested in understanding more about how London was viewed by foreigners at a time when it was both the capital of a great empire and the site of enormous poverty and degradation.

Lancaster University MICHAEL HUGHES

Grant, Susan. *Soviet Nightingales: Care Under Communism*. Cornell University Press, Ithaca, NY and London, 2022. xvii + 314 pp. Illustrations. Notes. Archives and libraries consulted. Index. $125.00; $24.95.

SUSAN GRANT's monograph on the profession of nursing in the USSR represents an innovative and necessary addition both to the history of medicine and to women's history in the Soviet Union. By drawing upon under-utilized sources, including archives and online interview repositories, as well as films and other products of visual culture, Grant's study provides the first full-length account of Soviet nursing. In so doing, she also exposes the central paradox that plagued

Soviet nurses: while the Communist state charged nurses with delivering the highest standard of compassionate care to its worker-citizens, nurses themselves did not receive the support necessary to fulfil this pledge. Moreover, they often endured harsh living and working conditions with little pay or advanced training opportunities, while concurrently receiving demoralizing criticism from their supervisors, the media and even the Party. These conditions gave rise to a sharp disjuncture between the Communist state's official narrative of nursing care and the lived experiences of nurses and their patients. As Grant convincingly demonstrates, this contradiction persisted throughout the lifespan of the USSR, and although the latter may no longer exist, problems of equity and provision for nurses have yet to be resolved.

Grant's trajectory starts with the advent of nursing in Russia, the origins of which may be traced to The Crimean War (1853–56) and the first Russian Sisters of Mercy community at Saint Troitsky, and ends with the fall of the USSR. Over the course of nine chapters, as well as an epilogue and a coda, Grant traces nurses' attempts to advance their skills and professional identities, as well as to distinguish themselves as a separate professional category from other so-called middle medical workers, such as feldshers and midwives. By taking collective action, nurses were on occasion able to advocate for their material and personal interests in the burgeoning socialist state's ideological landscape. At the same time, however, nurses were expected to be moral heroes to their patients and provide them with political enlightenment as well as exemplary care. Grant's analysis situates the development of nursing in a larger historical context, demonstrating how events such as war, revolution, economic crises and political cataclysms left their mark on Soviet healthcare. As may be unsurprising, the book focuses on nursing and treatment facilities in Russia, but there are also significant discussions of care work in cities such as Kyiv, Odesa and Baku.

A particular strength of Grant's study is its unique and in-depth contribution to women's, gender and sexuality studies in the Soviet context. As in most parts of the world, most nurses in the Soviet Union were women. Beginning with a discussion of the Woman Question in Russia in the nineteenth century, when Russian intellectuals began in earnest to debate the role of women in a rapidly developing, post-serfdom society, Grant demonstrates how thoroughly entrenched sexist views of female care work were in Soviet nursing. From a lack of their own proper textbooks to a state apparatus that emphasized the innate kindness and gentleness of female health workers, instead of their intelligence and specialized acquired knowledge, nurses were often marginalized due to their gender. While similar situations exist in many countries, the Soviet case was unique. As Grant convincingly argues, 'nurses were crucial symbols of the new Soviet state' (p. 3), which meant that the government was especially invested in propagating stereotypes of idealized feminine nurturing, particularly when individual healthcare workers had to make up for the systemic gaps in equipment and supplies caused by Soviet officialdom.

Impressive, too, is Grant's investigation of the representation of healthcare workers in visual culture such as cinema and photographs. In this latter category special mention should be made of her enlightening treatment of the photos in an unpublished manuscript from the Odesa Psycho-Neurological Institute, which shows remarkable similarities between Soviet care and progressive techniques for treating psychiatric patients in other countries. While at times the study would benefit from more robust background information on certain topics in Soviet culture, such as what is meant by 'medalists' (p. 21) who have entered nursing school, the 'war scare of 1927' (p. 71) and the precise meaning of 'cadres' (p. 7) in the Soviet work environment, this is a minor drawback in an otherwise excellent work. Overall, Grant's ambitious and ground-breaking study will prove useful not only to specialists in the history of medicine and scholars of women's, gender and sexuality studies, but also to social scientists, students and health professionals, as well as anyone who is interested in healthcare.

Department of German and Russian
Colby College

Melissa L. Miller

Rieber, Alfred J. *Stalin as Warlord*. Yale University Press, New Haven, CT and London, 2022. xiv + 360 pp. Illustrations. Chronology. Glossary. Abbreviations. Notes. Bibliography. Index. $38.00: £25.00.

Stalin as Warlord is a sweeping, detailed, meticulously documented and clearly written assessment of Stalin's use and abuse of power by one of our most distinguished scholars of Russian and Soviet history. Alfred Rieber commenced his critical scrutiny of the Soviet dictator in 1959 in a doctoral dissertation on Stalin and the French Communist Party. The thesis of his latest work is that creative and destructive impulses coexisted within Stalin to produce a 'paradox of power'. In this paradox (which Rieber sometimes terms — more accurately in the opinion of this reader — a 'contradiction'), the destructive impulses were far more prominent and impactful. To win the war against Nazi Germany, Stalin had to allow a measure of scientific, technological and cultural autonomy, but these creative elements were 'barely unfettered for four years' and were 'suppressed or stifled' after 1945. Stalin's successors 'failed to break the dead hand of Stalinism', the legacy of which extends to today (p. 268).

Rieber demonstrates a remarkable and wide-ranging knowledge of scholarly studies and published documents and diaries pertaining to Stalin. Coverage in this study is broad, thematically and temporally. In casting Stalin as 'warlord' (rather than as 'military commander', as Albert Seaton did in his work on Stalin from 1976), Rieber emphasizes the multiple roles that the *vozhd′* performed. He devotes relatively few pages to strictly military history of the Soviet-German War. Moreover, almost the first third of the book focuses on events prior to June 1941, but does not describe the Soviet invasions of Poland or Finland, and the final couple of chapters cover the post-war decades.

Rieber shows that in introducing violent collectivization of agriculture, rapid industrialization and forging a powerful military force in the 1930s, Stalin 'neutralized every real, potential and imagined opposition to his policies in the army, diplomatic corps, technical intelligentsia, nationalities and international communist movement' (p. 82). During the war, however, 'the heavy reliance on coercion [...] yielded to a [...] greater degree of latitude in what was permitted. But the agencies of repression also increased their authority' (p. 213). Rieber devotes significant attention to the contribution of the scientific and technical intelligentsia to the war effort. He invokes the fate of Sergei Korolev and Valentin Glushko to support his thesis of the 'paradox of power'. Both were promising researchers in the field of rocket artillery and were sentenced to eight years' imprisonment in 1938 as part of a mass purge of their institute. Korolev was initially slated for execution, and Glushko was subjected to torture. Both, however, conducted research on rocketry during the war, albeit in an NKVD-supervised *sharashka*.

Another of Rieber's key interests is Stalin's wartime flexibility in political messaging. He charts the rapid growth of Russo-centrism, in which Russians were cast as the leading group in the multi-ethnic Soviet friendship of peoples. 'Marxism-Leninism was muted, Rieber observes, 'though never absent' (p. 164). In international relations, the dissolution of the Comintern in 1943 ushered in a brief era of Communist polycentrism. At the end of the war, Stalin shoved the pendulum back toward coercion, his preferred method of rule. The Communist Party of the Soviet Union rebuilt its ranks, and 'reforms were drafted to raise the ideological awareness of the leading party officials' (p. 229). The formation of Cominform in 1947 once again subjected several European Communist parties to Moscow.

The short-lived existence of the Jewish Anti-Fascist Committee also bolsters Rieber's central thesis. Stalin's extension of 'an unprecedented degree of autonomy' to Soviet Jews, prompted largely by his desire to gain support in the West for the Soviet war effort, stood in sharp contrast to his criticism of the Jewish Bund before 1917 (p. 182). Stalin reverted to persecution with the murder of JAC chairman Solomon Mikhoels in January 1948, which preceded the dissolution of the JAC the following November.

One topic that is under-acknowledged in this otherwise comprehensive treatment of Stalin's wartime record is the impact of Lend-Lease aid in the

Soviet victory — especially in the areas of communication (radios, telephones and telephone wire), transportation (locomotives, trucks and jeeps), combat aircraft and aviation fuel, tanks and food — and Stalin's expressed appreciation of that aid. Although almost two-thirds of Lend-Lease aid arrived after the battle for Kursk in July 1943, as early as the end of 1941, nearly a quarter of all medium and heavy tanks in service in the Red Army had been provided by Britain. Donald Filtzer has calculated that Allied food deliveries to the USSR were sufficient to have fed the entire Red Army for 509 days.

This criticism aside, *Stalin as Warlord* is a magisterial study from which general readers and specialists alike will greatly benefit.

Washington and Lee University RICHARD BIDLACK

Shkandrij, Myroslav. *In the Maelstrom: The Waffen-SS 'Galicia' Division and Its Legacy.* McGill-Queen's University Press, Montreal, QC and Kingston, ON, London and Chicago, IL, 2023. xxx + 424 pp. Maps. Illustrations. Glossary. Notes on political and military figures. Notes. Bibliography. Index. $140.00; $44.95: £120.00; £37.99.

THE Ukrainian Waffen-SS Division 'Galicia' has been at the centre of public debates since the 1980s, especially in Canada and the United Kingdom, over Nazi perpetrators and collaborators among post-war East European immigrants. But in the immediate post-war years, the division was already being referred to as proof of Ukrainian nationalist collaboration with Nazi Germany and Ukrainian participation in mass crimes during the German occupation.

The division, set up in the second half of 1943 with Ukrainian volunteers and the support of some segments of Ukrainian society in the 'Galicia' district of the German-occupied General Government, had been mostly a combat unit in the German war against the Soviet Union. It was one of numerous non-German divisions subordinated to the Waffen-SS, the military arm of the SS, that the Germans raised as front-line combat units in the later phases of the war. The division fought its most important battle at Brody in July 1944 where it suffered a high number of casualties. At the end of the war it surrendered to British troops in Austria. Its members were interned in a British internment camp in Italy before they were brought to the UK in 1947. In 1950, the Canadian government allowed them to immigrate, which many took advantage of.

The fact that the 'Galicia' division became a focus of debates about war criminals and German collaborators was not a consequence of actual crimes of the division, but rather of its designation as an SS unit and because of stereotypical depictions of Ukrainians as German collaborators. Such allegations have been regularly repeated even though official investigations in Canada and the UK at the end of the 1980s concluded that the division had neither committed mass murders nor were there a large number of perpetrators among its former members.

Myroslav Shkandrij's book starts from the two questions at the centre of the debates during the 1980s, namely the possible crimes of the division and the motives for its support among Ukrainian political actors and its members, most of whom had volunteered for service. Shkandrij clearly shows that the motive for volunteering was not sympathy for Nazi Germany, but the aim of establishing a Ukrainian armed force as a basis for Ukrainian state-building, or at least for protecting the Ukrainian population. Another motive among the volunteers was to avoid deportation to Germany as forced labour.

The idea of creating a Ukrainian army had been the aim of various political factions since the beginning of the war. There had been some support for this also from the German side, but Hitler had initially rejected the idea, only agreeing to it after Germany's defeat at Stalingrad. Meanwhile, the Bandera wing of the 'Organization of Ukrainian Nationalists' (OUN) withdrew from the plans, instead creating the 'Ukrainian Insurgent Army' (UPA) at the end of 1942 which initiated the anti-German uprising in Volhynia in February 1943.

The question of crimes is, as Shkandrij shows, complicated by the fact that, in addition to the actual division, the Germans set up units known as Galician SS Volunteer Regiments, which recruited personnel from the same group of volunteers. However, the regiments were, despite protests from the Ukrainian side, subordinated to the German Order Police before being integrated into the division in the second half of 1944. Most of the crimes that are discussed in relation to the division were committed by these units, most notably the involvement in the destruction of the Polish village of Huta Pieniacka and the murder of several hundred residents in February 1944.

Generally, the book offers a balanced and nuanced account. Nevertheless, Shkandrij's engagement in countering overly negative notions of the division leads him in rare instances to rather uncritical treatment of either the very dubious (p. 112, on Huta Pienacka) or patently wrong positions of other researchers, as in his discussion of the Ivan Demjanjuk case as a Soviet fabrication (p. 295n.).

Nevertheless, there are clear indications that propagandistic Soviet publications had an impact on public discussions of the division in the 1980s (p. 284n.). They propagated the Soviet enemy image of Ukrainian nationalists as fascist collaborators and henchmen of the Germans during World War Two in the West. There is a direct line that links these Soviet depictions with Vladimir Putin's recent claim that Ukraine is ruled by a 'Nazi' regime, which he used to justify the invasion of Ukraine in 2022. This makes a critical reappraisal of older discussions about Ukrainian nationalist forces and German rule in World War Two urgent and timely, to which Myroslav Shkandrij's book makes an important contribution.

Martin Luther University
Halle (Saale), Germany
KAI STRUVE

Exeler, Franziska. *Ghosts of War: Nazi Occupation and Its Aftermath in Soviet Belarus*. Cornell University Press, Ithaca, NY and London, 2022. xvi + 344 pp. Maps. Illustrations. Notes. Bibliography. Index. $35.95; $17.99 (e-book).

WITH *Ghosts of War*, Franziska Exeler has established herself as a major voice in the history of the Soviet Union. Based on a 2013 Princeton doctoral thesis, the award-winning book recounts the history of Belarus before, during and after the war. Well theorized but not burdened with jargon, the book reads smoothly. The title is somewhat misleading, as the volume covers much more than just 'Nazi Occupation and Its Aftermath'. In fact, it is a history of Belarus in the twentieth century with a focus on the war as one of the most defining moments of this experience.

Chapter one recounts the making of Belarus between crumbling empires and their feuding successors: abandoned by the tottering Russian empire in World War One it was occupied by the victorious German empire, only to be embroiled in the wars of the Romanov succession after the Germans were beaten at the western front and retreated in 1918. In the violent upheaval that followed the fall of the Romanovs, 'Belarusian statehood [...] was announced no less than six times' between 1918 and 1920 (p. 32). By 1921, however, the fighting subsided and Belarusian lands were divided between two of the successor states of the Russian empire: the west went to Poland, the east to Bolshevik Russia. By 1922, the latter had reconfigured itself as the Soviet Union, with Belarus as one of the foundational republics. Borders were re-drawn again in 1939, when the Soviets joined Nazi Germany in a new division of Poland, which transformed parts of eastern Poland into western Belarus. It was this expanded republic which the Germans would occupy in 1941, opening the most bloody chapter in modern Belarusian history.

Chapter two turns to this 'heart of darkness': the years of Nazi occupation. Exeler focuses on the 'choiceless choices' people faced in a landscape of war and genocidal violence. Like much of recent writing on collaboration and resistance, *Ghosts of War* questions the glib black-and-white image this dichotomy implies and stresses the complexity of motivations instead, and the often impossible situations in which local actors made decisions. Chapter three analyses the return of Soviet power and chapter four turns to the Soviet politics of retribution, which took no heed of such complexities, but instead saw behaviour in war and occupation as a litmus test for loyalty to the Soviet cause. As others before her, Exeler stresses the changing severity of Soviet 'justice', but is at pains to point out that such variations are no evidence for a liberalization of the Soviet project. Soviet justice, she stresses repeatedly, remained 'illiberal'.

Chapter five is the most original contribution to the literature. It covers individual and collective responses to the ghosts of war, uncovering the complexities of such reactions and disproving many common-sense assumptions about what could and could not be believed, thought, said, or remembered after the war. This exploration then sets the scene for the final chapter, which turns to the official memory narratives and the way they were both received and shaped by individuals and groups.

Exeler's excellent book follows the trend away from 'all-Soviet' interpretations, which often enough turned out to be mostly about Russia, towards regional studies. Some landmarks include the books by Katrin Boeckh on Ukraine (2007), Olaf Mertelsmann on Estonia (2012), Johannes Due Enstad on northwest Russia (2018), Roberto Carmack on Kazakhstan (2019), or Nicole Eaton on Königsberg/Kaliningrad (2023). With her book on Belarus, Exeler closes an important gap in this literature.

Like much recent historiography on this war, *Ghosts of War* is based on multi-archival research. Gone are the times when a book could be based on a research stay in Moscow alone. Exeler has worked in archives in Belarus, Poland, Ukraine, Russia and the United States. In addition, she read published sources and conducted oral history interviews. The result is a finely textured account of Belarusian and Soviet history in the twentieth century, which avoids direct engagement with the more extreme positions in a sometimes polarized historiographical debate. It also eschews the artificial divisions between social, cultural and political history, which so agitated an older generation of historians of the Soviet experience. Her book is a major contribution to our understanding of this war and its place in twentieth-century history. It is highly recommended for any serious student of World War Two.

The University of Melbourne MARK EDELE

Torigian, Joseph. *Prestige, Manipulation, and Coercion: Elite Power Struggles in the Soviet Union and China after Stalin and Mao.* Yale University Press, New Haven, CT and London, 2022. xvi + 296 pp. Chronology. Notes. Index. $65.00.

THIS is an original and ambitious comparative study of the elite conflicts that took place in the Communist Party of the Soviet Union and the Chinese Communist Party over party leadership following the deaths of Iosif Stalin and Mao Zedong. It is deeply researched and makes particularly good use of memoirs in Russian and Chinese. The body of the book comprises four chapters on: the defeat of Lavrentii Beria by a putative 'collective leadership' in 1953; the struggle by the real victor, Nikita Khrushchev, against the 'anti-party group' in 1957; two longer chapters on the fall of the Gang of Four in 1976; and Deng Xiaoping's defeat of Hua Guofeng, complete by 1978. The author sensibly opts to conduct the comparison through parallel historical narratives and he has much to say about the conduct of the power struggles that is fresh and stimulating. In general he paints a grim picture of these struggles, showing persuasively that they were enacted in terms of personal prestige and political cunning, backstairs intrigue, score settling, and with the threat of military force always in the background. The common context in which these power struggles took place was one in which institutions were weak and rules insufficient to allow a politics of policy deliberation and exchange. The latter point is persuasive, although it is arguably more true of China than the Soviet Union where Khrushchev championed 'party revivalism'.

The analysis in each chapter draws on a typology that is set out in the introduction. This consists of three pairs of alternative hypotheses drawn from the political science literature. These relate, respectively, to an 'economic model', in which a leader wins power struggles by providing patronage or policy platforms; an 'authority model', where formal and informal rules are unclear and where those who select a leader compete for prestige rather than fight over policy; and a 'power ministries model', where the army and the political police exercise differing levels of influence while the ultimate arbiter remains the party. The models and their attendant hypotheses are not as clearly defined as one might like, but they generate a set of empirical questions that are fruitfully pursued in each of the four chapters. The issues concern political style, policy differences, historical legacies and compromising material, concrete deliberations, the body that makes decisions, the legitimacy of behaviour displayed, the threat of violence, the significance of institutions, and the inferences that may be drawn from each case. Torigian's analysis of the power struggles draws on elements in all three models, but it is the 'authority model' that proves to have the greatest explanatory power. The general features thrown up by the comparison are thought-provoking, and stress similarity rather than difference between the two parties. In both parties, the author argues, the outcome was shaped more by policy consensus than by policy difference; in both the position of competitors was often misrepresented, sometimes with devastating effect; in both historical antagonisms and 'kompromat' played a key role; and in both the selection of a new leader involved much underhand manoeuvring. In one crucial respect, the outcome in the two countries differed, insofar as the older generation was sidelined in the Soviet Union after 1953, whereas in China, in spite of the rejuvenating aim of the Cultural Revolution, members of the older pre-1940 generation reasserted their power. There is much to ponder although, in my view, a serious weakness derives from the author's Realpolitik approach. Most immediately, policy issues are given short shrift, so the reader is not able to assess their importance. More fundamentally, this derives from the author's radical downplaying of the role of ideology in Communist politics. For example, when Molotov apologised in September 1955 for falsely claiming that the 'foundations of socialist society are already built', Torigian dismisses it as an inconsequential detail; but it enabled Khrushchev to lay out a radical reformist vision. In China politics after 1962 was galvanized by Mao's obsession with Soviet-style 'revisionism'. Yet the author dismisses the Cultural Revolution as 'primarily a political struggle about status and hierarchy not about whether the system would be fundamentally changed' (p. 85); the 'two whatevers' (Hua Guofeng's defence of whatever Mao had said) are mentioned, but are not seen as touching on fundamental principles. If the winners in these power struggles were simply those with the most aggressive political styles, it is hard to explain why Khrushchev and Deng went on to push through fundamental change. But this is a disagreement about the nature of Communist politics, and does not detract from the novelty, analytical rigour and excellence of what is a demanding comparative study.

All Souls College, University of Oxford S. A. Smith

Kostovicova, Denisa. *Reconciliation by Stealth: How People Talk about War Crimes*. Cornell University Press, Ithaca, NY and London, 2023. xiv + 246 pp. Figures. Tables. Notes. Appendix. Bibliography. Index. $51.95; $33.99 (e-book).

This is a great book. Physically, it is a wonderful object: haptically, I found the hardback's dustcover a sensation: visually, the jacket image of Nela Milić's art installation (generated collaboratively with the research) is dazzling; and olfactorially, the edition creates an aroma of quality. This is all in keeping with its remarkable content. Denisa Kostovicova is a 'Rolls Royce' among academics — by which I mean the epitome of elegance and quality, all of which gleams in this outstanding volume. She has produced an exceptional work on three levels: as a major interdisciplinary innovation in method; as an account of the RECOM process (explained below); and, most strikingly, of the perhaps surprising processes of how people from different sides of ethnic divides in post-conflict contexts in the Western Balkans talk to each other in deliberative processes, that reveals ambiguity and commonality. The last of these is the major finding that will be of interest to most readers. It is a world-beating contribution to the fields of conflict and post-conflict studies, broadly, and to the study of the former Yugoslav lands. But, before examining those findings, it is vital to consider those first two contributions that this volume makes.

As the first serious account of RECOM, this book has its place as a go-to point in the literature. RECOM was a unique, ground-up initiative developed by NGOs across the Western Balkans — that is the various countries that had emerged from the dissolution of the Socialist Federative Republic of Yugoslavia and the armed conflict that accompanied it. Kostovicova sets out the rise of RECOM, its process and the challenges it faced from within and without. Shaped as a form of truth commission for the investigation of atrocities — 'war crimes' — it was an attempt to provide a particular form of — and angle on — transitional justice. It was unique because it is, to date, the only transitional justice-war crimes-reconciliation-focused action in the Western Balkans — or anywhere in the world — to have region-wide reach and to emerge organically from within post-conflict communities, rather than as an externally induced process. The author's treatment of it is exemplary, noting the pitfalls, seeing how momentum was lost — and regained as the research prompted interest in it again — and how, ultimately, it failed in its mission to get prime ministers and presidents across the region to sign up (although in 2018, around the time of the London Western Balkans Summit there was considerable hope, expectation even in some circles, that this could happen). RECOM, this Regional Commission for Establishing the Facts about War Crimes and Other Gross Violations of Human Rights Committed on the Territory of the former Yugoslavia from 1 January 1991 to 31 December 2001, came together in a series of public consultations from 2006 to 2011. Organized at all levels — regional, national, local — these conversations involved over 6,000 individuals from every ethnic group in every part of what had been Yugoslavia. While there must be an element of self-selection in that group — those who participated were entirely volunteers, with no inducements — it can be assumed that most of those more closely aligned with sharp nationalist views and the commission of atrocities did not often come forward to join RECOM's consultations. The outcome was in the region of 7 million words of transcribed talk. By 2011, the NGOs that had been involved agreed a Draft

Statute for a fully established regional war crimes truth commission. This needed the buy-in of political leaders, but this was not forthcoming. The process faltered, was then resurrected as Kostovicova — and her interest was crucial — sought to interrogate the mass of untapped empirical material, but finally fell into mothballs in 2019. Along the way, however, even if in the final analysis there had been a failure to engage political leaders and to get the Draft Treaty adopted, a remarkable amount had been achieved. But without Kostovicova's ingenuity and astonishing efforts, all that had been achieved — aside from the process itself — would have gone ignored, unnoticed and unrecognized.

Kostovicova's methods — and sheer effort — in discovering the hidden treasure in the RECOM process need full acknowledgement. The volume displays an impressive and distinctive blend of methods mastered with originality and the greatest rigour, informed by — while critiquing and crucially going beyond — deliberative democracy theory. Even more than the salience of Kostovicova's account of RECOM itself, her methodological approach is a landmark contribution. She combines a range of quantitative and qualitative approaches in conducting analysis of 1,211 'speech acts' from twenty consultations, involving half a million words — an astonishing achievement that involved eight months of dedication to the boring, but necessary task of coding to be able to carry out the research. Her methodological ingenuity stretches the boundaries of knowledge and understanding, taking ethnographic-style discourse analysis beyond the capturing of phrases into the realm of serious, hard numbers, while confronting those normally obsessed with using quantitative methods to prove things already blindingly obvious to the qualitative researcher and demonstrating that something of serious qualitative insight can be produced through the numbers. This is ground-breaking work that makes an immense contribution methodologically and should be recognized as such. Each different method is used to examine the same empirical body of material from multiple perspectives which are then integrated through interpretation. This 'Kostovicova method' (she does not give it a name, so far as I discerned, but it should have one) makes a central contribution to post-conflict and peacebuilding studies, which also makes it by definition, axiomatically, a contribution to conflict and war studies. It is of course a major addition to studies of the South Slav lands, but it has enormous potential for use across political science, sociological and ethnographic studies, history and any number of sub-fields. This is work of global significance — it can be hoped that the world will notice this and make the most of it, rather than overlooking it because it has an empirical focus on the Western Balkans. Of course, chapters two and three dealing with the research methods will be demanding, difficult and dull reading for some (although not because of the way they are written): those readers can take it on trust that these chapters contain the best in research methodology, making the research as a whole more than reliable, and thus safely skip on to the empirical findings. The empirical findings are where the true breadth and impact of the methods can be found, which is testimony to the quality of the research process, a process that extends beyond the methods to provide the kind of analysis that will interest most readers, and which reveals how the deliberative processes of RECOM hid within them unexpected reconciliation by stealth.

This finding is the final — and most significant, overall — achievement of this stunning work. The essence of this remarkable finding is visually encapsulated on pp. 101 and 102 in two graphs. The second shows that which most would assume and which could be found in standard modes of qualitative discourse analysis: that there is a high level of viewpoint agreement within ethnic groups. The first, against all expectations, shows a high level of agreement (if not quite so high) across ethnic lines. In essence, those from different communities share understandings and agree on a surprising number of things in their conversations about what happened and on war crimes. By going beyond the more usual approaches that are fixed on what people say in inter-group deliberation, Kostovicova also targets how her conversants speak. And this is the key to the insights she reveals. As she concludes, her 'real-world' analysis of 'how people talk' uncovers the 'previously undiscovered' type of reconciliation — 'reconciliation by stealth' (p. 143). Her granular analysis shows that 'even the most sensitive issues are amenable to deliberative scrutiny in postconflict contexts' (p. 142). Kostovicova indicates several points of significance arising from this, which are worth noting. First, the ever strong criticisms of so-called 'liberal international' intervention to foster reconciliation and peacebuilding as illegitimate are profoundly misplaced — the whole of her work, based on the most rigorous analysis, demonstrates the deep and embedded legitimacy of NGOs working in this spirit within the region. Secondly, extending from this, it is vital to hold faith with these organizations and provide them with the lifelines that international interest and funding can provide. Finally, and most importantly, all of this points to the value of transitional justice consultations and, above all, holding them in pan-regional, cross-border settings — after all, the conflicts themselves were pan-regional and cross-border, so it is actually a simple logic to frame postconflict deliberations on the same basis. Kostovicova's innovative research makes the case more strongly than the advocates of RECOM ever did or could do for the innovative format they adopted in pursuit of truth, reconciliation and transitional justice.

The DNA-like finding of reconciliation by stealth is based on a stipulative and purpose-driven approach to the concept of reconciliation. In an excellent discussion of the term, she points to the problems of attempting a kind of classical, philosophically reasoned definition. Not only is this subject to problems at the analytical level at which the attempt to define is made but, even more so, because it is used in so many different contexts and for so many different purposes. She sensibly, therefore, proposes what I just labelled a 'stipulative' approach, letting the context shape understanding — in her case, 'mutuality in public communication' (p. 8). This is a sensible approach, which rests, as she shows, on the use of language, with interaction and mutuality key to a 'thicker', relational notion of, and enhancer of, reconciliation.

For all its outstanding quality, *Reconciliation by Stealth* is not beyond question. RECOM was unique. It provided an unbelievable research resource. It might be that Kostovicova's work is sui generis — there might never be another RECOM, so there might never be a similar context to mine. Yet, it would be a shame if such groundbreaking methodological insight were not useful in other situations. Perhaps it is not too much to hope that understanding of the significance in Kostovicova's findings will influence scholars and practitioners to push for deliberative democratic, cross-border, region-wide consultations in other parts of the world, thus generating comparable bodies of data to pursue theory, method and practice. Of course, that will be difficult: one of the stunning things about this research is the author's unique set of skills sets — all the relevant languages, mastery of both quantitative and qualitative methods, close and granular familiarity with the region and its history and culture, knowledge of and access to those who made RECOM and to the vast reservoir of empirical material it provided. Any attempts to follow this lead in other contexts will almost certainly require whole research teams and leadership that can bring the same degree of insight and integration as has Denisa Kostovicova. And, of course, without a continuing RECOM — or equivalent — process, we cannot know, or measure, how durable the remarkable outcomes identified in this book might be. None of that, though, should detract from the fabulous work in this book, which could — and should — inform all types of research on political community in the future, irrespective of particular discipline.

King's College London JAMES GOW

Sagramoso, Domitilla. *Russian Imperialism Revisited: From Disengagement to Hegemony*. Contemporary Security Studies. Routledge, Abingdon and New York, 2020. xvii + 368 pp. Maps. Tables. Notes. Bibliographies. Index. £120.00; £38.99; £35.09 (e-book).

HAS the Russian Federation been pursuing an imperialist policy consistently since it emerged from the USSR in 1992? That is the main question of Domitilla Sagramoso's volume, *Russian Imperialism Revisited*. In view of Vladimir

Putin's full-scale invasion of Ukraine in February 2022, the book is particularly timely.

Sagramoso's method is an extraordinarily thorough and detailed examination of the security and economic policies and integration initiatives conducted by the Kremlin in relation towards the countries that are or have been members of the Commonwealth of Independent States (CIS), from 1992 up to about 2018.

From the start of this period, Western specialists on Russia were constantly being told by some politicians and academics from Eastern Europe and the Baltic States that Russia would always be an aggressive and imperial-minded country. Most of us, certainly in Britain, rejected what seemed to be an ethnic or geographical determinism which had no place in comparative social science. The fact that Russia under Putin did come to interfere in a variety of regions and then unleash the bloodiest war in Europe since the Second World War requires us to re-examine the evidence.

The author speaks mainly of 'neo-imperialism' rather than imperialism when analysing Russia's policy. By 'neo-imperialism' the author means the attempt to create an area where the dominant state can influence foreign and domestic policies of some of its neighbours, and prevent the hegemony of other powers; a neo-empire instead of a formal one (p. 6). In summary, Sagramoso argues that 'there is clearly support for the "neo-imperialist" hypothesis, especially during Putin's third term as President of Russia'; but 'the evidence of a neo-imperialist conduct is not always overwhelming, and this is especially the case in the first decade of Russia's life as an independent state after the USSR disintegrated' (p. 342).

Sometimes, perhaps, the book is a little too ready to justify Russia's actions. Considering Russia's involvement in conflicts around its borders in the El´tsin period, Sagramoso argues that while 'Russia's actions in many respects [...] clearly fitted the neo-imperialist pattern', it 'also had a legitimate interest in finding a peaceful resolution to these conflicts, and this weakens, to a certain extent, the neo-imperialist argument' (p. 119). Similarly, concerning the military grouping created by Russia, the Collective Security Treaty Organization (CSTO), she argues that in the 2000s, since 'several countries welcomed Russia's military assistance and support [...] it is not possible, therefore, to talk of Russia establishing a "neo-empire" in the CSTO space, in the strict meaning of the word' (pp. 190–91).

It cannot be denied that Russia's military support for separatists in Moldova, Georgia and Azerbaijan, beginning in 1992, could only weaken these neighbours and thereby strengthen the Kremlin's influence — even though, as Sagramoso rightly says, there was considerable lack of clarity and conflict between different Russian state institutions in this period, especially in the early years. Where

Moscow put pressure on its neighbours to sell assets, Sagramoso argues that Russia had a 'powerful argument' (p. 64) to do so because these states were in debt to Russian companies for energy supplies.

It could be argued at the same time, however, that the reason why El′tsin did not pursue a stronger neo-imperialist policy than he did was simply that he could not. The state was weak, divided and dependent on Western loans for its functioning. The book shows a different dynamic after Putin came to power at the end of 1999, with attempts to push military and economic integration among states whose regimes were most willing to cooperate. After the war with Georgia in 2008, Dmitrii Medvedev recognized the independence of Abkhazia and South Ossetia, and openly proclaimed that Russia had an (undefined) sphere of 'privileged interests' (p. 238).

When Putin returned to the presidency in 2012, he proclaimed the distinctive nature of Russian civilization. He created the Eurasian Economic Union to try to bring some of the countries sharing the common imperial heritage under further Russian domination, using both soft and hard power instruments. His annexation of Crimea in 2014 strengthened the resistance of the other members to the Russian *diktat,* however, and the union never functioned in the way Putin had wanted. The author rightly sees the annexation of Crimea as reflecting 'an imperialist project' (p. 331) rather than a neo-imperialist one. The barbaric invasion of Ukraine in 2022 can only be seen as a fully-fledged act of Russian imperialism.

The author discusses all these topics in meticulous detail, using a myriad of Russian-language sources and her own interviews with Russians, which cover a period of decades. I highly recommend this book. Because of its encyclopaedic coverage of Russian actions, many researchers will find this helpful as a reference, and Routledge are to be commended for making it available in paperback.

UCL SSEES PETER J. S. DUNCAN

Gustafson, Thane. *Klimat: Russia in the Age of Climate Change.* Harvard University Press, Cambridge, MA, 2021. xiv + 312 pp. Map. Illustrations. Table. Notes. Bibliography. Index. $39.95: £31.95: €36.00.

WHEN Thane Gustafson was writing *Klimat,* his examination of Russia's past and future in an age of climate change, he worried that the Covid-19 pandemic might upset some of his predictions. Of course, shortly after the book's publication, the war in Ukraine — and particularly the sanctions on Russia's economy that followed — quickly emerged as a far more destabilizing factor.

Thanks to Gustafson's deep research into the topic, however, the book remains an indispensable guide to understanding Russia's post-1991 energy politics and offers a provocative, and plausible, roadmap of a future that is clearly tied to petroleum and the climate change it is producing.

Gustafson's central contention is that the world's changing relationship with oil and gas spells trouble for Russia's leaders and populace, despite some claims that they will benefit from climate change. His prediction is premised on the crucial assumption that global demand for petroleum will soon peak and begin to decline. Gustafson, relying on industry experts, foresees peak oil by 2030 or 2040, after which renewable energy will enjoy price advantages and Western anti-carbon policies will have real bite. Even some Russian experts — notably the former minister of energy Aleksandr Novak — have at times accepted the 'peak-oil' narrative and begun to grapple with that future. However, many in Russia dispute this future, and there have been many who have prematurely forecast peak oil. We will see.

Regardless of the future of global demand for oil, *Klimat* makes a convincing case that Russia's petroleum-subsidized present also contains some serious weaknesses. Since 1991, the Russian state has become ever more dependent on hydrocarbon exports to finance its activities. In 2019, oil constituted 44 per cent of Russian exports, and hydrocarbons as a whole 56 per cent. But, the vast Western Siberian oil reserves that have powered the industry since the 1960s are running out and development of possible offshore reserves in the Arctic has become even more difficult with the withdrawal of Western oil firms and their know-how. There is some hope that natural gas, which produces less CO_2 than oil, will replace some of the lost revenues. Cheap gas is providing a valuable subsidy to Russian consumers, while new pipelines have recently come online to bring some of that gas from Siberia to China. Still, Gustafson sees a future of declining global gas demand and growing local competition in Asia. The fact that both India and China have been buying Russian petroleum at discount prices since the invasion of Ukraine makes this prediction seem a bit less certain.

Klimat is particularly good at detailing the histories of other sectors that will be impacted by the uncertain oil future. Take, for example, the little-known, remarkable rebirth of Russian coal exports. As Gustafson details, coal nearly died with the Soviet Union, but after 2000, the industry, buoyed in part by World Bank loans, was rebuilt and by 2019 achieved record production. Most coal exports go to East Asia, which has strong demand in part — ironically — to produce the electricity needed to fuel a coming boom in electric cars. Still, coal revenues, however impressive, cannot make up for the coming shortfall in oil sales. The similarly impressive growth in Russian agriculture since 1991 also has a pessimistic coda. One of the Russian state's responses to the growing array of trade embargoes since 2014 has been to invest in local agriculture, which is now the country's third most important export industry. On the face of it, climate change should help Russian agriculture, since the country's cold climate has always plagued its crops. But, the problem lies in Russia's soils. Those more northerly regions that will indeed become warm enough for a variety of food crops have poor soils, while the very fertile southerly black earth belts will suffer increasingly from drought. Overall Russian food production will likely drop.

For various reasons, nuclear power, the celebrated opening of the Arctic sea route, renewable energy and other alternatives are unlikely to replace future lost oil revenues. By 2030, and for the first time since the 1960s, Gustafson claims, the Russian state will not be able to fund itself with oil revenues. Its single-minded investment in that sector may have been rational at the time, but it has left the country seriously vulnerable to a rapidly changing world. Of course, as Gustafson quotes a Russian saying, 'People are our second oil'. They mean that Russian expertise and ingenuity will find new solutions to these looming problems. Gustafson thinks that to unleash the potential of Russia's best and brightest the country will need to open its economy and invest in the high-tech sector. However, the best-educated and the most inventive Russians are exactly those that have left the country in droves since February 2022. In that way, *Klimat*'s pessimism looks all the more prescient.

Department of History
University of Oregon

RYAN JONES

Publications Received

Baghiu, Ştefan; Olaru, Ovio and Terian, Andrei (eds). *Beyond the Iron Curtain: Revisiting the Literary System of Communist Romania*. German Studies. Peter Lang, Berlin, Bern, Brussels, New York, Oxford, Warsaw and Vienna, 2021. £46.00 (hardback & e-book).

Bernstein, Seth. *Return to the Motherland: Displaced Soviets in World War II and the Cold War*. Battlegrounds: Cornell Studies in Military History. Cornell University Press, Ithaca, NY and London, 2023. $46.95; $30.99 (e-book).

Borenstein, Eliot. *Soviet Self-Hatred: The Secret Identities of Postsocialism in Contemporary Russia*. Cornell University Press, Ithaca, NY and London, 2023. $125.00; $22.95; $15.99 (e-book).

Búr, Gábor; Pál, István and Stempler, Ádám (eds). *Followed by the Affected Compassion of the Free World: The 1956 Revolution from Different Perspectives*. ELTE Faculty of Humanities and Eötvös University Press, Budapest, 2023. Open access.

Burry, Alexander. *Legacies of the Stone Guest: The Don Juan Legend in Russian Literature*. Publications of the Wisconsin Centre for Pushkin Studies. The University of Wisconsin Press, Madison, WI, 2023. $99.95.

Butler, William E. *Russian-English Legal Dictionary*. Second revised and expanded edition. Studies in Russian, East European, and Eurasian Law. Talbot Publishing, Clark, NJ, 2023. $150.00.

Caridi, Cathi. *Making Martyrs East and West: Canonization in the Catholic and Russian Orthodox Churches*. Northern Illinois University Press, Ithaca, NY and London, 2023. $125.00; $27.95; $17.99 (e-book).

Cherkaev, Xenia A. *Gleaning for Communism: The Soviet Socialist Household in Theory and Practice*. Cornell University Press, Ithaca, NY and London, 2023. $125.00; $26.95; $17.99 (e-book).

Clarke, Charles (ed.). *Understanding the Baltic States: Estonia, Latvia and Lithuania since 1991*. C. Hurst & Co., London, 2023. £22.50; £16.99 (e-book).

Cooke, Olga M. *'A Mind Purified by Suffering': Evgenia Ginzburg's 'Whirlwind' Memoirs*. The Real Twentieth Century. Academic Studies Press, Boston, MA, 2023. $129.00.

Daiber, Thomas. *Vita des Konstantin-Kyrill: Altkirchenslavischer Text – Übersetzung – Kommentar*. Harrassowitz, Wiesbaden, 2023. €89.00 (hardback & e-book).

Eaton, Nicole. *German Blood, Slavic Soil: How Nazi Köningsberg Became Soviet Kaliningrad*. Battlegrounds: Cornell Studies in Military History. Cornell University Press, Ithaca, NY and London, 2023. $35.95; $17.99 (e-book).

Edgar, Adrienne. *Intermarriage and the Friendship of Peoples: Ethnic Mixing in Soviet Central Asia*. Cornell University Press, Ithaca, NY and London, 2022. $54.95; $35.99 (e-book).

Emery, Jacob. *The Vortex that Unites Us: Versions of Totality in Russian Literature*. NIU Series in Slavic, East European, and Eurasian Studies. Northern Illinois University Press, Ithaca, NY and London, 2023. $54.95: $34.99 (e-book).

Estraikh, Gennady. *The History of Birobidzhan: Building a Soviet Jewish Homeland in Siberia*. Russian Shorts. Bloomsbury Academic, London, New York, Oxford, Delhi and Sydney, 2023. £45.00; £12.99 (paperback); £11.69 (e-book).

Evtuhov, Catherine; Lajus, Julia and Moon, David (eds). *Thinking Russia's History Environmentally. The Environment in History: International Perspectives*. Berghahn Books, New York and Oxford, 2023. £107.00; £27.95 (e-book).

Funahashi, Daena Aki. *Untimely Sacrifices: Work and Death in Finland*. Cornell University Press, Ithaca, NY and London, 2023. $125.00; $29.95; $19.99 (e-book).

Goodman, Brian K. *The Nonconformists: American and Czech Writers across the Iron Curtain*. Harvard University Press, Cambridge, MA and London, 2023. $45.00: £39.95: €40.95.

Grupińska, Hanka. *I Came Home and There Was No One There: Conversations and Stories about the Uprising in the Warsaw Ghetto*. Translated from the Polish by Jessica Taylor. Jews of Poland. Academic Studies Press, Boston, MA, 2023. $159.00; $45.00.

Hall, Stephen G. F. *The Authoritarian International: Tracing How Authoritarian Regimes Learn in the Post-Soviet Space*. Cambridge University Press, Cambridge and New York, 2023. £85.00: $110.00.

Hess, Maximilian. *Economic War: Ukraine and the Global Conflict between Russia and the West*. New Perspectives on Eastern Europe and Eurasia. Hurst Publishers, London, 2023. £30.00.

Hokanson, Katya. *A Woman's Empire: Russian Women and Imperial Expansion in Asia*. University of Toronto Press, Toronto, ON, Buffalo, NY and London, 2023. $80.00.

Iandolo, Alessandro. *Arrested Development: The Soviet Union in Ghana, Guinea, and Mali, 1955–1968*. Cornell Univetsity Press, Ithaca, NY and London, 2022. $55.95; $36.99 (e-book).

Jackson, Robert Louis. *Essays on Anton P. Chekhov: Close Readings*. Edited by Cathy Popkin. Ars Rossica. Academic Studies Press, Boston, MA, 2023. $139.00.

Kaiser, Claire P. *Georgian and Soviet: Entitled Nationhood and the Specter of Stalin in the Caucasus*. Cornell University Press, Ithaca, NY and London, 2023. $43.95; $28.99 (e-book).

Karp, Masha. *George Orwell and Russia*. Bloomsbury Academic, London, New York and Dublin, 2023. £65.00; £21.99 (paperback); £19.79 (e-book).

Kin, Ostap (ed.). *Babyn Yar: Ukrainian Poets Respond*. Translated by Ostap Kin and John Hennessy. Harvard University Press, Cambridge, MA and London, 2023. $16.00: £13.95: €14.95 (paperback).

Klots, Yasha. *Tamizdat: Contraband Russian Literuture in the Cold War Era*. NIU Series in Slavic, East European, and Eurasian Studies. Northern Illinois University Press, Ithaca, NY and London, 2023. $46.95: $30.99 (e-book).

Klumbytė, Neringa. *Authoritarian Laughter: Political Humor and Soviet Dystopia in Lithuania*. Cornell University Press, Ithaca, NY and London, 2022. $125.00; $32.95; $21.99 (e-book).

Kohut, Zenon E.; Sklokin, Volodymyr and Sysyn, Frank E. (eds). *Eighteenth-Century Ukraine: New Perspectives on Social, Cultural, and Intellectual History*. Canadian Institute for Ukrainian Studies and McGill-Queen's University Press, Montreal, QC and Kingston, ON, London and Chicago, IL, 2023. CAD$110.00.

Kokosalakis, Yiannis. *Building Socialism: The Communist Party and the Making of the Soviet System, 1921–41*. New Studies in European History. Cambridge University Press, Cambridge and New York, 2023. £85.00.

Kornat, Marek. *Poland and the Origins of the Second World War: A Study in Diplomatic History (1938–1939)*. Polish Studies – Transdisciplinary Perspectives, 35. Peter Lang, Berlin, Bern, Brussels, New York, Oxford, Warsaw and Vienna, 2021. £55.60; £54.00 (e-book).

Kostovicova, Denisa. *Reconciliation by Stealth: How People Talk about War Crimes*. Cornell University Press, Ithaca, NY and London, 2023. $51.95; $33.99 (e-book).

Lecke, Mirja and Sicher, Efraim (eds). *Cosmopolitan Spaces in Odesa: A Case Study of an Urban Context*. Ukrainian Studies. Academic Studies Press, Boston, MA, 2023. $149.00.

Lewis, Virginia L. *The Novels of Zsigmond Móricz in the Context of European Realism: A Thematic Approach*. Studies on Themes and Motifs in Literature, 140. Peter Lang, New York, Berlin, Bruxelles, Lausanne, Oxford, 2023. £60.00 (hardback & e-book).

Marantzidis, Nikos. *Under Stalin's Shadow: A Global History of Greek Communism*. NIU Series in Slavic, East European, and Eurasian Studies. Northern Illinois University Press, Ithaca, NY and London, 2023. $125.00; $32.95: $21.99 (e-book).

Martin, Barbara. *Roy and Zhores Medvedev: Loyal Dissident in the Soviet Union*. Modern Biographies. Academic Studies Press, Boston, MA, 2023. $149.00: $25.00

McGlynn, Jade. *Memory Makers: The Politics of the Past in Putin's Russia*. Bloomsbury Academic, London, New York and Dublin, 2023. £20.00; £18.00 (e-book).

Metslang, Helle; Norvik, Miina and Kalnača, Andra (eds). *Insights into the Baltic and Finnic Languages: Contacts, Comparisons, and Change*. Potsdam Linguistic Investigations, 36. Peter Lang, Berlin, Bern, Brussels, New York, Oxford, Warsaw and Vienna, 2022. £54.00 (hardback & e-book).

Muravyeva, Marianna (ed.). *The Foundations of Russian Law*. Hart Publishing, an imprint of Bloomsbury Publishing, Oxford, New York and Dublin, 2023. £85.00; £76.50 (e-book).

Naliwajek, Katarzyna. *Sounds of Apocalypse: Music in Poland under German Occupation*. Eastern European Studies in Musicology, 25. Peter Lang, Berlin, Bern, Brussels, New York, Oxford, Warsaw and Vienna, 2022. £38.00 (hardback & e-book).

Plokhy, Serhii. *The Russo-Ukrainian War*. Allen Lane, London and New York, 2023. £25.00; £16.99 (paperback).

Porter, Jillian and Vinokaur, Maya (eds). *Energy Culture: Work, Power, and Waste in Russia and the Soviet Union*. Literatures, Cultures, and the Environment. Palgrave Macmillan, Cham, 2023. £109.99: £87.50 (e-book).

Praspaliauskiene, Rima. *Enveloped Lives: Caring and Relating in Lithuanian Healthcare*. Cornell University Press, Ithaca, NY and London, 2022. $125.00; $24.95 $16.99 (e-book).

Pravilova, Ekaterina. *The Ruble: A Political History*. Oxford University Press, Oxford and New York, 2023. £30.99.

Proskurina, Vera. *The Imperial Script of Catherine the Great: Governing with the Literary Pen*. Ars Rossica. Academic Studies Press, Boston, MA, 2023. $119.00.

Przebinda, Grzegorz. *From Chaadayev to Solovyov: Russian Modern Thinkers Between East and West*. Eastern European Culture, Politics and Societies, 20. Peter Lang, Berlin, Bern, Brussels, New York, Oxford, Warsaw and Vienna, 2022. £54.00 (hardback & e-book).

Roth-Ey, Kristin (ed.). *Socialist Internationalism and the Gritty Politics of the Particular: Second–Third World Spaces in the Cold War*. Histories of Internationalism. Bloomsbury Academic, London, New York and Dublin, 2023. £85.00; £76.50 (e-book).

Schechter, Brandon M. *The Stuff of Soldiers: A History of the Red Army in World War II through Objects*. Battlegrounds: Cornell Studies in Military History. Cornell University Press, Ithaca, NY and London, 2023. $36.95; $28.95; $13.99 (e-book).

Sebestyen, Victor. *The Russian Revolution*. Apollo, an imprint of Bloomsbury Publishing, London and New York, 2023. £27.99; £9.99 (e-book).

Smola, Klavdia. *Reinventing Tradition: Russian-Jewish Literature between Soviet Underground and Post-Soviet Deconstruction*. Jews of Russia and Eastern Europe and Their Legacy. Academic Studies Press, Boston, MA, 2023. $139.00.

Sutherland, Suzanne. *The Rise of the Military Entrepreneur: War, Diplomacy, and Knowledge in Habsburg Europe*. Cornell University Press, Ithaca, NY and London, 2022. $44.95; $29.99 (e-book).

Sutton-Mattocks, Julia. *Cures for Modernity: Medicine in Interwar Russian and Czech Literature and Cinema*. Cultural History and Literary Imagination, 35. Peter Lang, Berlin, Bern, Brussels, New York, Oxford, Warsaw and Vienna, 2023. £48.00 (paperback & e-book).

Tabachnikova, Olga (ed.). *A Culture of Discontinuity? Russian Cultural Debates in Historical Perspective*. Cultural History and Literary Imagination, 54. Peter Lang, Lausanne, Berlin, Brusells, Chennai, New York, Oxford, 2023. £52.00 (paperback & e-book).

Teodor, Bogdan; Baev, Jordan; Crosston, Matthew and Teodor Mihaela (eds). *Old and New Insights on the History of Intelligence and Diplomacy in the Balkans*. South-East European History, 1. Peter Lang, New York, Berlin, Bruxelles, Lausanne, Oxford, 2023. £74.00 (hardback & e-book).

Ther, Philipp. *How the West Lost the Peace: The Great Transformation Since the Cold War*. Translated by Jessica Spengler. Polity, Cambridge, Oxford, Boston, MA and New York, 2023. £55.00; £12.99: €62.20; €20.40.

Uehling, Greta Lynn. *Everyday War: The Conflict Over Donbass, Ukraine*. Cornell University Press, Ithaca, NY and London, 2023. $125.00; $31.95; $20.99 (e-book).

Utkin, Roman. *Charlottengrad: Russian Culture in Weimar Berlin*. Wisconsin University Press, Madison, WI, 2023. $99.95.

Vaninskaya, Anna (ed.). *London through Russian Eyes, 1896–1914: An Anthology of Foreign Correspondence*. Translated by Maria Artomonova. London Record Society, 57. Boydell & Brewer, Woodbridge and Rochester, NY, 2023. £60.00; £19.99 (e-book): $85.00; $24.95 (e-book).

Wanner, Catherine. *Everyday Religiosity and the Politics of Belonging in Ukraine*. Cornell University Press, Ithaca, NY and London, 2022. $125.00; $24.95.

Zhadan, Serhiy. *Sky Above Kharkiv: Dispatches from the Ukrainian Front*. The Margellos World Republic of Letters. Yale University Press, New Haven, CT and London, 2023. $26.00.

Abstracts

Maria Renata Mayenowa and the Forgotten Legacy of Polish Theory of Literature and Poetics by Tomasz Zarycki
This article examines the figure of an outstanding Polish philologist — Maria Renata Mayenowa (1908–88) — attempting to interpret her life trajectory with the help of sociological tools. It is argued that Mayenowa's biography is significant in the context of the history of Polish, as well as Eastern European intellectual thought, for several reasons. First, it can be helpful in the reconstruction of the Polish involvement in the development of social theory in the twentieth century. Second, it provides insight into Polish-Russian, and more broadly, Polish-Eastern European intellectual relations in the twentieth century. Finally, the third reason is the non-obvious forms in which the history of Eastern European Jewish elites, and in particular the Jewish bourgeoisie, manifested itself in her biography.

Repetition, Ageing and End of Life in Liudmila Ulitskaia's *The Body of the Soul* by Benjamin M. Sutcliffe
Liudmila Ulitskaia's 2019 volume of stories, *The Body of the Soul* (*O tele dushi*), humanizes the end of life and counters harmful mythologies about ageing as well as dying in Russian culture. Ulitskaia, one of the nation's most prominent living authors, was the first woman to receive the Russian Booker Prize. *The Body of the Soul* repeats scenes and images from her previous fiction to explore how *telesnost′* (corporeality) is its own cosmos of meaning. This contradicts assumptions dominating Russian culture over the past century and connects her older characters to the intelligentsia, which struggled to survive in the Soviet era and its aftermath. *The Body of the Soul* represents how the individual, often apolitical lives of older characters quietly contradict state ideals.

Addressing the Public in Eighteenth-Century Russian Letter Collections by Kelsey Rubin-Detlev
This article offers the first scholarly overview of original and translated letter collections printed in eighteenth-century Russia. Through a close reading of the publication history, structure and paratexts of correspondence editions, it argues that the proliferation of such collections under Catherine the Great (1762–96) reflects an expanding definition of publicness and a related eagerness on the part of editors and translators to reconfigure relationships within the public. Editors widened state- and church-centred concepts of publicness to encompass an array of letter writers from cultural figures to ordinary citizens. Simultaneously, horizontal relationships of exchange between writers, editors, texts and readers came to rival vertical hierarchies in motivating and shaping epistolary publicity. A previously overlooked element in Catherinian print culture, letter collections provide unique insights into late eighteenth-century Russian thinking about what it meant to be (a) public.

The Strange Case of the Disappearing Soviet Waiter by Diane P. Koenker
This article explores the phenomenon, causes and attempted solutions to the problem of poor restaurant service in the 1960s Soviet Union. It discusses the role of the restaurant in the dining options of the Soviet urban population, the organization of restaurants, the culture of service and the low status of the waitering trade and economic reforms. It also reconstructs the perspective of the Soviet waiters themselves to examine how they justified the behaviours decried by officials and customers. This exploration reveals a paradox between competing ideals of the 'good life': one of technologically driven satisfaction of biological needs, and the other of promotion of a psychologically rounded good life, in which the whole person merited respect. Lacking that respect and compensated with low wages, Soviet waiters responded with indifferent service.

THE SLAVONIC & EAST EUROPEAN REVIEW

The *Slavonic and East European Review*, the journal of the UCL School of Slavonic and East European Studies, is published quarterly by the Modern Humanities Research Association (MHRA). Issues are numbered serially, the four annual issues constituting a volume. Up to and including 1965 an even-numbered issue (published in December) together with the following and odd-numbered issue (published in June) constituted a volume.

Scholarly contributions are invited on all subjects related to the field of Slavonic and East European Studies. Articles should be between 8,000 and 12,000 words, although contributions falling outside this range may also be considered. Book reviews should be no longer than requested. Other contributions (review articles/essays, marginalia, obituaries, summary notes) should aim at a corresponding and proportionate brevity. Original documents are specially welcome. No correspondence is published in the *Review*.

Contributions should be submitted in English in a form ready for publication and in the final state intended. Contributors should study the leaflet, 'Guide for Contributors', obtainable on request from the Managing Editor, SEER Office, UCL SSEES, Gower Street, London WC1E 6BT (seer@ucl.ac.uk), or online at www.ucl.ac.uk/ssees/publishing/slavonic-and-east-european-review. All contributions must adhere to the *Review*'s house style.

Contributions and other editorial communications should be sent to the Managing Editor. While the editors take every possible care with regard to typescripts, they advise authors to retain duplicate copies. The editors do not consider themselves responsible in the event of the loss of a contribution.

Further information about the activities of the Modern Humanities Research Association and individual membership may be obtained from the Membership Secretary, email: membership@mhra.org.uk, or from the website at: www.mhra.org.uk. For institutional subscription rates and information, contact subscriptions@mhra.org.uk.

ISSN 0037-6795 (print); ISSN 2222-4327 (online)

Printed in the USA
CPSIA information can be obtained
at www.ICGtesting.com
LVHW022331171123
764260LV00009B/103

9 781839 542749